FLIPPING TABLES

The Seven Deadly Sins

and

Stories of Redemption

Collected by Naomi's Street People

Copyright © 2022 by Luanne Nelson

All rights reserved. No part of this book may be reproduced or transmitted in any form or by any means, electronic or mechanical, including: photocopying, recording, or by any information storage and retrieval system, without permission in writing from the copyright owner. This work is based on the experiences of individuals. Every effort has been made to ensure the accuracy of the content.

Flipping Tables
The Seven Deadly Sins and Stories of Redemption

Contributing Authors: Michael C., Vidal Cisneros, Jr., K. M. Fleming, Patricia Freeman, Rev. Michael DeShane Hinton, Daniel Holly, Dn. Dennis Kudlac, Thomas M., Vicki Manuel, James Mumaugh, Dr. David Nelson, Luanne Nelson, Jamie P., Robert Schultz, Verissa Walber, Steve West

Stories collected by Naomi's Street People
Editor: Marla McKenna
Associate Editors: Luanne Nelson, Griffin Mill, Lyda Rose Haerle
Cover Design Luanne Nelson & Michael Nicloy
Interior Layout: Michael Nicloy

Bible verses are taken from Biblegateway.com
©1995-2017, Zondervan Corporation, all rights reserved.

ISBN: 978-1-957351-18-6 (Paperback)
ISBN-978-1-957351-17-9 (Hardcover)
Published by Nico 11 Publishing & Design, LLC
Mukwonago, Wisconsin

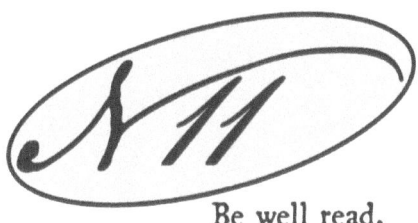

Be well read.

Quantity order requests may be emailed to:
mike@nico11publishing.com

Printed in The United States of America

A Compilation of Conversations by:

Naomi's Street People

and

A few of their friends

PART ONE

Table of Contents

Dedication ...pg. 13

Redemption – Defined ...pg. 14

Preface ...pg. 15

Chapter One	Let's Talk ...pg. 17
Chapter Two	What the Eye Doesn't See ...pg. 25
Chapter Three	Remembering ...pg. 31
Chapter Four	He's Made It So Simple for Us ...pg. 37
Chapter Five	God Loves Us. Seriously ...pg. 45
Chapter Six	Please ...pg. 51
Chapter Seven	Slippery Slopes ...pg. 59
Chapter Eight	This World We're in Today ...pg. 75
Chapter Nine	Redemption ...pg. 83
Chapter Ten	Following Directions ...pg. 91
Chapter Eleven	Forgiveness ...pg. 107
Chapter Twelve	Learning About Forgiveness in a Thunderbird ...pg. 113
Chapter Thirteen	Following Jesus ...pg. 121
Chapter Fourteen	A Few Holy Directives ...pg. 129

About Naomi's Street People ...pg. 137

Epilogue ...pg. 147

this is for all of us

Redemption

re·demp·tion
/rəˈdem(p)SH(ə)n/

noun

1. the action of saving or being saved from sin, error, or evil: "God's plans for the redemption of his world" synonyms: saving, saving/freeing from sin, vindication, absolution

2. the action of regaining or gaining possession of something in exchange for payment, or clearing a debt: "the peasants found the terms of redemption unattractive" synonyms: retrieval, recovery, reclamation, repossession, recoupment, return, rescue, repurchase, exchange, swapping, bartering, cashing in, conversion, return, trade-in, paying off, paying back, discharge, clearing, squaring, honoring, quittance, fulfillment, carrying out, discharge, making good, execution, performing, accomplishment, achievement, observance, honoring, meeting, satisfying, adherence to

(Oxford Dictionaries)

Preface

So, what is sin, anyway?

*R*ight or Wrong? Good or Bad? Holy or Evil? I know there's a line somewhere.

Courts of law are packed with people waiting for answers. People are paying lawyers, judges are sitting in the heavy seat of decision settling disputes. The gavel hits the metal with a heavy clack. Done. Over. Justice served. Or is it?

Appeal. Apply to a higher court for a reversal of the decision of a lower court.

Who is in charge?

Is there really and truly a God? Is He seeing everything? Is He in charge?

I am not going to church. They will want my money. They'll make me feel like crap. I will see my dirty rotten neighbor down the street there with the terrible kids who egged my house last year.

What happens when I die? I try to do good things for other people most of the time. What if there is life after this? I wonder if I am going to be reincarnated as an earthworm, get swept down a rain gutter, and that will be the end of me.

If there is such a thing as "sin," are some sins more serious than other sins? How do I get rid of sins that are piling up in the corners of my life, getting out of control, and seriously messing everything up? I really do need to stop smoking. My chest hurts. Drinking a bottle of wine a day can't be very good for my liver. I know, I'll drop off some clothing at the women's shelter! If there really is a God, He will see me doing that and maybe when I die, if there is life after this, He'll remember me doing some good stuff and cut me a break on a technicality.

Is there any hope for me? Should I care? Should I take another happy pill my doc prescribed for me and just forget about the whole thing? Where is that joint I rolled last night?

I wonder if Sally Struthers is still collecting money for orphans. Where is my checkbook? Where is her address?

Is anger a sin? I hope not because I am ticked off a lot. I remember Jesus was seen **FLIPPING TABLES** over in the Temple when He got angry, so it must be alright for me to be upset once in a while, too, right?

Am I really going to burn in hell if I shack up with my boyfriend? How many cookies are too many?

Chapter One

Let's Talk

Back in the olden days, not so long ago, ancient church ladies sat in wooden pews wearing lacy veils and dresses so soft you wanted to climb on them and sleep wrapped up in the folds. Their gnarled fingers were held together by delicate chains punctuated with beads; they mumbled on and on for hours. No matter the time of day or night, there were always one or two of them there, eyes closed, oblivious to the world, mumbling away.

Then, some deranged idiot knocked Mary's nose right off of her face with a hammer and tried to smash the Pieta to smithereens. So, they decided to lock the churches at dusk.

Damaging and stealing religious artifacts became de rigueur...after smashing the marble, they ran away with the gold. Churches were locked all day long.

Still, the heavy wooden doors were swung open for services. Big burly greeters in blue suits with striped ties cheerfully bellowed "good morning" to everyone passing through the marble archways; we knew they were armed guards put there to protect us.

Then, there were the gut-wrenching reports of clergy abuse and financial misappropriations. If there's one thing we can count on in this life, it's this: People can and will mess up just about everything and anything. Put someone in charge and you can bet it's going to be tainted with human error.

This didn't happen overnight. It took a few decades. Actually, quite a few. The ancient ladies holding the world together with their delicate lace of prayer died. The word "clergy" became interchangeable with the word "monster" and worse words than that. Nuns evaporated into thin air, either trading their black and white veils for cement hats or just plain not answering the call at all.

Oh, there still are a few cloistered nuns tucked away safely behind heavy iron gates, dead to the world, praying their hearts out for all of us - but that's about it. Recently, I read about a world-class basketball star who opted for that lifestyle. It's a captivating story; I read about her in the Sunday New York Times. She's definitely the exception these days.

Dead sheep file in and out of dead churches thinking they are keeping the Sabbath holy, only to lie cheat and steal on their way home. I stopped going to a building to pray a while ago after getting kicked out of three different churches.

Get this - I was uninvited to teach little children on Sunday morning because I told a holy roller big shot's kid to sit down until he was excused from class. I hurt his little itty-bitty feelings; he put his head down on the desk and sobbed until daddy big-bucks rescued him from meanie me. Yes, I was fired from a labor of love I was showing up and doing for free. Lesson learned. One must keep the donors happy, otherwise who will pay to keep the cavernous building heated so the dead sheep do not freeze? When the director of religious education dismissed me, I told him to "shove it." True, this is not holy speak; I do think I scored some extra points for effort and honesty in the long run, though.

Before you jump to any conclusions, please know this - I am completely and totally in love with Jesus, my Savior, Lord and King. I do recognize there is, however, a chasm of disconnect between Jesus' message for us and how that message is being carried out in the world today. It's become obvious there's a gully of gullibles and a wretched group of reprobates running amok at the helm of churches here on earth.

So, since I've been kicked out of so many churches, I've taken the message to the streets. I am not going to put my name on anything here because I think there's a little bit of me in every one. After all, we are His creation, made in His likeness and image; we are all searching for the truth and wondering what happened and what's going to happen next. I am pretty sure you'd rather be a sheep searching for your shepherd than a dead sheep; otherwise, you would not have picked up this book.

My God is found in the Trinity – the Father, the Son and the Holy Spirit. I learned this in the third grade. I was too afraid of Sister Theresa to not believe it. She truly terrorized us; I threw up every morning before school, begging my mother to let me stay home. Later in life, twenty years ago to be exact, I came to believe in the Trinity for real after I had messed up my life so badly I was seriously in need of and ready for a Savior. He delivered. I am His.

Let me clear something up here. You may be wondering about the other two debacles that got me tossed out on the street. You already know about my irreverence toward the religious education leader. That, of course, did not end well. Prior to that, I was banned from receiving the sacraments because I failed to give away enough free stuff to a priest who, since then, has been defrocked. Despite those two events, I continued to wander around in the proverbial religious desert searching for a church I could belong to.

I thought I had finally found spiritual nirvana in a nondenominational church out in the sticks. Trees surrounded this little Utopia, the lady-minister jumped around full of energy and happiness because Jesus is great, and everyone is happy or something like that. So far so good.

She had a white satin padded throne chair off to the side to rest on in between jumping around. The seven gifts of the Holy Spirit were carefully embroidered in the satin fabric; she claimed to have been given all seven gifts! Wow!

Before signing up, I ran this lady pastor through rigorous lunch interviews with my husband, who was skeptical about her. He was not convinced she was for real; he thought all the jumping around was a little over the top. That, and the fact she was dissing one of the guys who, as she put it, was "pretending to be a part of her church clergy" increased my husband's suspicions. She told us, over lunch, she wanted to remove this fake clergy guy because she was concerned he was trying to take over her church.

"Her" church. Hey, I'm all in for a good pilgrimage, but suddenly I realized I was holding the wrong road map – again. I attended a service there the very next day, and sure enough, the so-called fake-clergy guy was there. I confronted him. He lied to me three times and then claimed he didn't hear my questions anyway because I was not "speaking of the same spirit." Of course, I rebuked him in the name of Jesus, which got me hauled into pastor lady's office. Do you think she could tell the truth about what she had said to us about him the day before? Noooo. You can guess the outcome.

So, there I was – again – out in the spiritual desert once again getting stabbed in the back by fierce religious tigers, clawing at my soul, licking my blood off of the ground with their fierce gossipy lyin' scissor-shaped tongues.

One tends to have time to think a lot when roaming around. I decided to start searching again, this time asking questions since I realized I didn't have many answers at all. I found I was not alone. There were other pilgrims in the desert with me, describing similar experiences they'd had with fake churches, too.

I spent two long years approaching total strangers, asking them, "Do you believe there is life after this?" and "What is sin?" I dressed nicely and looked like the lady next door. People, for the most part, answered me. Some welcomed conversation, either out of loneliness or out of surprise someone was talking to them. I got bolder and bolder. There were times I put my face in between their cell phones and their faces to ask them questions. Most people thought the method of interruption was funny and took a smartphone break to talk to a human (me). On a few occasions, I schlepped a person to a coffee shop for a whole conversation on the subject. It became fun. Sahara Desert Pilgrim Coffee with a bagel, please.

I learned something big out there trudging the spiritual sand dunes. People are searching. They're lonely; many are afraid. A few people were just plain mean and would call me names because I had distracted them from their online Pet Rescue Game apparently causing them to lose a squirrel. I learned to look over shoulders and approach gamers on smartphones with caution.

One day, I invited an old college friend to have lunch with me at a local café so I could ask her what she thought about the whole thing. She had been the resident assistant on the dorm wing I resided in at college many years ago; I had always held her opinion in high esteem. Getting kicked out of three churches is a bit excessive, she'd have to agree. Maybe she would have some answers. I was looking forward to hearing what she thought.

I talked to her about the pope and how, despite my visit to the Vatican years ago, even going to Mass at the Sistine Chapel on the Feast Day of the Assumption, I was having serious misgivings about this particular pope's motives.

She reached into her purse, and I thought nothing of it. I figured she was getting a tissue to dab her nose.

I went on to explain to her Irish Catholic-ness why I thought this particular pope was a lunatic.

I caught her discretely "flicking" something at me under the table. It clicked! I smacked my forehead with my open palm and burst out laughing, asking her, "Are you trying to splash holy water on me?"

Her answer was, "Yes."

I could not stop laughing. God, help me. Sweet dear Jesus, help us all. Holy Spirit, enlighten us and guide us. Amen.

So, there I sat. Irreverent me. Forever in love with the Savior who rescued my sorry derriere many years ago. Churchless and still sinful; with a sinless man-God, Jesus, my best friend. He walks around the malls with me, He sits at the coffee shop table with me as I talk about Him. He covers me with His protection and never fails me. He told us all we should pray together. I just couldn't find a group to do that with no matter how hard I tried.

I search the streets. He's made it obvious He doesn't want me in a pew somewhere. That might be where He wants you, I don't know (shrugging shoulders). One thing I've come to know for sure: Jesus is not shy and He's turned me into a warrior. Street people are a tough bunch.

You may be wondering what some of those answers were during my two years in the desert asking total strangers one question after another.

Here are some of the answers people gave to the question: "What is sin?":

"I don't know. I haven't really thought about it."

"Something that makes you feel bad about yourself."

"Missing the mark."

"My ex-husband. He is walking and breathing sin."

"I don't think it matters any more. Does it?"

"Not showing yourself and the world the love of The Christ."

"It depends on the culture. What is a sin in one place may not be a sin in another place."

Sometimes I would ask, "So, if you rack up a lot of sins, how do you get rid of them?" Often, as an icebreaker, I would say, "You know, a kitty cat will preen itself and then throw up the fur ball. How do you get rid of the fur ball of sin? If they didn't back away and flee, their brave answers included:

"I would just put it out of my mind. Every day is a new day."

"I don't want to feel bad about myself, so I just forget about it."

"I am on meds that help me to feel better about myself."

"I apologize to the person I've hurt and go on from there."

"God loves me no matter what so it really doesn't matter."

Alrighty then ...

Most people I talked with admitted they had a Bible sitting at home "somewhere" collecting dust. Many agreed:

"It's too hard to read."

"It's outdated."

"It doesn't apply to today."

How did this happen? When did the most important book ever written become passe? How could it manage to travel through the centuries alive and well only to die a slow asthmatic death from collecting too much dust on bookshelves and in top drawers of hotels?

We're going to explore some questions together. I assure you, although I am now part of an army of warriors for Jesus Christ, we're are not going to ask you to send money or join a church or try to persuade you to do anything. Countless numbers of people have been destroyed by the church phenomena; no one wants to be made to feel worthless and un-save-able, no one wants to be scolded all the time, and few people are foolish enough to buy the line of the current prosperity gospel, "Give us 5 bucks and you'll get triple that amount back to you."

So many churches today are packed with fakers and thieves at the helm. If you go to a different kind, and you think I have a good chance of not getting thrown out, please, by all means, drop me a note.

Remember, I've been around the block and have gotten thrown out of three already. Plus, I've come to love being a street person, looking for Jesus in every person I meet.

I am going to share with you a heartfelt letter from a friend in the next chapter. His letter, both articulate and eloquent, hits dead center in questioning the nature and definition of "sin."

I think he speaks for so many of us.

Chapter Two

"What the Eye Doesn't See"
By Steve West

Sin. A word we all think we can perhaps easily explain. But what does it mean? It may be easily answered by stating that sin is any thought or action that defies God's law. The obvious solution is to not defy God's law. Resist temptations of the flesh in whatever form and have faith in the Lord. Strive for perfection (unachievable) and lead a good life (only God is good). We are all sinners to some degree, and none of us is sin free.

It is quite a contentious subject and has always been a thorny subject to me personally. If we adhered to the saying, "let he who is without sin cast the first stone," there would never in the history of mankind be any stones cast, and we would live in a perfect society. If only...

I must briefly add here that I have no real answers, only the one that I have just stated, and perhaps that is the only answer. I do have many questions however. Perhaps that is due to my lack of strength, willpower, faith, or whatever term we can use, or all.

I must also be honest here and let the reader know that established religion does not play a massive role in my life. But like many other people I have an "itch" if you like, about the whole subject. I do believe there is something more to life than birth, life, and death and instead of there being nothing either side of these things apart from the chemistry that we are formed from, there is something spiritual and special.

So, it is an itch that I often have to scratch at to try and gain understanding. Allow me also to say that the thought of returning to "stardust" isn't something that scares me particularly. What does worry me though is that I could be condemning myself to something unexplainable after this human existence is spent.

So, returning to the theme, "sin." The word troubles me. The word distracts me. It bothers me. Why? I like to think I live a good and honest existence. I detest violence and hateful acts. But they are extreme acts. What about subtle things that Humans do? It's easy for us to determine visual happenings, such as people stealing, bullying, hurting, terrorizing, killing, etc. But what about people who never do any of these things but in their minds don't condemn those who do, or it doesn't bother them, or perhaps may even do such things themselves if they knew they could get away with it?

In a religious sense, God knows everything. There is no hiding place, no deception available, but we, as mere mortals have no such insight, so we can never tell. How about the men or women who never cheat on their spouses? That is excellent, of course. But what if they thought about doing so? They are coveting their neighbor's wife as it were? Adultery is in their mind, even if it is never played out. But, according to Christ, it is sin nevertheless.

My point here is, temptation is like a worm eating into the brain. It can be resisted by will power and faith, but the sin is still there. It just doesn't put itself on display. I used this example because it's possibly the most prolific one that occurs in everyday living. But it can apply to anything that we are tempted by, but resist. We can hide our sins easily, but nevertheless we still sin.

An even worse thing in my opinion are the people who actually do bad (according to the Christian culture) things, but every Sunday turn up in church for the wafer and wine and believe that makes everything okay. Or is it just for show? Surely this is terrible in God's eyes? None of us is perfect, even though some people strive for it more than others. To pretend we are good human beings but in fact are amongst the worst sinners is beyond comprehension to my mind.

So, my question is a simple one, but at the same time throws up contradictions and complications. It's obvious we are all sinners to a lesser or higher degree, but how do we determine if we are living a good life? I know many people who I would consider good people and are lovely human beings, but I know for a fact in a biblical sense would never enter Heaven because they lead normal, everyday lives.

Is the answer then to live abnormal lives? Many folk play lotteries and gambling games, even if it's just a scratch card. We live in a capitalist society, which in my eyes is a good thing. But is wanting to live a life of wealth sinful? I admit I dream, perhaps even fantasize, about being wealthy. I also dream about giving much away in a philanthropic way to help other people with their dreams. So perhaps I am sinning to give other folk the opportunity to sin. According to the Bible, if we are wealthy, we should give our wealth away to those in need. This confuses me greatly and also begs the question why so many religious leaders and evangelists have fabulous wealth. My mind boggles.

Now I am going to touch on a subject that may make many readers very uncomfortable, but unfortunately is a major issue in society and is also growing: The Porn Industry. Please keep reading...

You may think that something like this doesn't belong in a Christian writing book, but I believe it is exactly the kind of issue that needs addressing. If you believe that porn is only a small problem in society, you would be very wrong. If you believe that watching porn is sinful, and is the work of Satan, then our world has a major problem. Literally millions of people in the USA alone visit porn sites every day. It is more popular now than it has ever been, and it's growing. I will decline to mention which are the most popular categories that are watched, but it isn't pleasant reading.

My point in mentioning this subject is that even though countless number of people watch porn as an everyday "normal" activity, only a tiny percentage actually try and act out what they see. Are they all sinners for taking part in such viewing? Many people would say no, as it's a normal part of life in our society now. Some people may say "yes," but in actuality do it themselves. Obviously, there are still many people who would never watch it or partake in viewing, but it's difficult to know who they are, which brings me back to the point that just because people display they are religious and have faith, this doesn't always ring true.

I live in Britain, and we have many problems too. Apart from social divides, which are huge, political divides are having an adverse effect on society, and I know it's the same in the USA. The hatred is tangible between differing viewpoints, and politics is so divisive at this time. It almost feels deliberate. Hypocrisy is rife, and lying seems to be an acceptable and acknowledged pastime. It is sin on a huge scale; a mass brainwashing, if you please.

The days of "Love Thy Neighbour" have almost long gone, and it is a case of loving the people you know, liking some others, and the rest of society can go to hell if they don't agree with your way of thinking. It is awful. How can we bring love, compassion, and caring back into society? It looks difficult. I actually believe it is by design, but that's a different discussion for another time.

Hatred, in my opinion, is a major sin, because it leads to many bad things that are happening in the world. If we can remove hatred, we remove many problems.

Let me go back to the religious view. Is Satan winning with his temptations? Are people sinning more now than they ever were? Is it easier to be tempted now because of the internet and social media?

I would like to believe that God has our backs on this and understands the pressures of our everyday lives and what we are exposed to. I would love to understand what God really wants from us. The Ten Commandments are useful, but I think barely scratch the surface of what is happening in the modern world. The attitude today, in the Western cultures at least, is that we are liberated and have freedom of speech, thoughts, and actions. But perhaps the "joys" of life that we can or do experience, rather than setting us free, are conversely trapping us, binding our souls to an inescapable destiny.

I think we need to know what "sin" really is and what we can do about it in our own lives. How do we escape from sinning, when we know that it is impossible not to sin, and how do we take control?

Redemption is a wonderful idea, and it surely works for many, but are most of us totally lost? Are we damned? Can we be saved? Nearly all of our sins can be forgiven, for surely that is why Christ made the ultimate sacrifice.

It is something that most of us take for granted.

We look at the imagery of Christ suffering and dying on the cross and for some it may mean nothing, for some it brings out feelings of sadness or humility. But how many of us feel shame? How many of us feel angry and sick that, because we are sinners, we were (and are) responsible for the suffering and torturous agony of this Man? The truth of it is, it was a terrible thing, and I personally abhor the idea that someone else should suffer for my sins.

We should also be in awe of the bravery it took to do such a thing. I hope it was worth it for most people that He did such a thing.

So, my final thoughts on this (for now) are this: We all sin because it is the human condition.

But is the "real sin" when we are aware that we are repeatedly doing so, probably hurting someone in the process, yet doing so anyway, unashamedly. I know that blasphemy and denial of the Holy Spirit are deemed the unpardonable sin in the religious context, but without religion does sin even exist?

They are intertwined, and it is and has been a power struggle between good and evil since time immemorial. Sin, in my opinion, can never be completely overcome but can be physically controlled.

However, controlling the mind is a different story. But we can ALL be better. Whether religious or not, we can all improve who and what we are, and then we can only hope that God gives us His Grace.

Flipping Tables - Part One: What Is Sin?

Steve West says, "I have been retired for a year now and it still feels strange. I worked in a school and I miss it dearly. My life consists of my family, my beautiful and funny granddaughter Thea and a few special friends. I am a gardening addict! I love life."

Chapter Three

Remembering

Everyone's story is different; it doesn't matter.
We all are born into this world blameless babies;
every one of us given the beautiful gift of free will.
As we progress through this precious life of ours,
we have choices given to us.
Ultimately, we get to decide our own fate.

Every morning, a blue and white giraffe stood at attention next to me, patiently waiting for me to wake up. My little pink rose-speckled robe hung on one of her furry pegged horns. She had floppy, brown, leather ears and clear, plastic button eyes with little, black, paper dot pupils that jiggled when I bumped her.

Let's take a deep breath together, and while exhaling, close our eyes, decluttering our lives for just a moment. Let's pretend we're innocent children just waking up. Clean slates, rubbing our eyes in the white light of morning, getting rid of every trace of sand from the corners of our eyes. We feel deeply loved and completely cherished. We are pure, sinless, and safe.

We are, after all, His magnificent creation.

Did you know, in the innocence of childhood, some little ones see angels? Moms and Dads have shared lovely stories of overhearing their chatty toddlers talking to imaginary friends, baby fingers pointing and waving at the invisible person they're jabbering with "over there." Some grown-ups will admit remembering seeing angels when they were children.

Take another deep breath, and think of some of the happiest days of your life. I am guessing most memories are filled with times surrounded by people you loved. The ones who nurtured you, who feed your soul, those with whom you felt the most cherished, the most protected, the most trusted of all. Birthday celebrations, weddings, dinner parties, and even funerals – those dreaded days when you kissed a beloved goodbye, then crumpled into the arms of the ones you loved who were left behind.

Thinking back, one of my happiest days was my First Communion at Divine Providence Alpha School. I remember brushing my teeth until Mother said they were shiny as pearls. I recall every detail of walking down the processional aisle of the chapel, because I was going to receive my best friend, Jesus, for real! I was seven years old. Yes, indeed. I was going to be a nun someday and marry this best friend of mine and spend every day of my life with Him. Sister Josephine would bake her delicious oatmeal cookies in the convent kitchen while I spent the day in conversation with Him in the chapel.

Then, I grew up. We all grow up. We get busy. We get realistic. We forget. I know I did. Big time.

What exactly happened between then and now? How did we fall so steadily from that grace, that innocence? The moments and feelings we just revisited; what happened to them? Maybe we were we so happy because we knew we were not alone? Could it be we were happiest and holiest in the midst of such Love? Divine Love?

What happens to that innocence; that safe, sinless space? Where does it go? I think I might know; at least I think if I am being as honest with myself as I possibly can be, I think I know.

I think what happened is this: I got in my own way. I edged out my best friend. I left Jesus behind in the distraction of bright, shiny objects. There was more of me and less of Him. "I can do it myself," became my mantra for living. Isn't that the very essence of pride? When we fall, we get back up more determined than ever to make our lives work out, proving we can do it ourselves. We jut our chin out and grit our teeth together convincing ourselves we are smart enough and strong enough to figure it all out on our own. We sign up for how-to classes. We work out at the gym. We pop pills to ease the pain of it all.

We get hurt over and over; we hurt ourselves over and over. Callouses form on our souls. Secular shrinks dispense happy pills. Our consciences evaporate into thin air, and we struggle to catch our breath.

Could that deadly sin of pride really be rooted in that very hurt, damaged soul desperately crying,

"I am the best, look at me, love me, be with me because I am better than anything or everything else?"

"Don't look over there, I am here!"

Did we somehow forget that God is Love, and there is no way we could ever take His place? How could we forget He never leaves us even when we try to push Him away?

Let's go back, way back, and look at the first couple of kids in the garden and their fall from favor. Adam and Eve were not tempted with food or sex or riches; the serpent did not tempt Adam and Eve to steal, kill, or commit adultery; he simply tempted them to question God's Word. The serpent seduced them into believing they could become Him; somehow be smarter than Him, love even better than Him.

So, they opted out. They chose that deadly mantra, "I am the best, look at me, love me, be with me because I am better than Him. I am smarter now. Don't look over there, I am here!"

Then, came the inevitable crashing loneliness. The separation. The fig leaves, the covering over the shame of pride and the disobedience toward the One who created them, the One who loved them the most, the tears.

The biggest sin of all is loneliness, Mother Theresa of Calcutta noticed. She said, "The biggest disease in the West today is not TB or leprosy; it is being unwanted, unloved, and uncared for. We can cure the physical diseases with medicine, but the only cure for loneliness, despair, and hopelessness is love. There are many in the world who are dying for a piece of bread, but there are many more dying for a little love. The poverty in the West is a different kind of poverty – it is not only a poverty of loneliness but also of spirituality. There is a hunger for love, as there is a hunger for God."

How did we get to this place of deep loneliness and despair? What happened? Loneliness and desperation permeate this world of ours. Sin rots us from the inside out.

Some time, one day we don't even remember, we ate "the apple." We've kicked Him out of what we thought was our garden.

Then, we wonder, *"What is sin, anyway?"*

Well, one thing I know for certain is this: We are all sinners. Every one of us. We're all in this boat together. In my days gone by, God was my last resort. Will He forgive me for that? Will He forgive me that He was the last One chosen from the bench called my life?

So, we come to this: If God is with us all the time, why do we ever feel lonely? Oscar Wilde penned, "To live is the rarest thing in the world, most people exist, that is all." Cell phones, iPods, TV, podcasts, smart phones – have we become the architects of our own misery? Are we a civilization doomed to living lives of quiet desperation? Is this self-imposed desperation the unforgivable sin? Is it in our moments of despair – those times when we feel completely isolated and alone, those times we feel there is "no way out" of our human misery, those times when we forget His Holy Spirit never leaves us or forsakes us – is it in those times of hopelessness that we are committing the highest act of emotional treason against our Creator?

Anger springing from injustice, overindulgence at a Thanksgiving dinner, enjoying a lazy afternoon; none of these things are sinful. Jesus was seen **Flipping Tables** in the synagogue when the money changers would not leave that sacred space. He was angry!

Anger is a God-given emotion no different from sadness, happiness, passion, or excitement. Of course, it's what we choose to DO with these emotions that makes the difference.

All too often, the many secular humanists choose to medicate in an effort to mask emotions as though there is something wrong with having them. A fidgety child? Medicate! A grieving adult? Medicate! It's almost as though we have become a nation of failed souffles. Meds slammed the door, stealing our fluff before we had the chance to rise. The side effects of many medications include the driving out the moral barometer called conscience. Feelings of guilt and shame are ironed flat and put in the back of the closet never to be felt again.

Years ago, I spent close to a year working in a semi-secure facility for juvenile delinquents partially funded by the State. Many children were prescribed a variety of medicines. They lined up at the nurse's station to receive their daily dosages. Some of those kiddos could not feel guilt or shame for the life of them. I don't know if this was a direct result of the medicines or if it was the result of a genetic predisposition - most likely, it was a combination of both.

Many of the children were administered pills to "stabilize" their mood, others were given pills to induce sleep, and so on. Practically every child was prescribed several medicines to take every day. Doctors checked on the children, psychologists worked with them, and counselors listened to them. The health care workers carefully charted notes gauging each child's progress. A tragic side effect was evident, whispered between us behind closed doors, "It's impossible to feel God-given emotions drugged up, whether the drugs are prescribed or illegally taken on the street."

Today, drugs are everywhere - in hospitals, treatment centers, in the valley, at the mall. What is the real cure? What is the real problem?

I've come to believe our soul-sickness is the result of placing our egos between God and ourselves. It's how we get ourselves into trouble. Our pride gets in the way, we truly believe we can handle everything ourselves. There's an acronym for "ego" – Edging God Out. Do we really think we can do anything without God? There was a time I thought so. Someone stopped me dead in my tracks one day saying, "Alright, smarty pants, make your own heart beat. Where do you think your breath comes from?" Now, that got my attention.

So, what is sin, really? Sin, forgiveness, redemption - let's explore these topics together.

There are marvelous, beautiful, true stories told in the second half of this book; new and old friends bravely sharing what happened to them as they traveled the distance, often in dangerous or difficult circumstances, toward forgiveness and redemption.

I've come to know for certain - we're all sinners in need of a great Savior. More than ever, now is the time to lean into the One who has never left us or forsaken us and Who never will.

"Put on the whole armour of God, that ye may be able to stand against the wiles of the devil. For we wrestle not against flesh and blood, but against principalities, against powers, against the rulers of the darkness of this world, against spiritual wickedness in high places. Wherefore take unto you the whole armour of God, that ye may be able to withstand in the evil day, and having done all, to stand."
Ephesians 6:11-13 AKJV

Chapter Four

He's Made It So Simple for Us.

"'Love the Lord your God with all your heart and with all your soul and with all your mind and with all your strength.' The second is this: 'Love your neighbor as yourself.' There is no commandment greater than these."
Mark 12:30-31

Let's think of how many ways we can complicate this simple directive. There are eight different types of love according to the ancient Greeks. Two thousand years later, the English language has over 36 definitions of love according to the Urban Dictionary. On top (or bottom) of that, we have the fluid peeps claiming over 100 variations of gender making me remember the good ole days when Kama Sutra was considered a dirty book for having at least that many love positions. Are non-binaries those who use only whole numbers or are they strictly zero and onesies? Love the one(s) you're with no longer is a swinging situation. Obviously, the father of confusion has authored the modern mess we share.

There were 613 laws in the Old Testament. God whittled it down to Ten Commandments. Then, Jesus made it super simple for us and said to love God, each other and ourselves. There are more difficult pancake recipes to follow, yet just about everyone seems to agree a good pancake is delicious. Try to add syrup to the cake, and there's a new controversy.

Jesus truly did make it that simple: Be nice, be kind. Love the people around you as you love yourself. Love your Creator. The basics. It's the starting point – and the ending point, too. Somewhere in between, we are actually handed the keys to the Kingdom of Eternal Life. Some of us accept them, yet, others startlingly refuse them.

Recently, a friend posted this on Facebook: "Sometimes we are just the collateral damage in someone else's war against themselves." So true. We do not know what someone else is going through. Wouldn't it be an interesting experiment to spend a whole day pretending every person we meet just found out their precious little doggy, kitty cat, or favorite pet turtle just got run over by a truck? Have you ever noticed how our own personal crabbiness dissipates directly in relation to another person's pain, unless, of course, one is a hard-hearted creep.

We are wired to comfort and to protect each other. In war, soldiers are paid to protect and defend. There are "sides" to take, troops to cheer. Those "sides" disappear when a soldier is injured; mothers do not care whose side that young person is on, she'll run to bandage and comfort; the person on the ground no longer is a soldier, he's someone's child.

There are times sick and hurting people will use us and slice our hearts until it feels like we are emotionally bleeding to death; we suffer at the hands and words of others. We cry, we search for answers. We open our hearts, we die a little bit. We do it again, anyway.

My dad had this poem on his desk under the protective glass covering. I grew up reading it:

Do It Anyway

People are illogical, unreasonable and self-centered.
Love them anyway.
If you do good, people will accuse you of selfish ulterior motives.
Do good anyway.
If you are successful, you will win false friends and true enemies.
Succeed anyway.
The good you do today will be forgotten tomorrow.
Do good anyway.
Honesty and frankness make you vulnerable.
Be honest and frank anyway.
The biggest men and women with the biggest ideas can be shot down by the smallest men and women with the smallest minds.

He's Made It So Simple for Us.

> Think big anyway
> People favor underdogs but follow only top dogs.
> Fight for a few underdogs anyway.
> What you spend years building may be destroyed overnight.
> Build anyway.
> People really need help but may attack you if you do help them.
> Help people anyway.
> Give the world the best you have and you'll get kicked in the teeth.
> Give the world the best you have anyway.
> ~Kent M. Keith

One of my dearest friends ever, Verissa Walber, reminded me of this story one day when I was feeling kicked in the teeth: Jesus healed ten men with leprosy. Lepers were "unclean" and rejected by society in Biblical times. They loudly called out to Jesus from a distance knowing He could heal them.

"As Jesus went to Jerusalem, He passed between Samaria and Galilee. As He entered a village, there met Him ten men who were lepers, who stood at a distance. They lifted up their voices, saying, 'Jesus, Master, have pity on us!'" (Luke 17:11-13).

Jesus showed his compassion and love for them, responding to their pleas.

"When He saw them, He said to them, 'Go, show yourselves to the priests'" (see Luke 17:14).

"And as they went, they were cleansed. One of them, when he saw that he was healed, returned with a loud voice glorifying God, and fell down on his face at His feet, giving Him thanks. And he was a Samaritan" (Luke 17:14-16).

All ten lepers were healed, but only one returned to thank Jesus.

"Jesus said, 'Were not the ten cleansed? Where are the nine? Were there not any found to return and give glory to God except this foreigner?'" (Luke 17:17-18).

Jesus faced thankless people daily. All He did all day long was help people, teach people right from wrong, love them, feed them, and then suffer through their lack of gratitude. Those were the wounds that didn't show. Despite all of his loving and kindness, they killed him anyway not knowing He wasn't going to stay dead for very long. Rising from death, He awakened every person who believed Him and brought them all into life forever with Him. He's still doing that to this day.

I have to ask myself: Do I, as a follower of Jesus, truly thank Him for what He has done? Do I really understand and value the significance of what He has done and is continually doing for me in my life? Or am I one of the other nine lepers who went on their merry old way not giving a second thought to saying "thank you" for the miraculous moments I've experienced daily? Do you? Do we just disappear after receiving what we ask God for until we need Him again in our next mess or crisis? I am as guilty as the next person for this: Bad manners. Rudeness. Often, we're rude to the person who loves us the most, whom we love the most.

The uncomfortable truth is we truly are more like the other nine who never said thank you than the one who returned to give thanks.

God doesn't ask much from us despite His generosity. He does ask us these very simple questions, though: Have we loved His other children? Do we love Him enough to remember to say "thanks" and do we love ourselves enough to even begin to realize His mercy? Do we love ourselves enough to take care of ourselves both physically and spiritually? Do we, really?

So much has gone awry over the past, oh, say, two thousand years since His Resurrection. The adversary (Satan) has been busy distracting and distorting; twisting God's message of love and His promise of eternal life. There are plenty of convincing reports of people experiencing life after this one here on earth; the people who have died and been sent back because their life mission is not finished. It's not hard to find them. I have a few to share with you, too, if you are interested. People are weirdly uncomfortable talking about this truth. Ask around. Ask strangers at the mall. You'll be surprised.

We are supposed to love the people around us as we love ourselves. Period. No exceptions. We do not have to agree with them, we do not have to have dinner with them. We do not even have to like them. We can't spout, "Love all around" when, in reality, we're only loving the people who agree with us.

"If you love those who love you, what credit is that to you? Even sinners love those who love them. And if you do good to those who are good to you, what credit is that to you? Even sinners do that. And if you lend to those from whom you expect repayment, what credit is that to you? Even sinners lend to sinners, expecting to be repaid in full. But love your enemies, do good to them, and lend to them without expecting to get anything back. Then your reward will be great, and you will be children of the Most High, because he is kind to the ungrateful and wicked. Be merciful, just as your Father is merciful" (Luke 6:32-36).

We are called to forgive others if they have offended us. We are forgiven according to how we forgive.

We are all sinners. *"For if you forgive men their trespasses, your heavenly Father will also forgive you. But if you do not forgive men their trespasses, neither will your Father forgive your trespasses" (Matthew 6:14-15).*

Somehow, Jesus' message of loving kindness, of treating each other as we would be treated, has gotten shoved aside. So many people told me they found His Word to be "too hard" to read. "It's stale" they say, "It puts me to sleep," I hear them say. To this, I respond, "Ask the Holy Spirit to give you new eyes to read, new ears to hear, and an open heart to understand." Ask! I am so serious. He never fails us.

Over the years, religious big shots seized this opportunity, hijacked the Word, dressed up like shepherds and started bullying the sleepy sheep. Self-proclaimed clergy, imposters, and modern day Pharisees filled with priss and pride lied to us and told us only they had the keys to the Kingdom and we would have to pay them to open spiritual doors for us. We were told we had to go through a hierarchy of holy humans to get to heaven.

Balderdash.

All of that nonsense is directly from the devil in an attempt to derail Jesus' message to us. The fundamental ethic to embrace as a follower of Jesus is love because God is love. The world misapplies this and confuses love with fake piety and consequently cascades a pile of lies on us disguising it as "truth." I've heard so many of these big shots braying, "MY church is the real one. MY church is the oldest one on earth. MY church is the true church." MY, my, my. It's nothing but a blob of self-promotion and wizardry behind the curtain.

Love God, love our neighbors, love ourselves. Simple. Forgive those who hurt us and do good to them anyway. We are commanded to seek loving relationships with others; but we are not commanded to do what God would not do. "Deliver us from evil" allows us to completely and totally forgive our neighbor without having to invite them over to our house for dinner. After all, they just might poison our dog or shove our silverware in their pockets on the way out. Forgive them, pray for them. Give the problem to Jesus to take care of while you're resting; He will figure it all out while we are sleeping. He tells us to do this: *"For my yoke is easy and my burden is light" (Matthew 11:30)*. He changes people's hearts. It's not our job.

So, when we are hurting from being misused, and we're waiting for that apology, or we're waiting for that "thank you" that we know is just plain never going to happen, we are told to pray for that person. It truly does make sense if you sit still and think about it for a minute. Praying for our transgressor's heart to be softened is asking God to pay special attention to one of His kids who is waging a war against themselves and probably cannot see past their own pain. In my humanness, I see praying for that person as kind of like tattling to God except we are hoping for a good outcome for them (we are hoping for a good outcome for the other person, *right*?). We've all been there.

"But I say to you who hear, love your enemies, do good to those who hate you" (Luke 6:27). "But I say to you, love your enemies and pray for those who persecute you" (Matthew 5:44).

You've been hurt by an evil reprobate? Well, pray for them anyway, too – from a distance, of course. God can change anyone's heart. He hears our pleas. Always remember: We are forgiven as we forgive.

My wise friend Mary Anne put it this way: "Would you kick the crutches out from under someone just because you didn't like them? Because they slandered you, hurt you, or abused you? Because they stole something from you? Really, would you kick the crutches out from under them in retaliation? Would you tip them out of their wheelchair and watch them flailing on the sidewalk? It might be tempting and the visual can be terribly gratifying to think about, but you know darned well you would not do it. Neither would I. Of course not."

"Well, my dear," she continued, "the person who hurt you is a sick person. No one in their right mind hurts someone on purpose – and if they are out of their mind, then pray extra hard for them because mental illness is a sickness you can't see. Pray for those who hurt you – from a distance – and let God do the healing as only He can."

Thanks, Mary Anne. You have prevented so many people from having the crutches kicked out from under them...Please God, heal them, cure them, and keep them away from me until You've fixed them for real. Amen.

One of my favorite verses in His Word is this one: *"And we know that in all things God works for the good of those who love him, who have been called according to his purpose" (Romans 8:28).*

When we love Him, put ourselves in His care, love ourselves and love the people around us the best we know how, it will all work out for the good. That's a comforting thought for me; I've actually seen it happen in my life.

In His care, we really can't go wrong.

Be the one to say "thank you" to Him for the blessings yet to be received.

He's made it so simple.

Chapter Five

God Loves Us. Seriously

In a perfect world, we would always give someone the benefit of the doubt. After all, we are all sinners in need of a Savior. We are all sinners in need of grace, forgiveness, and redemption. Free will. We've been making poor decisions from the beginning of time; pride and selfishness have been standard sins since Satan convinced Eve that she could be like God.

History is filled with examples of people committing horrific acts toward their fellow humans for their own gain. People are murdered in religious wars, in secular wars over oil and poppy plants; people are killed for others' political gain. The tongue is mightier than the sword; people's reputations and livelihoods are knocked over dead with gossip. We humans can be a mean bunch.

It's been this way since the beginning of time; people have acted selfishly, stupidly, and harshly throughout history consistently enough that every age has been marked by it.

Pride, the deadliest of all sins, causes us to think that somehow, on our own effort, we can lift ourselves out of sin. We reach a point, sooner or later, when we recognize some part of our life is broken, beyond our own ability to fix.

Parents do not teach toddlers how to be selfish or greedy. Often, a child's first word is "MINE!" Moms everywhere, of course, think their little cherub is saying "Mom." Teaching a child how to share takes years. Consider for a moment how many sins can be observed in the "innocence" of a child. Biting, kicking, scratching, temper tantrums, me, me, me.

A friend of mine gave birth to three children in three years. Her husband worked in a restaurant and rarely was at home nights or on the weekends. She kept a hologram postcard of a sea horse on her refrigerator to remind her that sea horses eat their young. It was her own private joke, and it made her laugh at her humanness amidst the mountains of diapers and "MINEs!"

Humanism attaches importance to personhood in the flesh rather than recognizing the divine. We all start out humanistic. Humanist beliefs stress the potential value and goodness of human beings, emphasizing common human needs, seeking rational answers to solve human problems.

We are born human; not knowing we were embraced by the Divine from the moment of that "spark" at conception. We are born with the need to search, to seek; we stop seeking, internal discord develops until we continue searching for the answer to:

What is my purpose?

Why am I here?

Is there life after this?

Is there really a God?

The testimony of Good Friday gives us the perfect example of humanism. Jesus, the example of perfect love, walked here on earth among us. People, living in the flesh, preferred darkness over His Light without even realizing it. They killed Him, not because they were wicked, rather, because they truly thought at the time they were doing the right thing. After all, Jesus proclaimed He was their King. They had to do something, so they chose to murder Him.

Jesus had been upsetting the elders for a few years leading up to His execution. He healed people on the Holiest Day of the week, His best friends were criminals and tax collectors. He cured lepers. They didn't know what to do with Him.

More importantly, they didn't know who He really was when they sentenced Him to death. It wasn't until He shook the earth at the moment of His death and then burst out of His grave a few days later that they began to realize what they had done. We know the story. We all have the benefit of Monday morning quarterbacking. Wouldn't we all have loved to see the expressions on the executioner's faces when the earth shook at the moment He died, and there He was, a few days later, walking around among them alive and well?

Remarkably, even though we know who He is today, we all continue to recrucify Him with our terrible thoughts, words, and actions all the time. Think about it: How much worse are we now, since we *know*, than the Roman soldiers who didn't know? So much for wanting to see the expressions on their faces – now, I want to go hide my own.

We all seem to cope with sin in one of three ways. Either we deny the reality of the problem, or we'll say "Humans are basically good," or personally, "I am fundamentally a good person." Or, we become self-deprecating messes, incapable of seeing how something could ever be resolved. We say to ourselves, "I am a terrible person, and nothing, not even God, could change that." Then, we give up.

We deny there is a problem with our behavior. Often, we decide to avoid the whole mess we've made. When those tactics don't work for us, sometimes we'll just blame it on someone else. Denial, avoidance and shifting of blame – seamlessly and effortlessly like changing gears in a Lamborghini.

The devil wants us to believe no matter what we do, it won't matter. We're toast. What we've done is so awful, God Almighty will never forgive us. This is a big lie. This clearly is not the message of the cruel cross Jesus gave His life up on. The Cross of Christ doesn't just show sin for what it is; it also shows us God's saving response. He loves us anyway in spite of ourselves; He loves us enough to say "I forgive you completely" in the moment we ask for forgiveness for the messes we make. Christ suffered every fury of the human heart and still loved us. God's response to sin always is always to remind us to love.

God's response to my sin and yours is to love us, not in a way that leaves the blemish of the sin with us, instead, He offers us a way out of the messes we've made and He even lights the way for us. We are created in His likeness and image, and we are called to love as He loves us. *"So God created mankind in his own image, in the image of God he created them; male and female he created them" (Genesis 1:27).* We are not seahorses. We are precious to Him just like my friend's children are precious to her.

It's in that perfect love for us that we come to know, deep in our hearts, that our own sins have no power over us - when we ask for forgiveness, even in our worst moments, we are met at the foot of the empty cross, we are met at the empty tomb; God meets us in the blazing Glorified Light of His Risen Son, Jesus.

Nonetheless, this world seems to be looking away from the chance to become holy and it seems to be becoming fleshier than ever. "Spirits" nowadays seem to be limited to conversations about alcohol or Halloween. People follow the lead of social media; their heads bent over their cell phones, posturing in what used to look like a deep state of prayer.

Who even prays anymore? Wait a sec, let me ask Siri. She knows everything.

Social media is blighting the different stages in the development of children and young people, who are experiencing a distorted sense of freedom through the neglect of their elders.

Are most parent(s) or caregivers even aware of the growing popularity of "Drag Queen" story time in many public libraries? It's a blatant attempt to desensitize a generation of children as young as four years old to weird, unholy behaviors. *"If anyone causes one of these little ones--those who believe in me--to stumble, it would be better for them to have a large millstone hung around their neck and to be drowned in the depths of the sea" (Matthew 18:6).*

The distortion escalates when women and men abandon their God-ordained identities and try to adopt the characteristics of the opposite gender. Men become like women, and women become like men. *"Furthermore, just as they did not think it worthwhile to retain the knowledge of God, so God gave them over to a depraved mind, so that they do what ought not to be done. They have become filled with every kind of wickedness, evil, greed and depravity. They are full of envy, murder, strife, deceit and malice. They are gossips, slanderers, God-haters, insolent, arrogant and boastful; they invent ways of doing evil; they disobey their parents; they have no understanding, no fidelity, no love, no mercy. Although they know God's righteous decree that those who do such things deserve death, they not only continue to do these very things but also approve of those who practice them" (Romans 1:28-32).*

This world, in the flesh, seems to be careening into hell on a fast track, doesn't it?

We are commanded to love our neighbor as Jesus loves us. Again, pray. Let God be God. Let God do His job. Our job is to pray. Pray. *"Pray without ceasing" (1 Thessalonians 5:17).*

This is one of my favorite passages from the *Big Book of Alcoholics Anonymous:*

"... When I am disturbed, it is because I find some person, place, thing, or situation—some fact of my life – unacceptable to me, and I can find no serenity until I accept that person, place, thing, or situation as being exactly the way it is supposed to be at this moment. Nothing, absolutely nothing, happens in God's world by mistake. Until I could accept my alcoholism, I could not stay sober; unless I accept life completely on life's terms, I cannot be happy. I need to concentrate not so much on what needs to be changed in the world as on what needs to be changed in me and in my attitudes.

"Shakespeare said, 'All the world's a stage, and all the men and women merely players.' He forgot to mention that I was the chief critic. I was always able to see the flaw in every person, every situation. And I was always glad to point it out, because I knew you wanted perfection, just as I did. A.A. and acceptance have taught me that there is a bit of good

in the worst of us and a bit of bad in the best of us; that we are all children of God and we each have a right to be here. When I complain about me or about you, I am complaining about God's handiwork. I am saying that I know better than God." (Page 417)

Chapter Six

Please

There are, thank you, Jesus, some ordained holy men and women bravely leading "awakened" congregations of people God has blessed. You will know them by their messages of love, forgiveness and redemption. You will know them because the world does not like them. The teachers of Truth are becoming less and less popular by the day. You will know them because they seek to serve, rather than to be served. They are fewer and fewer in numbers these days.

You will know them by their fruit. Oh, and by the way, the "fruit" is not the number of people in the congregation. Each person is not counted as an apple or a grape. *"Beware of false prophets, who come to you in sheep's clothing, but inwardly they are ravenous wolves. You will know them by their fruits. Do men gather grapes from thorn bushes or figs from thistles?" (Matthew 7:15-16).*

Stadiums are being filled every Sunday and some week days with sleeping sheep who are looking more to be accepted and entertained than led. These sheep are willing to give huge amounts of their money to these wolves in exchange for hearing the false promise that God is tolerant of sin. He's not. Don't be fooled. That money is not buying your salvation, it is, however, adding a jet or a summer home to the wolf's earthly collection of stuff.

Many of us stopped going to church because we got sick and tired of being asked for money, we got sick and tired of corrupt so-called clergy, we got sick and tired of listening to liars in the pulpit spewing corrupt messages ranging from phony tolerance to the fake gospel of earthy prosperity. Years ago, living in a rural community, a big-shot bishop told us we could not afford a parish priest because we wouldn't be able to support him. This wicked bishop went on to brag how, as a resident in a metropolitan area, he was gifted opera tickets and had his own chauffeur along with a generous monthly stipend to live on.

Where is the refuge? Where is a safe, holy place anymore? Certainly not in most churches, and not in schools or workplaces where prayer was banned a long time ago.

Anyone can scold, rant, and make empty promises from a pulpit. Anyone can throw wooden sliver-darts at someone, completely ignoring the plank in their own eye, including clergy. *"You hypocrite, first take the plank out of your own eye, and then you will see clearly to remove the speck from your brother's eye" (Matthew 7:5).*

Pray to find a place where the bravehearted tell the truth and offer good, holy direction.

The marriage rate has plummeted in this country since the sexual revolution in the 60s. Today, people shack up right and left instead of being married. Let's bring back the Gospel of Truth: *"Or do you not know that the unrighteous will not inherit the kingdom of God? Do not be deceived: neither the sexually immoral, nor idolaters, nor adulterers, nor men who practice homosexuality, nor thieves, nor the greedy, nor drunkards, nor revilers, nor swindlers will inherit the kingdom of God" (1 Corinthians 6:9-10).* Unpopular, yes. The truth, yes.

Let's have a conversation about religious greed. Let's have some conversations about how much wealth is accumulated in the Vatican and all the stuff that's stashed away in the mountainside at Mt. Athos. Let's talk about the monks walking around in circles chanting the same thing over and over while guarding all the stuff. So called "prayer" that is repetitive, in the sense that a person repeats the same phrase over and over as some sort of mantra or formula, is not biblical. Jesus says, *"And when you pray, do not heap up empty phrases as the Gentiles do, for they think that they will be heard for their many words" (Matthew 6:7 ESV).*

While we're at it, let's all talk about the billion-dollar cosmetic industry and certain underwear stores selling stuff to tweenies to enhance their sexiness. Let's talk about the ads peddling mascara to young girls who have already been conditioned to think looking like a little sexpot is alright. If they have relations with a boy and become pregnant, they can go kill the "clump of cells" and move on. They do not even need parental consent to have an abortion. We need to have conversations and put a stop to that, too.

And how about the gossipers murdering people with their words! They can kill a business, ruin a reputation, and they're proud of it! Oh! The power of the tongue – stronger than a sword. *"And the tongue is a fire, a world of unrighteousness. The tongue is set among our members, staining the whole body, setting on fire the entire course of life, and set on fire by hell" (James 3:6). "If anyone thinks he is religious and does not bridle his tongue but deceives his heart, this person's religion is worthless" (James 1:26).* Let's hear some brave truth and direction about that!

We need brave, holy direction – not more nonsense about how alright it is to roll over dead after being shot at with the false gospels of tolerance and prosperity. Let's talk about sin and what to do about it. *"As you enter a house, wish it peace. If the house is worthy, let your peace come upon it; if not, let your peace return to you. Whoever will not receive you or listen to your words—go outside that house or town and shake the dust from your feet" (Matthew 10:12-14).* The same applies to entering most modern day churches. If Jesus' message of Truth is not there, is not being lived by the leaders of the church, if it is not lovingly taught to the congregation – *shake the dust from your feet* and move on!

Is one sin worse than the another? No. God abhors them all equally. Jesus did not suffer more or less for the dirty little liar than for the murderer or for the pedophile.

Thunder claps from the heavens, and we are reminded…

We are ALL sinners in need of a Savior!

Flipping Tables - Part One: What Is Sin?

When we come to know and accept the love and mercy of Jesus, then, we *make a decision* to *stop living in sin*. We seek the Truth. We surround ourselves with others who are trying to do better, too; we are graced with an attitude to help others to know about God's saving grace and redemption. We learn to do this with love and affection for each other. We serve.

We try harder every day to do better than the day before. We grow in love, we become warriors of His Word. We become *"bold as lions" (Proverbs 21:11)*. We become *"wise as serpents and gentle as doves" (Matthew 10:16)*.

I love the following example of how Jesus, instead of scolding the sinner, chooses to love her. He scolds the Pharisees for their unloving, holier-than-thou behavior. We all know clergy who behave like the Pharisees. We are called to be like Jesus. See what He does here:

Jesus went to the Mount of Olives.

At dawn he appeared again in the temple courts, where all the people gathered around him, and he sat down to teach them. The teachers of the law and the Pharisees brought in a woman caught in adultery. They made her stand before the group and said to Jesus, "Teacher, this woman was caught in the act of adultery. In the Law Moses commanded us to stone such women. Now what do you say?" They were using this question as a trap, in order to have a basis for accusing him.

But Jesus bent down and started to write on the ground with his finger. When they kept on questioning him, he straightened up and said to them, "Let any one of you who is without sin be the first to throw a stone at her." Again he stooped down and wrote on the ground.

At this, those who heard began to go away one at a time, the older ones first, until only Jesus was left, with the woman still standing there. Jesus straightened up and asked her, "Woman, where are they?

Has no one condemned you?"

"No one, sir," she said.

"Then neither do I condemn you," Jesus declared. "Go now and leave your life of sin."

When Jesus spoke again to the people, he said, "I am the light of the world. Whoever follows me will never walk in darkness, but will have the light of life."

The Pharisees challenged him, "Here you are, appearing as your own witness; your testimony is not valid."

Jesus answered, "Even if I testify on my own behalf, my testimony is valid, for I know where I came from and where I am going. But you have no idea where I come from or where I am going. You judge by human standards; I pass judgment on no one. But if I do judge, my decisions are true, because I am not alone. I stand with the Father, who sent me. In your own Law it is written that the testimony of two witnesses is true. I am one who testifies for myself; my other witness is the Father, who sent me."

Then they asked him, "Where is your father?"

"You do not know me or my Father," Jesus replied. "If you knew me, you would know my Father also."

He spoke these words while teaching in the temple courts near the place where the offerings were put. Yet no one seized him, because his hour had not yet come (John 8:1-20).

Love. Choose love.

I also think it's interesting to note this is the only time Jesus was seen writing anything. I wonder what He wrote on the ground that prompted everyone to leave one by one. He had already challenged them to throw the first stone if they were innocent, so it wasn't that. I wonder what it was.

Jesus told her to go and "sin no more." I'm guessing she did her best to follow His loving command.

Sooner or later, by the grace of God, we come to KNOW the salve that cures the heap of hellish messes we all cause...it's the love of Jesus Christ.

Followers of Jesus are not pushovers playing with butterflies preaching serenity all the time; we are called to be noisy servants of God, too. Noisy, not mean. Jesus is specific in instructing us in how to help His children – all of them.

Jesus gives us holy directions with The Spiritual Works of Mercy from His Sermon on the Mount:

1. Instruct those who do not know (teach): *"But what about you?" he asked. "Who do you say I am?" (Matthew 16:15).*

2. Counsel the doubtful: *"Peace I leave with you; my peace I give you. I do not give to you as the world gives. Do not let your hearts be troubled and do not be afraid" (John 14:27).*

3. Admonish sinners: *"All Scripture is inspired by God and profitable for teaching, for reproof, for correction, for training in righteousness" (2 Timothy 3:16). "He even issues us a holy break, saying, 'Remember this: Whoever turns a sinner from the error of their way will save them from death and cover over a multitude of sins'" (James 5:20).*

4. Bear wrongs patiently: *"But to you who are listening I say: Love your enemies, do good to those who hate you, bless those who curse you, pray for those who mistreat you" (Luke 6:27-28).*

5. Forgive offenses willingly: *"And forgive us our debts, as we forgive our debtors" (Matthew 6:12).*

6. Comfort the sorrowful: *"Come to me, all you who are weary*

and burdened, and I will give you rest" (Matthew 11:28).

7. Pray for the living and the dead: *"Father, I want those you have given me to be with me where I am, and to see my glory, the glory you have given me because you loved me before the creation of the world" (John 17:24).*

Jesus continues, giving us specific directions in the Corporal Works of Mercy:

1. Give food to the hungry, give drink to the thirsty, shelter the homeless: *"For I was hungry and you gave me something to eat, I was thirsty and you gave me something to drink, I was a stranger and you invited me in" (Matthew 25:35).*

2. Clothe the naked, visit the sick, visit the imprisoned: *"I needed clothes and you clothed me, I was sick and you looked after me, I was in prison and you came to visit me" (Matthew 25:36).*

3. Bury the dead: *"And the King shall answer and say unto them, Verily I say unto you, Inasmuch as ye have done it unto one of the least of these my brethren, ye have done it unto me" (Matthew 25:40).*

God looks at every sin as equal. Jesus suffered no more or no less for the fornicator than for the murderer or for the thief or for the little liar. There is not one person on the face of this earth who will get through their life unscathed. We are all sinners. We are all forgiven when we ask for forgiveness and saved when we become His.

Yes, there is an antidote. A holy antidote. Jesus said to him, *"I am the way, and the truth, and the life. No one comes to the Father except through me" (John 14:6).*

Chapter Seven

Slippery Slopes

"Love must be sincere. Hate what is evil; cling to what is good. Be devoted to one another in love. Honor one another above yourselves. Never be lacking in zeal, but keep your spiritual fervor, serving the Lord. Be joyful in hope, patient in affliction, faithful in prayer. Share with the Lord's people who are in need. Practice hospitality."
Romans 12:9-13

Our loving Creator wants us to do well, He wants us to choose love, choose goodness, choose Him. He's the loving parent cheering us on, giving us everything we need to get through this life. All we have to do is ask Him.

Sin trips us up; free will gives us the ability to decide between good and evil. If you've never read the Story of Job in the Bible, please do. It's the oldest Book in His Word, a story of faithfulness, loss, grace, and redemption.

The writer of this gorgeous Psalm describes how our decision to sin saddens our Creator:

> *For you are not a God who is pleased with wickedness;*
> *with you, evil people are not welcome.*
> *The arrogant cannot stand in your presence.*
> *You hate all who do wrong; you destroy those who tell lies.*
> *The bloodthirsty and deceitful you, LORD, detest.*
> Psalm 5:4-6

Flipping Tables - Part One: What Is Sin?

In my two-year journey on the streets, I met people who were not interested in learning what sin is, who shut down any conversations about end time judgment and the need to change what they were doing (repentance). They had become desensitized to their own ruinous behavior, not seeing the endgame of pain and suffering they were setting up for themselves. I've been there, by the way.

Some of the more startling conversations had to do with "Guilt" and "Shame." Just yesterday, I had lunch with a lovely young woman who told me she thought the feelings of guilt and shame were from the devil. She explained since they were "bad feelings," they could not be from God. I gently explained to her – yes, absolutely they were from God! When we do something unloving, when we sin, we should feel guilty. I explained further, the guilty feelings will linger and turn to shame until we ask for forgiveness.

Later in the day, I ran into a woman I hadn't seen for a few years. Sharing with her the conversation earlier in the day, she, without skipping a beat, said, "Good God Almighty, help us! We are turning into a nation of sociopaths and psychopaths who think we're supposed to feel good about everything we do!"

How many times has someone told you to "Move forward, don't look back" after hurting you and then getting caught? It seems as though apologies have become a thing of the past; if we don't "move forward" fast enough and without an apology, then there must be something wrong with us.

The first time I experienced this skewed view was about 10 years ago. A co-worker gossiped about me, damaging my reputation. Instead of telling the truth to the higher-ups in the MLM company where she was a big-shot, she decided to continue to make it look like I was a thief, chiding me to just "move forward." Still hurt and angry about the whole thing, the higher-ups suggested I should get professional assistance because I seemed to have difficulty "moving forward." They said I seemed to be "stuck." Of course, I was stuck – I wanted my name cleared! Eventually, through prayer and more prayer, I was able to turn the whole thing over to God to take care of, which I should have done from the start; clearly, there was nothing I could do to fix the damage that was done.

"Moving forward" is the new mode of preferred secular behavior that allows us all to skip the guilt/shame part of our psyche that God intentionally equipped us with; instead of apologizing and asking for forgiveness, we are encouraged to move along, trampling over whoever or whatever is in our way. If you are the trampled upon, they'll tell you there is always medication, a handful of happy pills to help you to "get over it."

Yes, the friend I ran into yesterday is correct. There are more sociopaths and psychopaths in the world today than ever before. We have to remember this: There are angels among us, too. "Do not forget to show hospitality to strangers, for by so doing some people have shown hospitality to angels without knowing it" (Hebrews 13:2). Don't kid yourself. There are demons busy among us, too. It is more important than ever to stay close to God in prayer.

Sin is the opposite of love; it causes pain and suffering. Choosing to sin destroys us. Jesus often told people to quit sinning – *"go and sin no more" (John 8:11)*. God abhors sins for the simple reason it separates us from Him and everything that is good, everything that is holy.

It was the act of sinning that caused Adam and Eve to run away from God and hide *"among the trees in the garden" (Genesis 3:8)*. Sin always brings separation, and the fact that God loathes sin means he doesn't want to be separated from us, His children. His love brings restoration, which turns into holiness.

Sin has consequences; it enslaves us and will eventually destroy us.

Sin will lead to spiritual blindness and bondage. *"Don't you know that when you offer yourselves to someone as obedient slaves, you are slaves of the one you obey—whether you are slaves to sin, which leads to death, or to obedience, which leads to righteousness?" (Romans 6:16).* God is the source of life, and He extends life with Him eternally to all who believe in Him.

The Seven Deadly Sins

Pride

Pride is a deep pleasure or satisfaction derived from one's own achievements, the achievements of those with whom one is closely associated, or from qualities or possessions that are widely admired. Pride encompasses an unrestrained and improper appreciation of our own worth. Pride is named as the first of all the deadly sins because it is widely considered the most serious of the seven sins. Pride is evident in vanity and narcissism about one's appearance, intelligence, status, etc.

How often is it that pride keeps people from truly seeking meaningful relationships with both God and others? It is pride that causes us to seek power and control over others, often regardless of the costs - going way beyond monetary costs.

Pride has two antithetical meanings. The positive side is known as authentic pride, which emphasizes productivity, confidence, and accomplishments. The negative hubristic pride puts emphasis on arrogance, egotism, and conceitedness. The latter is considered by the Church to be a deadly sin.

Pride, according to Evagrius Ponticus, a Christian monk and ascetic, is the deadliest of the sin because it is like a tumor that festers and corrupts the soul. Lucifer, once one of God's angels, wanted to be as powerful as God and would not bow down to Adam. When he falls from God's grace, he brings about the fall of man by telling him that he can be as good as God. Instead of gaining wisdom from the tree of knowledge, man is destined to have a bitter future.

Pride was once two sins (vainglory and pride) until Gregory the Great combined the two. Vainglory is defined as excessive vanity, which asks for the opinion of others whereas in pride the individual focuses only on himself. In Dante's Divine Comedy those who have committed the sin of false pride are punished in hell by carrying crushing rocks on their backs, unable to look up. Working hard to be humble can also be seen as pride; it's the sin of false humility.

In America, by the 1850s, pride evolved into a secular twisted virtue. The Industrial Robber Barons made millions and led an opulent lifestyle. Some gave money to philanthropic organizations to justify their sins of greed and pride. Pride also includes narcissism, love of one self. People suffering from it cannot see others around them who are suffering. Vanity is another side of pride. In America today, hubristic pride has become a virtue. A trick of the devil, pride is so celebrated today that the sin seemingly is gone from it.

Pride is the slippery slope into: Disobedience (specifically, the refusal to obey authority), Boastfulness, Arrogance, Hypocrisy, Contention, Obstinacy, Discord, and False Humility.

The opposite of Pride is Humility. This virtue in its purest form is not self-hatred or humiliation of self, but rather a deep knowing that one does not need to prove themselves to anyone, knowing full well that I can do nothing without Him: *"I am the vine, you are the branches. If you remain in me and I in you, you will bear much fruit; apart from me you can do nothing" (John 15:5).*

Humility is not thinking less of yourself, it is thinking of yourself less. It is a spirit of self-examination; it is listening to and showing charity toward people you disagree with. It is the deep and profound giving credit where credit is due. It is being a person faithful to one's word. Of all the virtues, humility is the most important since it is the foundation that supports all of the other virtues. Humility makes me admit, "I am not perfect, and I am willing to learn from my mistakes."

Avarice (Greed)

Avarice is an obsession with money or covetousness, an excessive or insatiable desire for wealth or gain. Greed, which is also known as avarice or covetousness, is the overwhelming desire to attain earthly goods and power. It is a sin of excess. Greed can further inspire such sinful actions as hoarding of materials or objects, theft and robbery, trickery, and manipulation.

Greed is defined as the craving of wanting more, a selfish and excessive desire for more of something (such as money) than is needed. When governed by possessions, this sin, may lead to hoarding, theft, murder and other harmful behavior.

In the commandments we are warned against covetousness. According to Judaism and Christianity, individuals have a duty to the community. Those who have much are obligated to give to the less fortunate. Greed is also a subject in Buddhist teachings; suffering is born from craving earthly possessions. Those who were greedy in this life are reborn as starving spirits. They crave but are unable to eat anything because their throats are constricted.

Stories about greed abound in mythology. King Midas was able to turn everything he touched into gold. Unfortunately for him, his food and children also become gold. Aristotle taught that to have a good life one has to find a balance between excess and efficiency.

In Dante's 4th circle of hell, misers bombard one another with rocks while expressing their hatred for excessive hoarding and squandering. In the Medieval Ages Mammon (the word for possessions in Hebrew) became the demon of greed. By the time of the Renaissance, greed was everywhere. Even the Catholic Church had become infected. In his Wealth of Nations Adam Smith stated that self-interest and greed are good for the nation. Of course, this also brought about slavery. Twenty to thirty percent of the slaves died crossing the Atlantic before reaching the New World. Greed gave birth to the American Robber Barons of the 19th century who accumulated more than anyone could possibly need through unethical practices.

Avarice is also a slippery slope into: Treachery (the betrayal of trust), Fraud, Falsehood, Perjury, Restlessness, Anxiety, Violent Behavior involving physical force intended to hurt, damage, or kill someone or something to attain power over them, Insensibility for Mercy (a lack of concern or compassion for the plight of others). Avarice is the opposite of Charity.

The opposite of Avarice/Greed is Charity, which is having a generous spirit toward others – a willingness, a desire, to help others, no matter the cost to your personal self.

Gluttony

Gluttony, which comes from the Latin *gluttirei* – to gulp down or swallow, refers to the sin of overindulgence and over-consumption of food and drink. Gluttony is the consumption in excess of food, drink, pleasure, or possessions.

Gluttony is defined as the excessive desire to eat or drink. The Greeks worshipped the human body and took pleasure in eating. The Roman elite threw decadent banquets and pigged out on exotic foods. During drunken orgies, they would binge and purge to the point of exhaustion. In the Medieval Ages, gluttony was widely depicted in church paintings and literature. In his Divine Comedy, Dante depicted the circle of gluttony where a stinking slush falls down on naked gluttonous imbibers.

Modern science has discovered that humans may not have as much self-control as they should. The lack of the hormone leftin causes people to feel hungry and raid the fridge. Food is perhaps one of the hardest sins to avoid since we must eat or starve. Everything in moderation, they say, if we have the ability to control ourselves.

The manners in which gluttony manifests itself are eating too soon, eating too expensively, eating too much, eating too eagerly, eating too daintily, eating wildly, drinking to excess.

Gluttony is a slippery slope into: Vulgarity, Uncleanliness of Self,

Loquaciousness, Dullness of Mind in regard to understanding asceticism, Lack of Self-Discipline, Over Indulgence, and Hoarding.

The opposite of gluttony is temperance, the ability to control one's self. Restraint. Practicing selfcontrol, moderation, and delayed gratification are the hallmarks of temperance.

Lust

Lust is an overly strong sexual desire; or a strong passionate desire resulting from turning a blind eye on morality and acting on temptations. *"The acts of the flesh are obvious: sexual immorality, impurity and debauchery; idolatry and witchcraft; hatred, discord, jealousy, fits of rage, selfish ambition, dissensions, factions and envy; drunkenness, orgies, and the like. I warn you, as I did before, that those who live like this will not inherit the kingdom of God" (Galatians 5:19-21).*

According to His Word, sexuality is a gift and not inherently impure in itself. *"It is God's will that you should be sanctified: that you should avoid sexual immorality; that each of you should learn to control your own body in a way that is holy and honorable, not in passionate lust like the pagans, who do not know God" (1 Thessalonians 4:3-5).*

Defined properly lust is an intense wanting for any object or person, an overwhelming desire or craving. It can be lust for sex, money, power, and even food. But lust is mainly regarded as craving for sex. Lust, however, was celebrated in ancient civilizations. The Greeks depicted sexual acts and phallic symbols in artistic forms. Sex was part of their pagan religion. The word orgy actually meant "sacred ritual." The Romans also worshipped sexuality. In India, the Kama Sutra depicts 64 sexual positions.

In the Old Testament, however, two of God's commandments speak against lust: *"Thou shalt not commit adultery" (Exodus 20:14)* and *"Thou shalt not covet they neighbor's wife" (Exodus 20:17).* In the New Testament, Jesus also speaks against lust and fornicators. In Buddhism it is believed that suffering is caused by lust.

Sexual desire is good and considered part of God's plan. Fornication and adultery are sins that have dire consequences in the afterlife. Unfaithfulness causes great pain in this life, breaking hearts, and destroying marriages.

Lust refers to the impure thoughts and actions that misuse that gift, deviating from God's law and intentions for us. Lust is a slippery slope into Thoughtlessness (no consideration for the feelings or boundaries of others), Unfaithfulness, Impulsiveness, Smugness and Feelings of Superiority, Addiction to Pornography, Prostitution, Fornication, Adultery, Bestiality, Rape, Incest, and Human/Child Trafficking. Lust is a blatant and obvious hatred of God's love of His Creation.

Chastity, the opposite of Lust, allows us to be unhindered by worldly desires. Chastity gives us the ability to overcome temptation and have self-discipline. The manifestation of this virtue is not bred from the lack of temptation; rather, making a purposeful decision to better oneself instead of giving in and doing something that is morally wrong. Chastity encourages the practice of courtly love and friendship without physical sexual activity before marriage. Chastity calls for purity in all forms; cleanliness through good health and hygiene. A chaste person is honest with oneself, one's family, one's friends, and to all of humanity, embracing a moral wholesomeness and achieving purity throughout the course of his or her life. Chastity gives us the ability to stay focused and to refrain from being distracted and influenced by hostility, temptation, or corruption.

Sloth

Sloth is often described simply as the sin of laziness. However, while this is part of the manifestation of sloth, the central problem with sloth as a capital sin is spiritual laziness. Sloth is an aversion to seeking the spiritual disciplines which include: prayer, bible study, and working the corporal and spiritual works of mercy.

Sloth is a translation from the Latin "acedia" which means without care. It first referred to religious person who became indifferent to their obligation to God. Those afflicted by acedia show lack of feeling toward other people. They become bored and apathetic and are indifferent to work. They are lazy, indolent, and idle.

Acedia was accompanied by tristitia, which meant sadness or despair. Gregory the Great combined the two as one sin and it became sloth. Ancient civilizations denounced those who were too lazy to work. The Old Testament likewise speaks against laziness. In his psalms, Solomon praises the ant because it works so hard. Work is what kept people fed, and he who didn't work didn't eat. This was a moral for many societies.

Tristitia, another side of sloth, means despair, the antithesis of faith, when people turn away from the life that God had intended for them. In 500 B.C., however, Hippocrates, the father of medicine, called the affliction melancholia and considered it a disease. He defined it as an imbalance of bodily fluids.

In the Medieval Ages it was believed that depression was caused by an invasion of the soul and that it was the work of the devil. In Psalm 91 it was called the noonday demon, which had to be exorcised. Dante saw acedia as an impediment to love. As he travels to hell he encounters the wrathful fighting each other in the River Styx while slothful people lie gurgling in the water.

Dorothy Sayers, English writer and poet, describes the slothful as one "who believes in nothing, cares for nothing, seeks to know nothing, interferes with nothing, enjoys nothing, hates nothing, finds purpose in nothing, lives for nothing, and remains alive because there is nothing for which it will die."

Sloth is a slippery slope into: Malice, Spite, Faintheartedness, Timidness, Cowardice, Sluggishness, and Wandering of the Mind, Spiritual Apathy, and Indolence.

The opposite of sloth is diligence, the ability to be steadfast and focused on the completion of tasks at hand. Despite any problems that surface, one with this virtue stays true to the finish line in accomplishing their goal, and stays true to their beliefs. If there is work to be done, diligent people will be the ones to finish the task properly. The virtue of diligence allows us to stay true to one's convictions at all times, especially when no one else is watching. Diligent people have integrity. You can count on their word as gold.

Envy

The sin of envy is more than merely one person wanting what another person has; the sin of envy means one feels unjustified sorrow and distress about the good fortune of someone else. The law of love leads us to rejoice in the good fortune of our neighbor, jealousy is a contradiction to this.

Envy is defined as a feeling of discontented or resentful longing aroused by someone else's possessions, qualities, or luck, desire to have a quality, possession, or other desirable attribute belonging to someone else. It manifests itself as a feeling of resentment a person experiences when he or she lacks talent or possessions that another has in virtue or possessions.

In Greek and Roman mythology, the goddesses Nemesis and Invidia represent envy. The goddesses poison everything they touch. What Envy cannot possess, she destroys.

Some Christian theologians believe that Satan (the fallen angel) was expelled from heaven because he was envious of Adam and Eve. The Old Testament has numerous stories of the treachery caused by envy: Cain was envious of his brother Abel because God preferred his gifts. Ishmael was resented and mocked by his brother Isaac because he was Abraham's favorite son. Esau resented Jacob. Saul was so jealous of David that he attempted to kill him.

In his Divine Comedy, Dante paints spirits of envious creatures wandering a wasteland with their eyes sewn shut. Some civilizations have actually given in to envy. In Germany, the concept of envy is expressed in one word, "schadenfreude," which literally means "the feeling of being joyous when others are miserable or suffering or have lost something."

In ancient Greece when the elite were envious of someone, they would write the person's name on a piece of shard and cast their votes to ostracize them. The ostracized would have to leave Athens for 10 years.

Envy was a subject in Snow White; the envious queen in this Grimm fairy tale turned yellow and green with envy. Cinderella had three stepsisters who envied her looks. According to demonologists, envy has the face of a demon, his name is Leviathan, a giant sea monster that only God can control.

During the French revolution the poor, envious of the aristocrats, gave themselves reason to behead them in the name of equality. By doing so, they attempted to get rid of envy but failed since it is a human emotion that lives within all of us until we are released from its deadly grip on our lives.

Today, ads promote envy. Buy such and such a car and you will be the envy of the world. We seem to live in an "envy culture."

Envy is a slippery slope into: Gossip, Detraction (which is reducing or taking away worth or value of a person or thing), Malicious Feelings toward Neighbor's Successes, and Blind Jealousy over other's prosperity or admiration.

Compassion is the opposite of envy. Compassion offers a sympathetic consciousness of others' distress together with a desire to alleviate it. Whether times are good or tough, those holding this virtue true to heart will look for ways to help others. Fred Rogers, of "Mr. Roger's Neighborhood," often told this story about when he was a boy and would see scary things on the news: "My mother would say to me, 'Look for the helpers. You will always find people who are helping.' To this day, especially in times of disaster, I remember my mother's words, and I am always comforted by realizing that there are still so many helpers – so many caring people in this world." Compassionate people have empathy without prejudice or resentment, they are unselfish in their love for others; they inspire kindness and compassion in others.

Wrath

Wrath is defined as uncontrollable feelings of anger, hostility, and even hatred. Wrath springs from indignation, the annoyance that is provoked by what is perceived to be unfair. Wrath produces the strong desire for vengeance. Anger itself is not considered a sin in most religions. If we lose control of our anger, it turns to wrath, and we take vengeance on an innocent person, then it turns into a sin.

It is an abomination for one person to kill another person. The fifth commandment directs us not to kill. In the New Testament, King Herod is enraged when he hears that a child born in Bethlehem would become king. He has his soldiers kill every baby boy under two years of age. Such an act of rage was demonic. In the New Testament, Satan emerges as the source of wrath and vengeance.

So, what are humans supposed to do with our anger? Jesus teaches us how to use our God-given emotion of anger and instructs us to avoid wrath. "Be angry and do not sin; do not let the sun go down on your anger" (Ephesians 4:26). He directs us to turn the other cheek and to not resist evil, "But I tell you, do not resist an evil person. If anyone slaps you on the right cheek, turn to them the other cheek also" (Matthew 5:39).

Even as He died on the cross, He asks God to forgive His killers. All religions condemn vengeance as an abomination. Man will find any justification to avenge himself either through religion, nationalism, or personal reason. Christ and other teachers ask us to rise above our anger. "Beloved, do not avenge yourselves, but rather give place to wrath; for it is written, 'Vengeance is Mine, I will repay' says the Lord" (Romans 12:19).

The definition of *anger* is "a strong feeling of displeasure or hostility." This is in direct contrast to *wrath* defined as "uncontrollable feelings of anger, hostility, and even hatred."

Its ethical severity depends upon the act of retaliation and the extent of the passion. When these are in conformity with the elements of balanced reason, then it is "anger" and not "wrath." This is one reason that the Apostle Paul can faithfully say *"Be ye angry, and sin not" (Ephesians 4:26)*. We are called to be angry in cases of injustice or immorality.

There is nothing wrong with getting angry! Jesus **TIPPED TABLES** in anger!

"When it was almost time for the Jewish Passover, Jesus went up to Jerusalem. In the temple courts he found people selling cattle, sheep and doves, and others sitting at tables exchanging money. So he made a whip out of cords, and drove all from the temple courts, both sheep and cattle; he scattered the coins of the money changers and overturned their tables. To those who sold doves he said, "Get these out of here! Stop turning my Father's house into a market." (John 2:13-16 NIV).

Anger becomes sinful when it is sought to wreak vengeance upon one who has not deserved it, or to a greater extent than it has been deserved, or in conflict with the dispositions of law, or from an improper motive contrary to justice and charity. Because anger can be just, and due to the common usage of the word anger, anger is often confused with the sin of wrath. Wrath is a slippery slope into: Blasphemy, Quarrels, lack of Forgiveness.

Patience is the opposite of Wrath, possessing the ability to be peaceful in attaining goals. Patience incorporates the willingness to forgive and show mercy. Patience as a virtue endorses stability, rejects revenge, and accept the faults of others. Patient people resolve conflicts and injustice peacefully, as opposed to resorting to violence. Mercy and grace go together hand in hand with patience and perseverance.

We are all sinners in need of forgiveness and redemption. *"If we confess our sins, he is faithful and just and will forgive us our sins and purify us from all unrighteousness. If we claim to be without sin, we deceive ourselves and the truth is not in us" (1 John 1:8-10).*

When we get over ourselves and realize we need God's help to get through this life, we change. Our hearts change. We…

Repent

1.: to turn from sin and dedicate oneself to the amendment of one's life

2. a : to feel regret or contrition

   b : to change one's mind

Then, we turn to the one who is the source of Holiness and make a commitment, continually working to become holy.

One of the fondest memories I have of my dad is being in the car with him, gabbing together while driving the beautiful hillsides of western Pennsylvania. Occasionally, we would pass a cemetery. Dad would always say, "They're out of chances." I never gave it a second thought until one day I realized, each day offers another chance for each one of us – I really don't know how many chances I have left…do you?

Chapter Eight

This World We're in Today

*The biggest lies of the 20th century:
Hell doesn't exist, and the devil isn't real.*

These two lies have pushed the world into the realm of the ridiculous. We are all faced with challenges resulting from the decay of morality, the direct result of the abandonment of Holy teachings. Think about it for a sec: Why bother learning about sin and forgiveness and mercy and redemption if there's nothing after this life anyway? Boy oh boy, the devil has been busy wrecking the world. It's gotten to the point where right is called wrong; what is immoral is celebrated.

In many parts of the world, Jesus' followers must either renounce Him or be persecuted. The Resurrection, that Divine event that changed the world, is being disregarded and replaced with an "anything goes" religion of acceptance. "Love all around" is the mantra for the new secular religion of the world – unless, of course, you disagree with the "loving" person saying it.

Turning against parents, disrespecting elders, fornication, murdering of innocent children in the womb, gossiping, and slandering have become the new social norms. Drag queens and fluid genderless beings have become the new cutting edge heroes championing the perversions of the day.

"People will be lovers of themselves, lovers of money, boastful, proud, abusive, disobedient to their parents, ungrateful, unholy" (2 Timothy 3:2).

There is that restless spirit deep within each one of us that seems to always beg for an answer amidst chaos. We have become a world filled with people demanding proof that God is real. We often hear, "Show me some proof and maybe I will believe!" Living in such a broken world, it's understandable why non-believers and those who have fallen away would want to see evidence of God's loving mercy.

The proof can be found in every letter of His Holy Word. The proof can be found when we open our hearts to receive Him. The proof is in the calling to serve Him and answering that call with a "yes!" The proof is in the beautiful traditions passed down from generation to generation, practiced with faith and love in His Holy Name. *"Now faith is the realization of things hoped for, the confidence of things not seen" (Hebrews 11:1).*

We get to decide! Our Creator gave us that spectacular gift. We get to decide for ourselves. Free will.

How much of our sinfulness revolves around pride? It certainly appears to have been the case with Eve's temptation — believing that she could become "like God." She thought she could have all of the knowledge and power God has simply by disobeying Him and eating fruit from a tree He had forbidden her to consume.

Turning our backs on God, living in sin, and justifying it is nothing new. Let's face it, we, at our core, often believe we know better than God. Today, how sinful are we, really? Be honest. Our supposed intellectual superiority and social awareness cause us to commit Eve's sin over and over. We think we are smarter than our Creator; we think we are intellectually superior. Right? We know better. Or do we? We think we can bend the rules, we can take spiritual shortcuts. Little white lies, a cheat here, a cheat there. No one will know. Right?

Let's use human sexuality as an example. Same sex marriage is now recognized as the law of the land. Today, all Americans, regardless of where they live, have the lawful right to get married to another person, regardless of gender. No state can pass a law that violates this Constitutional right. Yet, His Word clearly says, *"Therefore shall a man leave his father and his mother, and shall cleave unto his wife: and they shall be one flesh" (Genesis 2:24).*

The World We're in Today

The purpose of marriage is clearly spelled out in *Genesis 1:26-28*

God spoke: "Let us make human beings in our image,
make them reflecting our nature
So they can be responsible for the fish in the sea,
the birds in the air, the cattle,
And, yes, Earth itself,
and every animal that moves on the face of Earth."
God created human beings;
he created them godlike,
Reflecting God's nature.
He created them male and female.
God blessed them:
"Prosper! Reproduce! Fill Earth! Take charge!
Be responsible for fish in the sea and birds in the air,
for every living thing that moves on the face of Earth."

Let's break into small, imaginary groups and discuss this for a few minutes...

The adversary (Satan) can do everything God can do, except create LIFE - that spark of the Divine. By the way, recently it was discovered sparks truly do fly at the moment the egg is fertilized. A scientific team discovered that sparks of zinc explode at that exact point of conception.

Satan tries again and again; yet, he cannot produce that spark of the Divine. It infuriates him. He cannot create LIFE. He can clone it, mimic it, and pretend to cause it; there is no spark of the Divine for the enemy. This, of course, infuriates the evil one. So, since it cannot bring life forth, it is hell-bent on destroying it.

Satan and his evil minions kill, maim, and cause suffering and death. Drugs, alcohol, and cigarettes all maim, all can cause sickness and ultimately destroy. The adversary does not stop there, though. In his envious rage, not only does he maim and destroy life, the adversary also PREVENTS it from happening; the adversary does everything in its' limited power to PREVENT that spark of the divine from occurring.

Look no further than same-sex marriages to see the adversary's obvious plan to prevent life. Birth control prevents life, too; it interrupts the divine order included in that spark.

God considers sexual relations to be of utmost importance; after all, His Creation is perpetuated through it. We honor His Creation and continuation of it within the sacred bonds of marriage. Fidelity. Faithfulness to Him and to each other as husband and wife. We can easily see why it's in the evil one's first line of attack. Our Creator is specific in His instructions to us to abstain from sexual relations outside of the holy bond of marriage. *"For God wants you to be holy and pure and to keep clear of all sexual sin so that each of you will marry in holiness and honor" (1 Thessalonians 4:3-4).*

Further, when entering into marriage, *"Honor your marriage and its vows, and be pure; for God will surely punish all those who are immoral or commit adultery" (Hebrews 13:4).*

"Know ye not that the unrighteous shall not inherit the kingdom of God? Be not deceived: neither fornicators, nor idolaters, nor adulterers, nor effeminate, nor abusers of themselves with mankind, nor thieves, nor covetous, nor drunkards, nor revilers, nor extortioners, shall inherit the kingdom of God" (1 Corinthians 6:9-10).

"That is why I say to run from sex sin. No other sin affects the body as this one does. When you sin this sin it is against your own body" (1 Corinthians 6:18).

God is specific in his commands to us about protecting the holy perpetuation of His Creation.

There is no room for sexual recklessness and deviance in God's eternal Kingdom. The adversary has been diligently at work, chipping away at the gift of marriage, sexual intimacy, and family. The evil one is desperate to prevent that spark of the Divine and will go to any length to kill it if it does occur. Just look at the statistics on abortion, human trafficking, and pornography.

The enemy has convinced a huge part of humanity that it's alright to fornicate and kill the unborn child of the union if he or she poses an inconvenience or plainly is unwanted. Every time a child is sacrificed in the womb, it is a blood sacrifice to the evil one.

Abortion was legalized by judicial fiat. Few people are aware that Norma McCorvey, also known as Jane Roe of Roe v Wade, became a follower of Jesus after the infamous federal ruling went into effect as the law of the land. She spent the entire rest of her life in an effort to reverse the case that bears her (false) name. She said, "I think it's safe to say the entire abortion industry is a lie. I am dedicated to spending the rest of my life undoing the law that bears my name." She died in 2017, vociferous in her pleas to stop the killing of unborn children to the end of her days.

The abortion industry continues to thrive. Baby body parts are sold in the black market; some of the food we eat may contain aborted fetal cells as flavor enhancers. Aborted fetal cells are used as moisturizers for skin. We have unwittingly become a nation of cannibals. The adversary has temporarily won this battle for the time being, not the war, though. It's not over, yet.

Arguments abound about when life begins. Some say it's when you can hear the heartbeat, others say post-birth when still attached to the "host" (mother). Lord Jesus, have mercy! We know life begins at the moment of conception – the moment is visible by that spark of the Divine.

Disintegration of the family unit, emasculation of men, men used as "baby-daddies" for their sperm and then tossed aside, people "shacking up," playing house and fornicating their days away – all the work of the evil one to maim, pervert, prevent, and destroy life. All the fruit of the raging jealousy of the enemy.

Spiritual warfare is waged twenty-four hours per day. This battle is not only to capture the souls of individual believers, but to silence followers of Jesus from preaching the Word of Truth.

In 1965, Donald Grey Barnhouse wrote a book about what he called *The Invisible War*. In it he states, "this is the battle for our minds, and that battle is vicious. It is intense. It is unrelenting, and it is unfair because the enemy never plays fair."

Sin is the opposite of love; sin maims, harms, murders and/or prevents life.

Sin (Merriam-Webster definition)

1. a : an offense against religious or moral law

   b : an action that is or is felt to be highly reprehensible

   c : an often serious shortcoming : a fault

2. a : transgression of the law of God

   b : a vitiated state of human nature in which the self is estranged from God

"For though we live in the world, we do not wage war as the world does. The weapons we fight with are not the weapons of the world. On the contrary, they have divine power to demolish strongholds. We demolish arguments and every pretension that sets itself up against the knowledge of God, and we take captive every thought to make it obedient to Christ" (2 Corinthians 10:3-5).

The lesson from the above scripture is that in spiritual warfare, we don't fight with politics, we don't fight with money, and we don't fight with secular means. We prepare ourselves for spiritual battle. Jesus did not buckle under political pressure by accepting public opinion as the rule of law. As His followers, neither do we agree to participate in the evils of our day.

The World We're in Today

True followers of Jesus Christ become bold as lions in their faith, never afraid to speak out against evil. We need to seek and find the same Holy Spirit inspiration that filled Peter (Acts 2:14-36) with the boldness to speak out to the multitudes.

Chapter Nine

Redemption

What is it anyway?

For the time will come when people will not put up with sound doctrine. Instead, to suit their own desires, they will gather around them a great number of teachers to say what their itching ears want to hear. They will turn their ears away from the truth and turn aside to myths.
2 Timothy 4:3-4

Redemption in our day and age is a misunderstood word. What do we have to be redeemed from anyway? When asked, most of us will say we're basically pretty good. We haven't killed anyone (yet), we haven't knocked over a bank, and we don't pull the wings off of butterflies in our spare time. We mind our own business and plunk a few cans of pumpkin pie filling and brown gravy in a designated basket for the poor at Thanksgiving time. We're good, really. Right?

More often than not, we reject the idea that anything outside of us can, or should have any sway over our actions or choices. After all, we figure we're all in the same boat; let's get through the day and have enough to go around at the beginning of each month to carry us through to the end. The bigger the boat, the more we'll need. Simple.

So, exactly what is the "redemption" thing all about?

Remember: The greatest Commandment is to love God with our whole heart and being and to love our neighbor as we love ourselves.

"'Love the Lord your God with all your heart and with all your soul and with all your mind and with all your strength.' (Mark 12:30). The second is this: 'Love your neighbor as yourself.' There is no

commandment greater than these" (Mark 12:30-31).

So far, we've spent some time identifying sin. The reason is twofold; one, so that we can know how to avoid it, and two, so that we can get on track, repairing our individual broken relationships with God. So, why is this important?

There's an undeniable pit in our gut that gets bigger every time we do something nasty to ourselves or to the people around us. It's called feeling "guilty." Guaranteed, sooner or later, that pit will turns into a monster in our gut if we don't do something about it. Then, it's called "living in shame." We continue to carry our crappy deeds around with us whether we like it or not. Sooner or later, we have to deal with the consequences of our actions. We can choose to be a hopeless mess or decide to get help to rid us of our internal train wreck.

"How?"

Some people drink away the wreck, others get buzzed, yet others may shoot up to dull the sharp edges of misery. Others just get meaner, you know, the constant forever bad mood. Then, there are some who pretend it's not all so bad after all and put on a cheerful face until their world inevitably crashes in around them and they wonder what happened. There are the docs who will prescribe "happy pills" for a price – a very hefty price if you live in the USA. There's nothing quite like medicating misery. The minute we forget a dose or we sober up, we see the mess we've made is still there.

Fact: No matter how hard we try to clean anything here on earth, it's still going to get dirty again. We're all selfish creatures. "Self" is the root of all of our sins. Me, me, me. There's no room to love anyone or God Almighty Himself when we are so full of ourselves.

Let's take a quick look at some of the most common ways we mess up our lives:

Sensuality → inordinate selfish appetites for self

Lust, greed, depravity → selfish appetites satisfied without regard for others or God

Selfish desire → lusting for others' things for self

Avarice, covetousness → pursuing property for self

Ambition → pursuing power for self

Vanity, Haughtiness → pursuing esteem of self

Pride, arrogance → self-complacency, self-sufficiency, self-isolation springing from a selfish spirit that desires nothing so much as unrestrained independence

Love of Knowledge → selfish thirst for intellectual superiority and satisfaction

Self-righteousness → seeking righteousness or virtue for self above God

Self-sufficiency → based in pride, but denying the need for assistance from others or God by isolating yourself

Selfish affection → making others servants to your wishes

Malice, hatred, revenge → reactions of selfishness against those who stand or are perceived to stand in its way

Falsehood, lies → deception of others for selfish reasons

Nepotism, indulgence → because of the selfishness in the parents, they favor their children over others (nepotism), or indulge their children without regard to God's law or holiness

Unbelief, enmity toward God → selfishness leading to doubt, then unbelief, then ultimately hate

Ungrateful → selfishness even in gratitude

Witchcraft → using potions, spells, or magic to get for yourself something you don't have and want (always temporary gain)

Rebellion → placing self above God

(Reprinted with permission from "The Systematic Theology Syllabus," MLS, Inc. p. 56)

Self, self, self. Me, me, me. We truly are our own worst enemies. Over and over, we do the same things expecting different results. When totally into "self," there is always the need for more for me – more stuff, more thrills, more knowledge, more recognition, more of this, more of that, until we are forced to look at how we got to where we are and why we still have that hole in our gut that needs to be filled. Distractions are great until we run out of them and are forced to look in the mirror.

More laundry to do, the house is dirty again, we know how to clean everything except our souls. How do we get rid of those hurts we've caused ourselves and others?

Wouldn't it be fabulous if we could just trade our dirty souls in for a new one? Start over? Become like the innocent children we were before we became our own little know-it-all? Is it even possible that we could be feeling homesick for our "littleness," that we might be longing for a way to start over, to have a new beginning?

... And therein is the very heart of Redemption.

This is exactly what Jesus did for you and me. In His death, he wiped away all of our dirtiness and not only promised us a new beginning, He also, in His holy and miraculous rising from death, fulfilled His holy promise to us of a sparkling new eternal life with Him.

Let me explain a little further. Please stay with us on this one, it's everything:

REDEMPTION is a biblical word that means "a purchase" or "a ransom."

Redemption was used in reference to the purchase of a slave's freedom. A slave was "redeemed" when the price was paid for his or her freedom. God spoke of Israel's deliverance from slavery in Egypt in this way: *"I am the LORD, and I will bring you out from under the burdens of the Egyptians, and I will deliver you from slavery to them, and I will redeem you with an outstretched arm and with great acts of judgment" (Exodus 6:6).*

The use of redemption in the New Testament includes this same idea. Every person is a slave to sin; through the price Jesus paid on the cross, every sinful person (which is every one of us) is redeemed from sin and death. Our own debts wiped away, a clean slate, a new beginning. The hope for eternal life fulfilled.

Redemption is necessary for the simple fact *"all have sinned and fall short of the glory of God" (Romans 3:23)*. The following verse reveals we are "justified by his grace as a gift, through the redemption that is in Christ Jesus" (Romans 3:24). Jesus *"is the mediator of a new covenant...since a death has occurred that redeems them from the transgressions committed under the first covenant" (Hebrews 9:15)*.

Redemption provides everything for us:

"You are worthy to take the scroll and to open its seals, because you were slain, and with your blood you purchased for God persons from every tribe and language and people and nation. You have made them to be a kingdom and priests to serve our God, and they will reign on the earth" (Revelation 5:9-10).

Redemption provides the forgiveness of sins, *"In him we have redemption through his blood, the forgiveness of sins, in accordance with the riches of God's grace" (Ephesians 1:7)*. Redemption provides a good relationship with God, *"For if, by the trespass of the one man, death reigned through that one man, how much more will those who receive God's abundant provision of grace and of the gift of righteousness reign in life through the one man, Jesus Christ!" (Romans 5:17)*.

Redemption brings peace with God, *"And he is the head of the body, the church; he is the beginning and the firstborn from among the dead, so that in everything he might have the supremacy. For God was pleased to have all his fullness dwell in him, and through him to reconcile to himself all things, whether things on earth or things in heaven, by making peace through his blood, shed on the cross" (Colossians 1:18-20)*.

Redemption brings to us the Holy Spirit to live within, *"Do you not know that your bodies are temples of the Holy Spirit, who is in you, whom you have received from God? You are not your own; you were bought at a price. Therefore honor God with your bodies" (1 Corinthians 6:19-20)*, and through Redemption, we are adopted into God's family, *"to redeem those under the law, that we might receive adoption to sonship" (Galatians 4:5)*.

Redemption promises to us, *"while we wait for the blessed hope — the appearing of the glory of our great God and Savior, Jesus Christ, who gave himself for us to redeem us from all wickedness and to purify for himself a people that are his very own, eager to do what is good" (Titus 2:13-14)*.

When we realize our lives have been redeemed, we are different – how could we not be different? We are new, cleaned up, filled with hope; we no longer are selfish brats with impossible messes.

When God redeemed Israel from slavery in Egypt, He made them a new nation and gave them a new land. Likewise, the follower of Jesus acquires a new identity through Him. We are no longer captives, or slaves to sin and death. Instead, we become citizens of God's kingdom spending some time here on earth. "Redeemed," we live in anticipation of our eternal home with our Creator.

Jesus paid a high price for our redemption with the ultimate sacrifice of His own life to free us from sin.

None of us is beyond redemption – the saving grace and mercy of our Lord and Savior Jesus.

We're including a story here that explains the significance of the Redemption that our Lord and Savior Jesus Christ wrought for us. We hope it pulls a string in your heart as it has in ours:

There once was a man named George Thomas, a pastor in a small

New England town. One Easter Sunday morning he came to the Church carrying a rusty, bent, old bird cage, and set it by the pulpit. Several eyebrows were raised and, as if in response, Pastor Thomas began to speak.

I was walking through town yesterday when I saw a young boy coming toward me, swinging this bird cage. On the bottom of the cage were three little wild birds, shivering with cold and fright. I stopped the lad and asked, "What you got there, son?"

"Just some old birds," came the reply.

"What are you gonna do with them?" I asked.

"Take 'em home and have fun with 'em. I'm gonna tease 'em and pull out their feathers to make 'em fight. I'm gonna have a real good time."

"But you'll get tired of those birds sooner or later. What will you do then?"

"Oh, I got some cats. They like birds. I'll take 'em to them."

The pastor was silent for a moment. "How much do you want for those birds, son?"

"Huh? Why, you don't want them birds, mister. They're just plain old field birds. They don't sing – they ain't even pretty!"

"How much?"

The boy sized up the pastor as if he were crazy and said, "$10?"

The pastor reached in his pocket and took out a ten-dollar bill. He placed it in the boy's hand. In a flash, the boy was gone.

The pastor picked up the cage and gently carried it to the end of the alley where there was a tree and a grassy spot. Setting the cage down, he opened the door, and by softly tapping the bars persuaded the birds out, setting them free.

Well, that explained the empty bird cage on the pulpit, and then the pastor began to tell this story:

One day, Satan and Jesus were having a conversation. Satan had just come from the Garden of Eden, and he was gloating and boasting.

"Yes, sir, I just caught the world full of people down there. Set me a trap, used bait I knew they couldn't resist. Got 'em all!"

What are you going to do with them?" Jesus asked.

"Oh, I'm gonna have fun! I'm gonna teach them how to marry and divorce each other. How to hate and abuse each other. How to drink and smoke and curse. How to invent guns and bombs and kill each other. I'm really gonna have fun!"

"And what will you do when you get done with them?" Jesus asked.

"Oh, I'll kill 'em."

"How much do you want for them?"

"Oh, you don't want those people. They ain't no good. Why, you take them and they'll just hate you. They'll spit on you, curse you and kill you! You don't want those people!"

"How much?"

Satan looked at Jesus and sneered, "All your tears, and all your blood."

Jesus paid the price.

The pastor picked up the cage, he opened the door, and he walked from the pulpit.

Jesus has paid the price for our redemption, well-being and wholeness with His blood and by laying down His life in replacement for all. That He has paid the ultimate price is not in doubt. The important thing is if you'll accept Him.

~ Author Unknown

Jesus said to him, "I am the way, and the truth, and the life. No one comes to the Father except through me" (John 14:6).

Chapter Ten

Following Directions

*N*ow that we know how and why JESUS came to earth to clear the clutter for us, let's work on how to get rid of the sins stagnating in the corners of each one of our lives. I know firsthand the freedom and the wonder you will feel when you do it. Here's the best part – when you invite Jesus into your life as your Redeemer, your life will be shaped into something you could never, ever imagine - for eternity. You are made in His image already, and you will carry yourself in the grace and glory of His walk so you will never want to live in the rot of sin again.

This does not mean you or I will be perfect; we're all still humans doing our best. It does mean, however, our walk will be so grace-filled together, we will avoid the near occasion of sin like the plague. We no longer live in the flesh of selfishness, we will live in the glory of His Holy Spirit. *"I have been crucified with Christ and I no longer live, but Christ lives in me. The life I now live in the body, I live by faith in the Son of God, who loved me and gave himself for me"* (Galatians 2:20).

… And if you think you don't have any clutter to clear, please go back to the previous chapter and review the me-me-me part. We all know that part extremely well.

Of course, we are all familiar with the Ten Commandments, which were presented to Moses by God on stone tablets. The first three Commandments focus on our relationship with God. Commandments 4 through 10 focus on our relationships with other people.

The Ten Commandments
(Exodus 20:2-17)

1. *"I am the Lord your God, who brought you out of the land of Egypt, out of the house of bondage. You shall have no other gods before Me."*

2. *"You shall not make for yourself a carved image, or any likeness of anything that is in heaven above, or that is in the earth beneath, or that is in the water under the earth; you shall not bow down to them nor serve them. For I, the Lord your God, am a jealous God, visiting the iniquity of the fathers on the children to the third and fourth generations of those who hate Me, but showing mercy to thousands, to those who love Me and keep My Commandments."*

3. *"You shall not take the name of the Lord your God in vain, for the Lord will not hold him guiltless who takes His name in vain."*

4. *"Remember the Sabbath day, to keep it holy. Six days you shall labor and do all your work, but the seventh day is the Sabbath of the Lord your God. In it you shall do no work: you, nor your son, nor your daughter, nor your male servant, nor your female servant, nor your cattle, nor your stranger who is within your gates. For in six days the Lord made the heavens and the earth, the sea, and all that is in them, and rested the seventh day. Therefore the Lord blessed the Sabbath day and hallowed it."*

5. *"Honor your father and your mother, that your days may be long upon the land which the Lord your God is giving you."*

6. *"You shall not murder."*

7. *"You shall not commit adultery."*

8. *"You shall not steal."*

9. *"You shall not bear false witness against your neighbor."*

10. *"You shall not covet your neighbor's house; you shall not covet your neighbor's wife, nor his male servant, nor his female servant, nor his ox, nor his donkey, nor anything that is your neighbor's."*

So, let's "break down" these Commands and see where we've gone wrong, and what we need to ask forgiveness for...in doing so, our personal Redemption is near. Go to a quiet place and take your time in reading them. Remember the most important Command of all:

"Teacher, which is the greatest commandment in the Law? Jesus replied: "'Love the Lord your God with all your heart and with all your soul and with all your mind.' This is the first and greatest commandment. And the second is like it: 'Love your neighbor as yourself'
(Matthew 22:36-39).

It's all He asks of us. Do we love? Do we truly, deeply, love?

How do we sin?

We don't love God, His creation and/or ourselves.

We refuse to hold tight onto simple guidelines. It really is that simple.

So, here we go...

> How to Live and Love the Lord, our God, as outlined
> in His Ten Holy Commandments:

First Commandment: "And God spoke all these words: 'I am the LORD *your God, who brought you out of Egypt, out of the land of slavery. You shall have no other gods before me'" (Exodus 20:1-3).*

Do I thank God for absolutely everything? Do I think I've created my own personal reputation, my status, my title all by myself? Do I remember everything comes from Him? With Him all things are possible? He gives and takes away according to His measure? Do I thank Him? Do I love Him for His generosity, His justice, His mercy? Does it make me sad, do I feel guilty, when I step back and realize I am being greedy, braggy or obnoxious?

Have I counted on people, places, or things to get me out of the problems I've made for myself instead of remembering to ask for His directions in my life?

Do I pray for the leaders of our Nation? Do I do my part in taking care of His earth and everything in it? Is God the source, center and hope of my life? Have I put myself, anyone or anything before God? Do I spend more time on my hobby than I do praying? Have I given to anyone or anything the love, honor and worship that belongs to God alone? Have I made a priority out of any person, idea, occupation or thing?

Do I trust in God, His love and mercy? Do I pray and worship Him faithfully? Have I been thankful for God's blessings? Do I thank Him? Have I tried to serve God and keep His Commandments faithfully? Have I murmured or complained against God in when things are not going the way I want them to go? Do I know that in His care everything works for the good and His glory?

Do I tell other people about God's love for us? Do I let others know His forgiveness, mercy, and compassion? Do I tell people about Jesus' life and death and resurrection and His promise of eternal life?

Do I read His Word in the Bible and do I know the Holy Spirit is with us? Do I use the gifts of the Holy Spirit to help others? Do I thank Him for every breath I take – for another chance to get it right with Him?

Second Commandment: "You shall not make for yourself an image in the form of anything in heaven above or on the earth beneath or in the waters below. You shall not bow down to them or worship them; for I, the LORD your God, am a jealous God, punishing the children for the sin of the parents to the third and fourth generation of those who hate me, but showing love to a thousand generations of those who love me and keep my commandments" (Exodus 20:4-6).

Have I become a slave to material things? Do I find more satisfaction and happiness in cars, boats, houses, clothing, and jewelry than I do in seeking His Truths? Do I spend more time figuring out how to get stuff than I do in prayer and thanksgiving for what He's already blessed me with?

Am I aware of spiritual generational curses and how to fight against them in His Holy Name? Do I ask my brothers and sisters in Jesus to help me, to pray with me?

Do I bow down in front of statues and give money to places that will spend it on gold, fancy things and elaborate robes for the leaders of the earthy, fleshy "church" instead of using that money to help my poor brothers and sisters who are struggling? Do I say repetitive prayers over and over, insulting Him by assuming He didn't hear me the first time?

Do I love God, truly love Him? Seriously love Him enough to read His love letters to us in His Word, seriously love Him enough to learn how to serve Him in this world? Do I serve? Do I seriously love Him enough to know His protection and mercy?

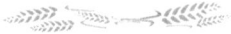

***Third Commandment:** "You shall not misuse the name of the LORD your God, for the LORD will not hold anyone guiltless who misuses his name" (Exodus 20:7).*

"If a man makes a vow to the LORD, or takes an oath to bind himself with a binding obligation, he shall not violate his word; he shall do according to all that proceeds out of his mouth" (Numbers 30:2).

Loving our Creator, loving our Lord and Savior Jesus, loving the Holy Spirit who enlightens our minds, provides wisdom and has the Power to part the Red Sea; this commandment goes way beyond the obvious misuse of His Holy Name.

Am I careful to think, speak, and live my life lovingly, respectfully, and faithfully obedient to God's laws and way of life? In my love for God, I am commanded to uphold the covenants made within legal and personal situations. God opposes perjury; He wants civil servants to keep their vows. Am I a faithful servant?

The LORD, our God, values keeping ordination vows and marriage vows between a man and a woman sacred. It is serious business to commit to a vow made in the name of God. Breaking the vow, the covenant made in His Holy Name, makes us liars of the worst sort. Do I honor my vows?

Do I have a deep and sincere respect for God and His Holy Name? Have I sworn a false oath? Have I broken any solemn promise or vow that was done before God? Have I cursed or used foul language? Have I lied and said God spoke to me when He didn't (false prophesying), or have I lied and said "God told me to do so and such" for my own personal gain?

False prophets say, "God told me this, God told me that …" to manipulate God's people. We must stay sober and vigilant and stay close to our loving Creator in navigating the treacherous waters of this world. There are plenty of false prophets in these days who will temporarily "wow" people into believing them. Be *"sober and vigilant" (1 Peter 5:8)*; they are the worst liars of all! Have I sought the help of fortune tellers, soothsayers, or clairvoyants? Do I stay away from anyone who claims to practice magic?

Fourth Commandment: "*Remember the Sabbath day by keeping it holy. Six days you shall labor and do all your work, but the seventh day is a sabbath to the LORD your God. On it you shall not do any work, neither you, nor your son or daughter, nor your male or female servant, nor your animals, nor any foreigner residing in your towns. For in six days the LORD made the heavens and the earth, the sea,*

and all that is in them, but he rested on the seventh day. Therefore the LORD blessed the Sabbath day and made it holy" (Exodus 20:8-11).

"The Sabbath was made for man, not man for the Sabbath" (Mark 2:27). Does God need to rest? No, of course not. God knows we do, though.

"When we are still and we know that He is God, here with us here on earth and among all nations" (Psalm 46:10), we come to know His love and His peace.

Do I spend quiet time in prayer to allow His Holy Spirit to continue creating me into the person He wants me to be? Do I help others to do this, too? Have I asked God to forgive my sins and have I forgiven myself? I have learned to love myself – do I truly, deeply recognize I am God's creation? Am I forgiving to others and am I loving toward all of His creation?

Fifth Commandment: "Honor your father and your mother, so that you may live long in the land the LORD your God is giving you" (Exodus 20:12).

Crystal McDowell, prolific Christian writer and teacher, sums it up beautifully: "Parents often get a bad rap. Blogs, memoirs, and made-for-TV movies reveal the ugly truths of family drama behind closed doors. As believers, we are the light of the world even in our own dysfunctional families. Our light brightly shines when we resist living in the negative past and pressing forward in our relationship with our parents. This isn't living in denial of past wrongs or hurts, but rather walking in freedom." She can be found at: https://crystalmcdowellspeaks.blogspot.com/

How do we accomplish this in our very broken world? It's difficult, that's for sure. More and more families are experiencing the painful splintering resulting in estrangement between parents and their children. We know dozens of families experiencing this split; grandparents not being allowed to see their grandchildren, children not speaking to their parents. It's heartbreaking. Studies confirm the heartbreak actually shortens the life of the grandparent.

Christian support groups are springing up across the country, God-centered gatherings praying for healing for the brokenhearted. Many have fallen away from God, becoming self-proclaimed atheists. Others have elected to bear children out of wedlock purposefully, more and more stay away simply because they do not want to be reminded of any "archaic moral code." My own daughter, according to one of her friends, simply does not want to have any communication with me because the conversation always "turns into a 'discussion' and she doesn't want that in her life anymore." Consequently, I have a granddaughter, who will be two, whom I have never seen.

It's wise to remember the times we are in and His Word regarding this growing problem: *"Do you think that I have come to give peace on earth? No, I tell you, but rather division. For from now on in one house there will be five divided, three against two and two against three. They will be divided, father against son and son against father, mother against daughter and daughter against mother, mother-in-law against her daughter-in-law and daughter-in-law against mother-in-law"* (Luke 12:51-53).

So, how do we cope with this growing problem in a holy way, satisfying God? Pray for our children, no matter what. Prayer moves mountains. He replied, *"Because you have so little faith. Truly I tell you, if you have faith as small as a mustard seed, you can say to this mountain, 'Move from here to there,' and it will move. Nothing will be impossible for you"* (Matthew 17:12).

Meanwhile, McDowell suggests:

Learn to respectfully disagree. *"Do not rebuke an older man harshly, but exhort him as if he were your father...older women as mothers"* (1 Timothy 5:1).

Patiently listen, *"Everyone should be quick to listen, slow to speak and slow to become angry" (James 1:19).*

Freely forgive. "I will forgive their wickedness and remember their sins no more" (Hebrews 8:12).

Regularly contact. *"See what large letters I use as I write to you with my own hand" (Galatians 6:11).*

Faithfully visit. *"I hope to visit with you and talk face to face, so that our joy can be complete" (2 John 1:2).*

Consistently love. *"May the Lord make your love increase and overflow for each other" (1 Thessalonians 3:12).*

To the extended family members: Encourage the estranged ones to call their parents; do not encourage wrongdoing. *"How blessed are those whose way is blameless, who walk in the law of the LORD. How blessed are those who observe His testimonies, who seek Him with all their heart. They also do no unrighteousness; They walk in His ways. You have ordained Your precepts, that we should keep them diligently" (Psalm 119:1-4).*

By showing honor and respect, we teach younger generations how to do the same.

Sixth Commandment: *"You shall not murder" (Exodus 20:13).*

God creates life; the devil will do anything it can to destroy it, maim it, injure it, or prevent it.

Murder's deep roots are cultivated in maliciousness. *"You have heard that it was said to those of old, 'You shall not murder; and whoever murders will be liable to judgment.' But I say to you that everyone who is angry with his brother will be liable to judgment; whoever insults his brother will be liable to the council; and whoever says, 'You fool!' will* be liable to the hell of fire" (Matthew 5:21-22). Murder, then, is any thought or feeling of deep-seated hatred or malice against another person.

Jesus tells us to forgive. There is no excuse for not forgiving the sins of others; in fact, a continual refusal to forgive shows a lack of the Holy Spirit in a person, a sign that they have not truly received Jesus Christ into their hearts as their Savior. We are forgiven, in the end, according to how we forgive those who trespass against us. *"And forgive us our trespasses, as we forgive them that trespass against us" (Matthew 6:12). "If you forgive others their trespasses your heavenly Father will also forgive you; but if you do not forgive others their trespasses, neither will your Father forgive your trespasses" (Matthew 6:14-15).*

Still holding that grudge? Fanning the flames of hatred for another person by gossiping about them? Murdering their reputation with your tongue? *"Likewise, the tongue is a small part of the body, but it makes great boasts. Consider what a great forest is set on fire by a small spark. The tongue also is a fire, a world of evil among the parts of the body. It corrupts the whole body, sets the whole course of one's life on fire, and is itself set on fire by hell" (James 3:5-6).*

Instead of holding onto that grudge, we are specifically instructed to do this: *"If your brother or sister sins, go and point out their fault, just between the two of you. If they listen to you, you have won them over. But if they will not listen, take one or two others along, so that 'every matter may be established by the testimony of two or three witnesses.' If they still refuse to listen, tell it to the church; and if they refuse to listen even to the church, treat them as you would a pagan or a tax collector" (Matthew 18:15-17).*

And, *"If it is possible, as far as it depends on you, live at peace with everyone. Do not take revenge, my dear friends, but leave room for God's wrath, for it is written: 'It is mine to avenge; I will repay,' says the Lord. On the contrary: 'If your enemy is hungry, feed him; if he is thirsty, give him something to drink. In doing this, you will heap burning coals on his head.' Do not be overcome by evil, but overcome evil with good" (Romans 12:18-21)*.

Jesus defeated sin, conquered death, and now comes to us and gives us life, love, and peace. Keeping the Sixth Commandment means that, for love of Jesus, we should strive to do the same.

Seventh Commandment: "You shall not commit adultery" (Exodus 20:14).

"God created man in his own image, in the image of God created he him; male and female created he them" (Genesis 1:27). The devil attacks this Commandment with a vengeance; dismantling the family unit, the foundation of a God-centered society, piece by piece. The devil knows it, and we are seeing it happen.

Am I faithful to my marriage vows in thought and action? Do I engage in any sexual activity outside of marriage? Have I been emotionally unfaithful, seeking refuge in outside friendships and relationships that violate the sanctity of the intimacy granted to me within the vows of marriage?

Do I seek to control my thoughts and imaginations? Pornography is one of the devil's most effective tools in ruining a marriage. Porn is one of the most destructive weapons in Satan's arsenal. Pornography literately destroys a marriage. It pollutes the eye, destroys the mind, changes a personality, weakens the soul, destroys marriages, hurts your relationship with others, destroys sex, and will destroy your desires for a real relationship with the opposite sex. Porn kills love. *"Every other sin that a man commits is outside the body, but the immoral man sins against his own body. Or do you not know that your body is a temple of the Holy Spirit who is in you, whom you have from God, and that you are not your own? For you have been bought with a price: therefore, glorify God in your body" (1 Corinthians 6:18-20). "But I tell you that anyone who looks at a woman lustfully has already committed adultery with her in his heart" (Matthew 5:28).*

"Put on the full armor of God, so that you can take your stand against the devil's schemes. For our struggle is not against flesh and blood, but against the rulers, against the authorities, against the powers of this dark world and against the spiritual forces of evil in the heavenly realms. Therefore, put on the full armor of God, so that when the day of evil comes, you may be able to stand your ground, and after you have done everything, to stand" (Ephesians 6:11-13).

Marriage is holy. The Bible teaches in Hebrews 13:4, *"Marriage should be honored by all, and the marriage bed kept pure, for God will judge the adulterer and all the sexually immoral."*

God created Eve from the nearest thing to Adam's heart, which is his rib. God didn't create the woman from man's foot to be trodden upon. Nor did God create a woman from man's head to argue with him and rule with him. Rather, God created a woman from man's rib to protect his heart. That's what the ribs do, they protect the heart. A wife's job is to protect her husband's heart. Marriage is two people making a life for each other.

God is specific in giving these instructions for Christian Households: *"Submit to one another out of reverence for Christ. Wives, submit yourselves to your own husbands as you do to the Lord. For the husband is the head of the wife as Christ is the head of the church, his body, of which he is the Savior. Now as the church submits to Christ, so also wives should submit to their husbands in everything. Husbands, love your wives, just as Christ loved the church and gave himself up for her to make her holy, cleansing her by the washing with water through the word, and to present her to himself as a radiant church, without stain or wrinkle or any other blemish, but holy and blameless. In this same way, husbands ought to love their wives as their own bodies. He who loves his wife loves himself. After all, no one ever hated their own body, but they feed and care for their body, just as Christ does the church — for we are members of his body. For this reason a man will leave his father and mother and be united to his wife, and the two will become one flesh.' This is a profound mystery — but I am talking about Christ and the church. However, each one of you also must love his wife as he loves himself, and the wife must respect her husband" (Ephesians 5:21-33).*

Eighth Commandment: *"You shall not steal" (Exodus 20:15).*

We are each called to love our neighbors as we love ourselves. Obviously, this means not taking anything belonging to someone else and claiming it as your own. Do unto others as you would have done unto you.

If I've taken something that wasn't mine, have I returned it? Have I apologized to the person I've gossiped about, stealing or tarnishing their reputation with my word?

There is a story about a dad who was called to his son's grade school because his son was caught stealing. He met with the principle. "What was he stealing," asked the dad. "Supplies, you know, like paperclips, pencils, pens, and markers," replied the Principle. "That's impossible," retorted the father, "he knows I can get that stuff from work." Stealing becomes a deadly generational attitude springing from gross entitlement.

"Anyone who has been stealing must steal no longer, but must work, doing something useful with their own hands, that they may have something to share with those in need" (Ephesians 4:28).

Ninth Commandment: "You shall not give false testimony against your neighbor" (Exodus 20:16).

False testimony is lying. Lying about one's self to gain confidence or pity from someone for one's own personal gain. Do I check my sources when receiving information, making sure it is true and correct? Have I betrayed the confidence of another person?

Do I lie? Do I tell half-truths? Do I try to make myself look injured or innocent all the time? Do I delude myself with an attitude of perfection? Conversely, do I put myself down and behave like a victim to manipulate people to feel sorry for me?

"Their tongue is a deadly arrow; It speaks deceit; With his mouth one speaks peace to his neighbor, But inwardly he sets an ambush for him" (Jeremiah 9:8).

"Their throats are open graves; their tongues practice deceit. The poison of vipers is on their lips" (Romans 3:13).

Tenth Commandment: "You shall not covet your neighbor's house. You shall not covet your neighbor's wife, or his male or female servant, his ox or donkey, or anything that belongs to your neighbor" (Exodus 20:17).

This is God's commandment to us to guard our thoughts. To covet is to desire wrongfully, inordinately, or without due regard for the rights of others. Obsessing over what is not ours is not a healthy, holy, or loving thing to do. The world of marketing and advertising wants us to desire things. We will not be judged by our possessions. Not by God, not by people who love us.

We do not have to worry. *"Therefore I tell you, do not worry about your life, what you will eat or drink; or about your body, what you will wear. Is not life more than food, and the body more than clothes?*

Look at the birds of the air; they do not sow or reap or store away in barns, and yet your heavenly Father feeds them. Are you not much more valuable than they? Can any one of you by worrying add a single hour to your life? And why do you worry about clothes? See how the flowers of the field grow. They do not labor or spin. Yet I tell you that not even Solomon in all his splendor was dressed like one of these. If that is how God clothes the grass of the field, which is here today and tomorrow is thrown into the fire, will he not much more clothe you—you of little faith?" (Matthew 6:25-30).

How important are material things to me? Do I seek riches on earth? Am I jealous of what other people have? Am I greedy or selfish? Do I share?

"Woe to them that devise iniquity, and work evil upon their beds! when the morning is light, they practice it, because it is in the power of their hand. And they covet fields, and take them by violence; and houses, and take them away: so they oppress a man and his house, even a man and his heritage" (Micah 2:1-2).

Do I love God enough to thank Him for everything?
Do I love the unlovable enough to pray for them?
I am so unlovable at times. Do I even see it?
Do I love myself enough to know – really know – He forgives me when I ask?
Do I truly forgive others? Do I truly forgive myself?

Be kind and compassionate to one another, forgiving each other, just as in Christ God forgave you.
Ephesians 4:32

Prayer for Forgiveness

*Create in me a pure heart, O God,
and renew a steadfast spirit within me.
Do not cast me from your presence
or take your Holy Spirit from me.
Restore to me the joy of your salvation
and grant me a willing spirit, to sustain me.*

Psalm 51:10-12

Chapter Eleven

Forgiveness

Christianity is different from other world views in that it stands by itself in forgiveness, redemption and salvation; eternal life is promised through the death and the Resurrection of Jesus Christ.

"*For if you forgive other people when they sin against you, your heavenly Father will also forgive you*" (Matthew 6:14).

"*If my people, who are called by my name, will humble themselves and pray and seek my face and turn from their wicked ways, then I will hear from heaven, and I will forgive their sin and will heal their land*" (2 Chronicles 7:14 NIV).

"*Whoever conceals their sins does not prosper, but the one who confesses and renounces them finds mercy*" (Proverbs 28:13 NIV).

"*And forgive us our debts, as we forgive our debtors*" (Matthew 6:12).

One of the most staggering truths of the Scriptures is this: We do not "earn" our way to heaven with special works and offerings; however, God does not want a faith that is empty and hypocritical. He tells us in James 2:24: "*You see that a man is justified by works, and not by faith alone.*" This passage is talking to those who "say" that they have faith but have no works, nothing to show for it. Therefore, the world cannot tell if they are followers of Jesus or not, because there is nothing to show for it. That kind of a faith is useless and is not a saving faith. True faith brings forth good works like these:

We forgive those who trespass against us.

We help others because we want to share the joy of true forgiveness and saving grace we have come to know!

We become grace in action.

Once we are saved by grace, we become a breathing, walking demonstration of having received God's forgiveness. We do not wear grace as a merit badge, sitting around doing nothing. *We want to help others; we have a deep desire to do good!*

God's forgiveness gives us a fresh start. We become beacons of JOY, enthusiastic to share the fabulous news of eternal life. We are not stuck in a human world of misery forever. We know our flesh will fall away; our Spirits are safe with Him. We walk in confidence, and do good things in His Holy Name.

The forgiveness that comes through the grace of Jesus Christ gives each day a new beginning. Our soiled past does not stain our lives forever. We ask for forgiveness, and we are forgiven. It really is that simple. He tells us to go forth and sin no more; and in that glorious release of our past transgressions, we work on doing better every day. We *want* to change. We *want* to do better.

Ravi Zacharias, a modern day evangelist, snared this story from an elementary school teacher:

He came to my desk with a quivering lip, the lesson was done. "Have you a new sheet for me dear teacher? I have spoiled this one." I took his sheet all soiled and blotted, gave him a new one all unspotted, and into his tired heart I cried, "Do better now my child."

In the same way, I went to the throne with a trembling heart, the day was done, "Have you a new day for me dear Master I have spoiled this one." He took my day all spoiled and blotted and gave me a new one all unspotted and into my tired heart He cried, "Do better now my child."

Jesus' handpicked students, His apostles, were sent out to spread the Word of their Holy Teacher's horrible death and Glorious Resurrection. Their lessons were not to spread a confining new law created to enslave people to guilt and a church hierarchy. Jesus did not summon a new batch of Pharisees to walk around making people feel "less than." Jesus, as a matter of Scriptural fact, loathed the way the Pharisees behaved with their condescending better-and-holier-than-thou attitudes. "Look at me, dressed up all fancy in the front of this or that church! Look at how important I am! Look how much I know!" No, Jesus handpicked a bunch of smelly fishermen, a tax collector and regular people on the dusty roads He traveled to be his students and future teachers of His Word. He chose everyday people – people like you and like me. J*esus said, "For those who exalt themselves will be humbled, and those who humble themselves will be exalted" (Matthew 23:12).*

You can read about Jesus' students in Scripture in the Acts of the Apostles. Jesus instructed them to heal the sick, raise the dead, cleanse those who have leprosy, drive out demons through Him. *"Freely you have received; freely give" (Matthew 10:8).*

In Matthew 19:16-30, Jesus is specific about what to do:
Just then a man came up to Jesus and asked, "Teacher, what good thing must I do to get eternal life?"

"Why do you ask me about what is good?" Jesus replied. "There is only One who is good. If you want to enter life, keep the commandments."

"Which ones?" he inquired.

Jesus replied, "You shall not murder, you shall not commit adultery, you shall not steal, you shall not give false testimony, honor your father and mother, and love your neighbor as yourself."

"All these I have kept," the young man said. "What do I still lack?"

Jesus answered, "If you want to be perfect, go, sell your possessions and give to the poor, and you will have treasure in heaven. Then come, follow me."

When the young man heard this, he went away sad, because he had great wealth.

Then Jesus said to his disciples, "Truly I tell you, it is hard for someone who is rich to enter the kingdom of heaven. Again I tell you, it is easier for a camel to go through the eye of a needle than for someone who is rich to enter the kingdom of God."

When the disciples heard this, they were greatly astonished and asked, "Who then can be saved?"

Jesus looked at them and said, "With man this is impossible, but with God all things are possible."

Peter answered him, "We have left everything to follow you! What then will there be for us?"

Jesus said to them, "Truly I tell you, at the renewal of all things, when the Son of Man sits on his glorious throne, you who have followed me will also sit on twelve thrones, judging the twelve tribes of Israel. And everyone who has left houses or brothers or sisters or father or mother or wife or children or fields for my sake will receive a hundred times as much and will inherit eternal life. But many who are first will be last, and many who are last will be first."

This is why it says in Ephesians 2:8, *"For it is by grace you have been saved, through faith, and this is not from yourselves, it is the gift of God."* It is in donning this new cloak of faith that we want to do holy works in His Name. *"By this everyone will know that you are my disciples, if you love one another"* (John 13:35). Then, they will know us by our love.

"Is anyone among you in trouble? Let them pray. Is anyone happy? Let them sing songs of praise. Is anyone among you sick? Let them call the elders of the church to pray over them and anoint them with oil in the name of the Lord. And the prayer offered in faith will make the sick person well; the Lord will raise them up. If they have sinned, they will be forgiven. Therefore, confess your sins to each other and pray for

each other so that you may be healed. The prayer of a righteous person is powerful and effective" (James 5:13-16).

When we follow God's Word and His Holy directions, we realize when our sins are remitted, they are forgiven by God Himself. *"And it shall come to pass, that whosoever shall call on the name of the Lord shall be saved" (Acts 2:21).* In bearing witness to Jesus Christ, we become new again.

So, who forgives sins? The Apostles were sent out to spread the Good News of salvation, not to enslave people to guilt and a church hierarchy. "All the prophets testify about him that everyone who believes in him receives forgiveness of sins through his name" (Acts 10:43). In first Timothy 2:5 it is declared; "For there is one God, and one Mediator between God and men, the man Christ Jesus."

Jesus clarifies what sin is, and makes it easy for us to confess our sins. Jesus summed up the 10 Commandments with this: "Love the Lord your God with all your heart and with all your soul and with all your mind and with all your strength. The second is this: Love your neighbor as yourself. There is no commandment greater than these" (Mark 12:30-31).

Thank you, Jesus. You are the Master Teacher. You have made it so easy for us to be good students. If we've hurt someone? Yes, that's a sin. If we've hurt ourselves? Yes, that's a sin. In other words, be loving, and if you aren't loving, ask God for forgiveness and start over, working on being more loving.

We are all in need of forgiveness. Jesus looked at his murderers as he was suffering horribly at their hands, and said, *"Father, forgive them, for they do not know what they are doing.' And they divided up his clothes by casting lots" (Luke 23:34).*

"Therefore, confess your sins to each other and pray for each other so that you may be healed. The prayer of a righteous person is powerful and effective" (James 5:16).

"Have nothing to do with the fruitless deeds of darkness, but rather expose them. It is shameful even to mention what the disobedient do in secret" (Ephesians 5:11-12).

One last thing about forgiveness: When God forgives you, forgive yourself!

When I don't forgive myself after God has forgiven me, I walk in false humility. After all, if we don't fully accept His forgiveness, aren't we saying we are greater than He is? Please always remember what He tells us: In His forgiveness, we become new again! It's our job to do better, not beat ourselves more. We are forgiven!

"If we confess our sins, he is faithful and just to forgive us our sins and to cleanse us from all unrighteousness."

1 John 1:9

Chapter Twelve

"Learning About Forgiveness in a Thunderbird"

A True Story

Totally relieved that the crumpled part was facing the garage wall instead of the garage door, I knew I had a few extra minutes to figure out how to deal with the mess I'd made. No one could see it...yet.

A few minutes earlier, I stood next to it on the dusty gravel berm of the country road, accessing the damage. The wheel well was kissing the tire. French kissing. I mean, they were really into each other. Literally. I pulled as hard as I could to release the fender so I could drive it without shredding the rubber. I considered never going home again. I did have transportation, after all, and I easily could drive away, never to return.

Crime and punishment. The wheels of justice were going to roll over my derriere like never before. This time, I had really done it. How could I be forgiven for wrecking my mother's brand new icy blue Thunderbird, her twenty-fifth anniversary gift from my dad? Dad had beamed with joy handing her the shiny silver keys at dinner. She threw her head back, giddily looked up at the heavens, and raced to the driveway. Their marriage was a serious one; I witnessed a rare moment of child-like exuberance. It was a happy moment.

Sorrow and fear ebbed and flowed deep in my gut. I felt like throwing up.

Life had not unfolded easily for my father. The oldest of twelve children, he had often missed school. Working alongside his dad at the family garden center, he chipped in to keep the family afloat. His nine brothers joined them year after year; one of his sisters joined a convent at sixteen and another sister often stayed at home to help her mother with household chores. It was a different time back then. Families stayed together and never dreamed of asking for outside help. Can-do was the universal theme in life.

Dad was smart and studied hard. His classmates came from rich families. The private high school he attended was a stepping stone toward college. Admission to North Catholic High School was reserved for the best and the brightest boys in the city. In his spare time, he played the saxophone. He dreamed of owning a Pontiac with the cool fins over the tail lights. Dad worked hard all of his life and never did get that Pontiac. The Thunderbird was a splendid replacement for his dream car, he said.

My heart sank. How was I going to tell him I - wrecked - the - car?

He would find out soon enough. Mother would soon need to run an errand, get in her car, and drive off to pick up a gallon of milk or a loaf of bread. She wouldn't notice the damage until returning to her shiny new anniversary gift, glittering in the summer sun, awaiting her between the two white stripes on the parking lot.

I could suggest perhaps a meteor had struck her car while she was in the store, as she shopped for a ripe cantaloupe next to the bananas framed by the columns of cracker boxes. No, better yet, I know! It must have been a hit and run, Mother. Did you hear any loud crunching of metal sounds while you were in the store? I'll bet a crazy driver plowed into the right side causing a real mess! Too bad they drove away, Mom, now we'll never catch them!

I breathlessly created scenarios to avoid responsibility. This was not just any car. This was her special gift, a dream fulfilled, a milestone. Spending the rest of my life living in the corner of a barn eating leftover horse grain straight from the old, cracked concrete floor seemed like a better option than fessing up to the truth.

The truth is, I had been daydreaming while driving. Who does that? A real nitwit. Which would be worse for them? A wrecked car or realizing one of their daughters is a serious idiot?

"Learning About Forgivness in a Thunderbird"

It was a gorgeous summer day, midafternoon, when my mom handed me her car keys to drive to my old high school to visit my piano teacher, Sister Veronica. The hills of western Pennsylvania offered weathered gray strips of country highway adventure punctuated with long yellow double stripes of caution, reminding drivers how Amish buggies drawn by horses could be over the next crest. I drove carefully, winding past farm fields of new corn and deep green alfalfa. It was a beautiful little road trip, about 50 miles round trip in all.

The front door of an Amish house is painted blue if there is a daughter available to be wed. I wondered if I would marry any time soon. I was a junior in college and my first real love had slipped away between my heartstrings the year before. I crossed over a rickety bridge with rusted trusses, saying a quick prayer to make it safely over the river to the other side. Breathing a sigh of relief, I continued on my journey.

Alongside the river were old railroad tracks used to carry coal to neighboring towns where factories produced steel. The coal-rich landscape of western Pennsylvania was dotted with old wooden farmhouses where lazy cows grazed in pastures reaching far past the horizon. Sons and daughters of farmers saw the steel factories as their ticket out of the bucolic life into cities where shopping was easy and where they thought life was better.

I flipped though the radio stations and settled on Roberta Flack's beautiful ballad of lost love, "Killing Me Softly." I thought of my own love lost and was jolted back to reality by the awful scraping sound of metal against metal. Steadying the car back onto the shoulder, I realized I had gone off road in my reverie, the guard rail catching me from falling onto the railroad tracks below, next to the river.

I sat there for a minute or two, heart pounding, praying the car had suffered only a few scratches.

Making matters worse, this was not my first wreck. Three years earlier, shortly after getting my driver's license, I detoured a car into the woods after hitting an ice patch on a 90 degree turn. My dad's Ford LTD was destroyed. I stumbled through the snow-covered woods toward the nearest farmhouse and knocked on the door. Using their telephone, I called my father's best friend. I figured Dad would be more merciful to me if I went through a buffer zone. Turned out, Dad was over the moon I was not hurt. Nary a scratch on his little chicken, as he affectionately called me. I cried, he teared up, life went on.

Oh, that's not all. A year later, I had another mini-mishap of sorts. It was a little accident, resulting in a few scratches on the front bumper. I was parked to the left of a glass greenhouse with a car parked behind me and a building a few feet in front of me. It looked to me like I had enough clearance to back the car out. As I looked over my right shoulder – backing up ever so slowly to not hit the car behind me – the front right corner of the car angled right into the greenhouse. It wasn't until I heard the faint groaning of metal that I realized the front bumper was cruelly bending the metal frame of the glass house. I ever so slowly inched the car forward, detaching the car from the metal. That day, I learned geometry applied in real life, even though I remained convinced algebra didn't apply at all.

The Thunderbird had more than a few scratches. It was a disaster. Seriously. The entire right side was metal-swiped in addition to the front tire being held hostage by the wheel well. After manually freeing the tire, I got in the icy blue anniversary present and drove home. Shaking.

When I got home, I carefully parked the car in the garage, got out and paced. Paced and prayed. Paced and prayed more. Time was up. I knew the allotted time was up. Oh, I think I wandered around the desert of my guilt for about three hours. Each and every minute in those hours lasted another entire Stone Age.

"Learning About Forgivness in a Thunderbird"

I knew the moment of reckoning had arrived. There was no more place to pace. I knew I had to fess up. There were no meteor strikes, no hit and run criminals, no buffer friends. It was just Dad and me.

Oh, God. Please give me the words.

As with any serious pain, the memory of the moment is blurred. I remember walking to the garage with Dad. I remember showing him the car. I distinctly remember feeling like I had shrunk to the size of a five-year-old. I remember saying how sorry I was and how I was willing do anything to fix it and make up for it. I remember crying and shaking. I remember bracing myself for the punishment of a lifetime.

What happened next, I remember vividly as though it happened today. Dad looked at me and said, "Are you hurt?" It never dawned on me. Aside from being terrified, I never relaxed my muscles enough to know if I was injured. "No, I am alright, I am not bleeding or broken." Then, he hugged me. He hugged his little chicken tight and told me I would not be driving for a while until I retook some driving classes. He told me he loved me more than any car on earth.

Insurance fixed the Thunderbird, and Dad bought me a big, heavy Ford Bronco to get around in. He told me he would have gotten me an Army tank, lamenting the fact that tanks were not allowed on the street. To this day, if I am driving and Roberta Flack's "Killing Me Softly" happens to start playing on an oldies radio station, I cannot turn it off quickly enough.

God, I love my dad.

Why confess our sins to another person when we can go directly to God for forgiveness?

Good question.

"Is anyone among you in trouble? Let them pray. Is anyone happy?

Let them sing songs of praise. Is anyone among you sick? Let them call the elders of the church to pray over them and anoint them with oil in the name of the Lord. And the prayer offered in faith will make the sick person well; the Lord will raise them up. If they have sinned, they will be forgiven. Therefore confess your sins to each other and pray for each other so that you may be healed. The prayer of a righteous person is powerful and effective. Elijah was a human being, even as we are. He prayed earnestly that it would not rain, and it did not rain on the land for three and a half years. Again he prayed, and the heavens gave rain, and the earth produced its crops. My brothers and sisters, if one of you should wander from the truth and someone should bring that person back, remember this: Whoever turns a sinner from the error of their way will save them from death and cover over a multitude of sins" (James 5:13-20).

Do we not go to a trusted person for advice? Do we not seek direction from those with wisdom and insight? Is it not prudent to go to a person educated and blessed in the ways of human frailty and forgiveness? Of course it is.

"Confess your trespasses to one another, and pray for one another, that ye may be healed. The effective, fervent prayer of a righteous man avails much" (James 5:16 NKJV).

If you sin against each other, you must first get it right with you brother" (Matthew 5:23-24).

Step Five in The Big Book of Alcoholics Anonymous is: "Admitted to God, to ourselves, and another human being the exact nature of our wrongs." Why do that? Because we learn how to be humble. We experience humility. There is a big difference between humility and humiliation. Admitting we are wrong to another person and changing our ways (repenting) is a vital step in healing.

In seeking a clean relationship with God, in opening our hearts to receive His forgiveness, there is a deep and profound healing that comes when we admit the exact nature of our wrongs to one another first. Apologize, correct our errors with our brothers and sisters in

Jesus Christ. Seek a trusted person for advice and direction. We are all sinners in need of our Savior and His holy, saving grace.

Jesus said in Matthew 18:3-4, *"Truly, I say to you, unless you turn and become like children, you will never enter the kingdom of heaven. Whoever humbles himself like this child is the greatest in the kingdom of heaven."*

RELIGION: "I messed up. My dad is going to kill me."

GOSPEL: "I messed up. I need to call my Dad."

Chapter Thirteen

Following Jesus

*"But just as he who called you is holy,
so be holy in all you do; for it is written:
'Be holy, because I am holy.'"
1 Peter 1:15-16*

The Beatitudes from Matthew 5:3-12

Blessed are the poor in spirit, for theirs is the kingdom of heaven.

Blessed are they who mourn, for they shall be comforted.

Blessed are the meek, for they shall inherit the earth.

Blessed are they who hunger and thirst for righteousness, for they shall be satisfied.

Blessed are the merciful, for they shall obtain mercy.

Blessed are the pure of heart, for they shall see God.

Blessed are the peacemakers, for they shall be called children of God.

Blessed are they who are persecuted for the sake of righteousness, for theirs is the kingdom of heaven.

Blessed are the poor in spirit, for theirs is the kingdom of heaven. The poor in spirit recognize the need for Jesus as Savior. The poor in Spirit know the brokenness caused by sin; unable to contribute anything to their salvation. Being poor in spirit is recognizing my total spiritual bankruptcy. I understand I have absolutely nothing of worth to offer God in my state of sin. Being poor in spirit is admitting that, because of my sins, I am completely destitute spiritually and can do nothing to deliver myself from my own circumstances. Jesus is saying that, no matter our status in life, we have to recognize our spiritual poverty before we can come to God in faith to receive the salvation He offers. I ask myself: Have I recognized and joyfully accepted my complete dependence on God? Have I been proud, arrogant, and/or self-righteous? Have I been selfish, greedy, possessive, and self-seeking? Have I sought after status, recognition, power, material possessions, and wealth?

Blessed are those who mourn, for they shall be comforted. Sin is offensive to God. When we sin, we are saying to God, "I believe that my ways are better than your ways, and I am going to do it my way instead of your way." When we sin, we hurt God and break his heart, and so we mourn. Yet, there is also a loving promise for us in our mourning. Jesus promises that God himself will comfort us when we mourn over our sin. I ask myself: Have I endured difficulties and afflictions with faith and patience? Have I truly been sorrowful for my sins and faults? Do I defer to God's way over my own?

Blessed are the meek, for they shall inherit the earth. The Greek word translated "meek" is praeis and refers to mildness, gentleness of spirit, or humility. Other forms of this Greek word are used elsewhere in the New Testament, including (James 1:21) and (James 3:13). Meekness is humility toward God and toward others. *"Be completely humble and gentle; be patient, bearing with one another in love" (Ephesians 4:1-2).* Meekness is found in the humility of Jesus. As (Philippians 2:6-8) says, *"Being in very nature God, did not consider equality with God something to be used to his own advantage; rather, he made himself nothing by taking the very nature of a servant, being made in human likeness."* Followers of Jesus Christ are called to share the gospel message in gentleness and meekness." 1 Peter 3:15 tells us to, *"Always be prepared to give an answer to everyone who asks you to give the reason for the hope that you have. But do this with gentleness and respect."* I ask myself: Do I treat unbelievers with kindness and answer their questions with love? Do I find ways to serve my brothers and sisters in Christ? Do I act like a know-it-all? Have I been impatient, resentful, bitter, unforgiving or insulting, and abusive to others?

Blessed are they who hunger and thirst for righteousness, for they shall be satisfied. Hunger and thirst are two of the most powerful forces in the human body. There are few physical sensations as compelling as an empty, growling stomach or a parched throat in need of water. Hunger and thirst drive us to take prompt and decisive action. When we are truly hungry and thirsty, we are eager to fill that need. The hunger reaches the point where it consumes our every waking thought. There is no way to ignore such hunger and thirst, and so we naturally experience a drive to satisfy the need to eat and drink as soon as possible. With our hunger and thirst for God's righteousness, we are to act with the same urgency. Those who make the commitment to God's way of life and change their old sinful ways (repent), are baptized and have the laying on of hands, will receive the Holy Spirit (Acts 2:38). When we receive the Holy Spirit, we begin to be filled with a living water that will continue to flow as long as we eagerly drink of it (John 4:14). When we look at the first three Beatitudes, after pronouncing a blessing upon those who recognize their emptiness and grieve over it and don't try to justify or defend themselves, Jesus now makes a transition from emptiness to fullness by saying that hunger and thirst for righteousness is also blessed. How beautiful, isn't it? I ask myself: Do I work on myself in an attempt for holiness? Do I truly yearn for God's will to be done, in my life and in all things? Do I thank God for filling me up spiritually with His Truths?

Blessed are the merciful, for they shall obtain mercy. Have I been merciful to others? Have I turned away from someone who needed my help? Have I refused to forgive? Have I forgiven myself after God has forgiven me? Have I turned my back on someone poor, hungry, rejected, lonely, and needy? Have I tried to *understand* and pardon those who I've perceived hurt me? Have I been indifferent? Judgmental?

Do I pray for my enemies? Have I defended people who I know were right for fear of humiliation or persecution? Have I had the courage to stand up for the truth despite criticism, ridicule, or persecution? Do I wholeheartedly witness my faith in Christ Jesus?

Blessed are the pure in heart, for they shall see God. Do I strive for holy purity and honesty? Have I been dishonest in my speech or actions? Have the motives or intentions of my actions been evil or selfish? Have I given way to lust, impure thoughts, words, or deeds? Have I been guilty of prejudice? Have I been hypocritical, pretentious, or self-indulgent to sinful passions?

Is this a contradiction? Moses (Exodus 33:20), John (John 1:18), and Paul (I Timothy 6:16) all say that no one can see God here on earth. God is hidden. But Jesus says the pure of heart shall see God! To be pure of heart means to be free of all selfish/prideful intentions and self-seeking desires. What a beautiful goal! How many times have any of us performed an act perfectly free of any personal gain? Such an act is pure love. An act of pure and selfless giving brings happiness to all.

Blessed are the peacemakers, for they shall be called children of God. Am I at peace with God? Do I have His peace in my heart? Have I been aggressive or impatient? Do I foster peace at home, work, church, and community? Have I been irritable? Have I caused division and discord? Is my criticism harmful and disruptive? Do I know the difference between constructive criticism and destructive complaining?

Jesus gives us peace, *"Peace I leave with you; My peace I give to you" (John 14:27).* Peace is also a fruit of the Spirit (Galatians 5:22). Peacemakers not only live peaceful lives but also try to bring peace and friendship to others, and to preserve peace between God and man. But one cannot give another what one does not possess oneself. Praying for peace will help change your heart. The Lord wants you first to be filled with the blessings of peace and then to pass it on to those who have need of it. By imitating God's love of man, the peacemakers become children of God.

Blessed are those who are persecuted for righteousness sake, for theirs is the kingdom of heaven. When they revile you and persecute you on my account, rejoice and be glad, for your reward is great in heaven. This is critical for today's followers of Jesus. The biblical passage continues to elaborate: *"Blessed are you when men revile you and persecute you and utter all kinds of evil against you falsely on my account. This should serve as a reminder that even in the midst of persecution we can find reason to rejoice and be glad, for your reward is great in heaven, for so men persecuted the prophets who were before you" (Matthew 5:11-12).* Jesus said many times that those who follow Him will be persecuted. *"If they persecute me, they will persecute you" (John 15:20-21).*

Before his heart was softened and changed, Saul persecuted the early Church in Jerusalem, which scattered the Christians throughout the regions of Judea and Samaria (Acts 8:1). St. Peter advised *"Whoever is made to suffer as a Christian should not be ashamed but glorify God because of the name" (I Peter 4:16).*

Is the joy of Christ in my heart, even in trying moments? Do I give thanks to God in all circumstances, or do I complain often? Have I been pessimistic, negative, despondent, or despairing? Have I truly delighted in the promise of God's treasures in heaven?

"And be ye kind one to another, tenderhearted, forgiving one another, even as God for Christ's sake hath forgiven you" (Ephesians 4:32). Jesus was in this world, He was not of this world. In living a life filled with the imitation of Jesus, in trying each day to be more like Him. The message of Jesus is the same today as it was 2,000 years ago when he walked this earth.

As followers of Jesus, treating every person with kindness, mercy, and compassion is our hallmark. People truly know us by our love. Love, as we've come to see, does not demand acceptance of sinful behavior. Our love also includes gentle discipline to help a wayward soul to a state of grace.

We sin. We mourn how our own actions have separated us from His holy place of grace. We've offended the One who has given us everything that's good in our lives. We mourn because we've hurt the One we love, the One who loves us the most.

In the midst of our busy and often messy lives, sometimes we forget that we are indeed loved by God, and that we are not beyond redemption. No matter how far we may think we have fallen away, God is still there, offering to lift us up, or offer us a shoulder to cry on. He entered boldly into the human experience and suffered both physical and emotional trauma. Jesus knows our struggles and His mercy knows no bounds. We are to remain in the world, but remaining within the world's sin is something we need to abandon.

"My dear children, I write this to you so that you will not sin. But if anybody does sin, we have an advocate with the Father – Jesus Christ, the Righteous One. He is the atoning sacrifice for our sins, and not only for ours but also for the sins of the whole world" (1 John 2 1-2).

"Therefore put on the full armor of God, so that when the day of evil comes, you may be able to stand your ground, and after you have done everything, to stand. Stand firm then, with the belt of truth buckled around your waist, with the breastplate of righteousness in place, and with your feet fitted with the readiness that comes from the gospel of peace. In addition to all this, take up the shield of faith, with which you can extinguish all the flaming arrows of the evil one. Take the helmet of salvation and the sword of the Spirit, which is the word of God" (Ephesians 6:13-17).

The Holy Bible never contradicts itself. *"Jesus answered, 'I am the way and the truth and the life. No one comes to the Father except through me'" (John 14:6).*

"For what is a man profited, if he shall gain the whole world, and lose his own soul? Or what shall a man give in exchange for his soul?" (Matthew 16:26).

In striving to live the Beatitudes, our own lives become freer from sin, and others are able to see our individual transformation. They will see Jesus Christ in us, and want what we have, too.

Chapter Fourteen

A Few Holy Directives

There is Hope for Us:

"For all have sinned and fall short of the glory of God" (Romans 3:23).

"Because, if you confess with your mouth that Jesus is Lord and believe in your heart that God raised him from the dead, you will be saved" (Romans 10:9).

"Put on then, as God's chosen ones, holy and beloved, compassionate hearts, kindness, humility, meekness, and patience" (Colossians 3:12).

"Correcting his opponents with gentleness. God may perhaps grant them repentance leading to a knowledge of the truth, and they may come to their senses and escape from the snare of the devil, after being captured by him to do his will" (2 Timothy 2:25-26).

"So then it depends not on human will or exertion, but on God, who has mercy" (Romans 9:16).

"If you love me, you will keep my commandments" (John 14:15).

If we go to a place and we are greeted with hostility, this is what we are to do:

"If the home is deserving, let your peace rest on it; if it is not, let your peace return to you. If anyone will not welcome you or listen to your words, leave that home or town and shake the dust off your feet" (Matthew 10:13-14).

"Let nothing be done through selfish ambition or conceit, but in lowliness of mind let each esteem others better than himself. Let each of you look out not only for his own interests, but also for the interests of others" (Philippians 2:3-4).

We are called to love each other, even when we don't like each other:

"A new commandment I give to you, that you love one another: just as I have loved you, you also are to love one another. By this all people will know that you are my disciples, if you have love for one another" (John 13:34-35).

"You have heard that it was said, 'You shall love your neighbor and hate your enemy.' But I say to you, love your enemies, bless those who curse you, do good to those who hate you, and pray for those who spitefully use you and persecute you, that you may be sons of your Father in heaven; for He makes His sun rise on the evil and on the good, and sends rain on the just and on the unjust. For if you love those who love you, what reward have you? Do not even the tax collectors do the same? And if you greet your brethren only, what do you do more than others? Do not even the tax collectors do so? Therefore you shall be perfect, just as your Father in heaven is perfect" (Matthew 5:43-48).

God changes hearts, we don't. It's not our job. It's our job to tell people about Jesus, His love, His mercy, and Eternal Life through Him.

"Therefore, if anyone is in Christ, he is a new creation. The old has passed away; behold, the new has come" (2 Corinthians 5:17).

"Create in me a clean heart, O God, and renew a right spirit within me" (Psalm 51:10).

"Therefore, you have no excuse, O man, every one of you who judges. For in passing judgment on another you condemn yourself, because you, the judge, practice the very same things. We know that the

judgment of God rightly falls on those who practice such things. Do you suppose, O man—you who judge those who practice such things and yet do them yourself—that you will escape the judgment of God? Or do you presume on the riches of his kindness and forbearance and patience, not knowing that God's kindness is meant to lead you to repentance? But because of your hard and impenitent heart you are storing up wrath for yourself on the day of wrath when God's righteous judgment will be revealed" (Romans 2:1-25).

"I will give them a heart to know that I am the Lord, and they shall be my people and I will be their God, for they shall return to me with their whole heart" (Jeremiah 24:7).

"Do not be conformed to this world, but be transformed by the renewal of your mind, that by testing you may discern what is the will of God, what is good and acceptable and perfect" (Romans 12:2).

"Pray then like this: Our Father in heaven, hallowed be your name. Your kingdom come, your will be done, on earth as it is in heaven. Give us this day our daily bread, and forgive us our debts, as we also have forgiven our debtors. And lead us not into temptation, but deliver us from evil" (Matthew 6:9-13).

"Jesus answered, 'Truly, truly, I say to you, unless one is born of water and the Spirit, he cannot enter the kingdom of God'" (John 3:5).

"Peace I leave with you; my peace I give to you. Not as the world gives do I give to you. Let not your hearts be troubled, neither let them be afraid" (John 14:27).

"Therefore, confess your sins to one another and pray for one another, that you may be healed. The prayer of a righteous person has great power as it is working" (James 5:16).

"The heart of man plans his way, but the Lord establishes his steps" (Proverbs 16:9).

"Jesus said to them, 'I am the way, and the truth and the life. No one comes to the Father except through me'" (John 14:6).

Flipping Tables - Part One: What Is Sin?

Beware of wolves in sheep's clothing.

"Beware of practicing your righteousness before other people in order to be seen by them, for then you will have no reward from your Father who is in heaven. Thus, when you give to the needy, sound no trumpet before you, as the hypocrites do in the synagogues and in the streets, that they may be praised by others. Truly, I say to you, they have received their reward. But when you give to the needy, do not let your left hand know what your right hand is doing, so that your giving may be in secret. And your Father who sees in secret will reward you" (Matthew 6:1-4).

"Not many of you should become teachers, my brothers, for you know that we who teach will be judged with greater strictness. For we all stumble in many ways. And if anyone does not stumble in what he says, he is a perfect man, able also to bridle his whole body. If we put bits into the mouths of horses so that they obey us, we guide their whole bodies as well. Look at the ships also: though they are so large and are driven by strong winds, they are guided by a very small rudder wherever the will of the pilot directs. So also the tongue is a small member, yet it boasts of great things. How great a forest is set ablaze by such a small fire!" (James 3:1-5).

"A joyful heart is good medicine, but a crushed spirit dries up the bones" (Proverbs 17:22).

"For John came to you in the way of righteousness, and you did not believe him, but the tax collectors and the prostitutes believed him. And even when you saw it, you did not afterward change your minds and believe him" (Matthew 21:32).

"Beware of false prophets, which come to you in sheep's clothing, but inwardly they are ravening wolves" (Matthew 7:15).

"Do nothing from rivalry or conceit, but in humility count others more significant than yourselves" (Philippians 2:3).

A Few Holy Directives

People won't understand you.

"But I say to you who hear, 'Love your enemies, do good to those who hate you'" (Luke 6:27).

"For God gave us a spirit not of fear but of power and love and self-control" (2 Timothy 1:7).

"But the fruit of the Spirit is love, joy, peace, patience, kindness, goodness, faithfulness" (Galatians 5:22).

"For the whole law is fulfilled in one word: 'You shall love your neighbor as yourself'" (Galatians 5:14).

"And we know that for those who love God all things work together for good, for those who are called according to his purpose" (Romans 8:28).

"The revelation of Jesus Christ, which God gave him to show to his servants the things that must soon take place. He made it known by sending his angel to his servant John, who bore witness to the word of God and to the testimony of Jesus Christ, even to all that he saw. Blessed is the one who reads aloud the words of this prophecy, and blessed are those who hear, and who keep what is written in it, for the time is near. John, to the seven churches that are in Asia: Grace to you and peace from him who is and who was and who is to come, and from the seven spirits who are before his throne, and from Jesus Christ, the faithful witness, the firstborn of the dead, and the ruler of kings on earth. To him who loves us and has freed us from our sins by his blood" (Revelation 1:1-5).

"Now faith is the assurance of things hoped for, the conviction of things not seen" (Hebrews 11:1).

"Again Jesus spoke to them, saying, 'I am the light of the world. Whoever follows me will not walk in darkness, but will have the light of life'" (John 8:12).

"Do not be conformed to this world, but be transformed by the renewal of your mind, that by testing you may discern what is the will of God, what is good and acceptable and perfect" (Romans 12:2).

"'Judge not, and you will not be judged; condemn not, and you will not be condemned; forgive, and you will be forgiven'" (Luke 6:37).

"'In the same way, let your light shine before others, so that they may see your good works and give glory to your Father who is in heaven'" (Matthew 5:16).

"'Enter through the narrow gate. For wide is the gate and broad is the road that leads to destruction, and many enter through it. But small is the gate and narrow the road that leads to life, and only a few find it'" (Matthew 7:13-14).

*Search me, God, and know my heart;
test me and know my anxious thoughts.
See if there is any offensive way in me,
and lead me in the way everlasting.*

Psalm 139: 23-24

About Naomi's Street People

"Go ye therefore, and teach all nations, baptizing them in the name of the Father, and of the Son, and of the Holy Spirit" (Matthew 28:19).

"And He said unto them, 'Go ye into all the world, and preach the gospel to every creature. He that believeth and is baptized shall be saved; but he that believeth not shall be damned. And these signs shall follow them that believe; in my name shall they cast out devils; they shall speak with new tongues they shall take up serpents; and if they drink any deadly thing, it shall not hurt them; they shall lay hands on the sick, and they shall recover. they shall take up serpents; and if they drink any deadly thing, it shall not hurt them; they shall lay hands on the sick, and they shall recover" (Mark 16:15-18 KJV).

"And this gospel of the kingdom shall be preached in all the world for a witness unto all nations; and then shall the end come" (Matthew 24:14 KJV).

"As you go, proclaim this message: 'The kingdom of heaven has come near.' Heal the sick, raise the dead, cleanse those who have leprosy, drive out demons. Freely you have received; freely give" (Matthew 10:7-8 NIV).

We are street teachers and preachers for the Glory of Jesus Christ. We are called to be His servants; followers who walk in faith, obeying His Word by preaching the Gospel. We teach. We preach. We baptize. We seek the blessed opportunity to lead people to salvation in the knowledge of Christ Jesus through the Holy Spirit; He gives the increase.

We are spiritual gardeners, continually sowing new seeds, watering and nurturing those seeds with the Word of God. Every day we pray we will have the opportunity to lead people to Jesus. We pray, we practice compassion. God is love, He knows the maps of our hearts. He knows the map of your heart. You are His beautiful creation.

Our ministry does not have a church building, we gather in homes, in restaurants, and on the streets to pray together. Jesus ministered outside, enjoyed dinner with friends at home, served dinner on mountainsides as described in Mark 8:1-9.

We are on the streets where you live—you'll find us in grocery stores, at the hardware store, at the post office—wherever you go! We know the power and the love of God and we want you to know, too!

We have been freely given His mercy, His Grace and we know His Love. Our God, the Creator of Justice and Mercy. Get to know Him. Seriously. Know His Goodness, Mercy, Forgiveness, and Love.

We are thankful to Jesus—He taught us how to truly love, how to serve, He promised us eternal life and delivered on this promise by His terrible death and Holy Resurrection. It's all spelled out specifically in His Holy Word.

His Holy Spirit is at work: He works through each one of us—we are His servants until He returns in Glory! Ask the Holy Spirit to give you eyes to read, ears to hear, and a heart to understand His Word. You'll discover how His Word replaces bitterness with joy, despair with hope, and doubt with faith.

Here is a partial list of the many documented Healings and Miracles we have witnessed recently:

- Jesus appeared to two women on separate occasions; they saw His beautiful face!
- Several men and women have audibly heard His voice.
- One woman has seen heaven.
- A neck was healed after years of pain following an auto accident.
- A shoulder was healed after years of pain from a work injury.
- A man saw the Light of Jesus and was given a specific message for his life.
- A woman was healed from chronic pain in her hips.
- An elderly man with withered legs got out of his wheelchair and walked for the first time in decades.
- A woman was cured of ovarian cancer.
- A man, in a hospital bed in a vegetative state with no hope for recovery, was restored to life and is now fully recovered.
- A service dog was completely healed from a soft tissue sarcoma.
- A spine that was bent and rotated from an injury was miraculously straightened.
- A healthy baby was born to a woman who was not supposed to have children.
- A lump in a neck disappeared instantly during prayer.

"These are some of the signs that will accompany believers: They will throw out demons in my name, they will speak in new tongues, they will take snakes in their hands, they will drink poison and not be hurt, they will lay hands on the sick and make them well."
Mark 16:15-18

Who is Naomi?

Naomi's life is a beautiful story of love, loss, and loyalty; it illustrates the power of God to bring goodness out of bitter circumstances. The story of Naomi appears in the Book of Ruth in the Holy Bible.

A man from Bethlehem named Elimelek fell in love with a woman named Naomi and married her. The name Naomi means "sweet, pleasant," which gives us an idea of Naomi's basic character. They had two sons, naming them Mahlon and Kilion.

There was a great famine in Israel, so Elimelek and Naomi traveled together to Moab with their sons to find food. After some time, they decided to stay in Moab. Elimelek died in Moab. After her husband's death, Naomi continued to live there with her two sons who married Moabite women named Orpah and Ruth. Then, tragedy struck again. Naomi's two sons died leaving Naomi with her two widowed daughters-in-law.

Naomi's heartache in Moab was more than she could bear; she decided to return to her homeland in Israel. She decided to go back to Bethlehem in Judah. Naomi blessed Orpah and Ruth and told them to stay in Moab to find new husbands. She kissed them and asked that the Lord deal kindly with them.

"Then Naomi said to her two daughters-in-law, 'Go back, each of you, to your mother's home. May the LORD show you kindness, as you have shown kindness to your dead husbands and to me. May the LORD grant that each of you will find rest in the home of another husband.' Then she kissed them goodbye and they wept aloud and said to her, 'We will go back with you to your people.'"

"But Naomi said, 'Return home, my daughters. Why would you come with me? Am I going to have any more sons, who could become your *husbands? Return home, my daughters; I am too old to have another husband. Even if I thought there was still hope for me—even if I had a husband tonight and then gave birth to sons— would you wait until they grew up? Would you remain unmarried for them? No, my daughters. It is more bitter for me than for you, because the LORD's hand has turned against me!' At this they wept aloud again. Then Orpah kissed her mother-in-law goodbye, but Ruth clung to her"* (Ruth 1:8-14).

Orpah agreed to stay in Moab and returned to her mother's home there. Naomi's daughter-in-law named Ruth loved her very much and told her mother-in-law that she would stay with her. She told Naomi her people's God in Israel would be her God, too.

When Naomi and Ruth arrived in Bethlehem, the women of the town greeted Naomi by name, but she said, *"Don't call me Naomi. Call me Mara, because the Almighty has made my life very bitter. I went away full, but the Lord has brought me back empty. Why call me Naomi? The Lord has afflicted me; the Almighty has brought misfortune upon me'"* (Ruth 1:20-21). The name *Mara* means "bitter."

The cup of affliction is a bitter cup, but Naomi understood that the affliction came from the God who is sovereign in all things. Little did she know at the time that from this bitter sorrow great blessings would come to her, her descendants, and the world through Jesus Christ.

Destitute and hungry upon returning to Bethlehem, Ruth went into the fields during the barley harvest to pick up leftover grains in a field belonging to a man named Boaz. Ruth had no idea Boaz was a relative of her deceased father-in-law, Elimelek.

When Boaz heard that Naomi had returned with Ruth and was told Ruth was gleaning the leftover grain, he went to Ruth and told her she could work safely in his fields and get a drink from his water jars when she was thirsty.

Ruth questioned his kindness. Boaz responded that he had heard of Ruth's kindness toward Naomi and that the Lord God of Israel would bless her and reward her. Ruth worked very hard in the fields to provide enough barley to sell and to keep some for her and Naomi. Naomi declared that the Lord *"has not stopped showing his kindness to the living and the dead" (Ruth 2:20).*

Seeing God's hand in these events, Naomi encouraged Ruth to meet Boaz on the threshing floor and to lie down at his feet when he was done working. This apparently was the customary way of asking a man to provide the protection of marriage. When Boaz awakened and noticed Ruth at his feet, he blessed her for her kindness and noble character. Boaz then gave Ruth six measures of barley for her to take home to Naomi.

Boaz went before his friends and elders to purchase the land that had belonged to Elimelek which was now Naomi's. He did this so that he could also acquire Naomi and Ruth, as was customary at the time. Boaz was then able to marry Ruth.

Boaz and Ruth married and had a son named Obed and a grandson named Jesse who would be the father of David and from whose genealogy would come the Savior Jesus Christ. *"He will renew your life and sustain you in your old age. For your daughter-in-law, who loves you and who is better to you than seven sons, has given him birth" (Ruth 4:15).* Naomi was no longer Mara. Her life again became sweet and pleasant, blessed by God.

When Naomi was an old woman, grief-stricken, poor and far from home, she held on to her faith, giving her courage. Little did Naomi know that from her bitter sorrow in the Land of Moab, great blessings would come to her, her descendants, and the world through Jesus Christ.

"Now faith is the substance of things hoped for, the evidence of things not seen" (Hebrews 11:1).

About Naomi's Street People

Statement of Faith

We believe the Bible is the mind of Christ and is the inspired, the only infallible, and authoritative Word of God. We believe that there is one God manifested in three personalities: Father, Son, and Holy Spirit.

We believe the reality of Satan and that his present control over unregenerate man does exist.

We Believe:

1. The deity and virgin birth of our Lord Jesus Christ; *"Behold, a virgin shall be with child, and shall bring forth a son, and they shall call his name Emmanuel" (Matthew 1:23 KJV).*

2. He came to earth as a man, and died for the sins of mankind, *"And the Word was made flesh, and dwelt among us, (and we beheld his glory, the glory as of the only begotten of the Father), full of grace and truth" (John 1:14 KJV).*

"Who his own self bare our sins in his own body on the tree, that we, being dead to sins, should live unto righteousness: by whose stripes ye were healed" (1 Peter 2:24 KJV).

3. Whoever calls upon the name of the Lord will be saved, no matter what station in life, the lowest of low, or the highest of high, *"For God so loved the world that he gave his one and only Son, that whoever believes in him shall not perish but have eternal life" (John 3:16 KJV).*

4. In the sacraments of communion, water baptism, and baptism of the Holy Spirit, *"And when he had given thanks, he brake it, and said, 'Take, eat: this is my body, which is broken for you: this do in*

remembrance of me.' After the same manner also he took the cup, when he had supped, saying, 'This cup is the new testament in my blood: this do you, as oft as ye drink it, in remembrance of me'" (1 Corinthians 11:24-25 KJV).*

"And now why tarriest thou? arise, and be baptized, and wash away thy sins, calling on the name of the Lord." (Acts 22:16 KJV)

"And they were all filled with the Holy Ghost, and began to speak with other tongues, as the Spirit gave them utterance" (Acts 2:4 KJV).

5. And the Gifts of the Spirit should function, flow, and operate within the confines of the church community; *"And He gave some, apostles; and some, prophets; and some, evangelists; and some, pastors and teachers; For the perfecting of the saints, for the work of the ministry, for the edifying of the body of Christ: Till we all come in the unity of the faith, and of the knowledge of the Son of God, unto a perfect man, unto the measure of the stature of the fulness of Christ." (Ephesians 4:11-13 KJV).*

6. Including miracles, signs and wonders. *"God also bearing them witness, both with signs and wonders, and with divers miracles, and gifts of the Holy Ghost, according to his own will" (Hebrews 2:4 KJV).*

About Naomi's Street People

Naomi Street Ministries is a daughter ministry of the Ministries of the Living Stones in Sterling, Alaska.

Epilogue

The Empty Tomb

Early on the first day of the week, while it was still dark, Mary Magdalene went to the tomb and saw that the stone had been removed from the entrance. So she came running to Simon Peter and the other disciple, the one Jesus loved, and said, "They have taken the Lord out of the tomb, and we don't know where they have put him!"

So Peter and the other disciple started for the tomb. Both were running, but the other disciple outran Peter and reached the tomb first. He bent over and looked in at the strips of linen lying there but did not go in. Then Simon Peter came along behind him and went straight into the tomb. He saw the strips of linen lying there, as well as the cloth that had been wrapped around Jesus' head. The cloth was still lying in its place, separate from the linen. Finally the other disciple, who had reached the tomb first, also went inside. He saw and believed. (They still did not understand from Scripture that Jesus had to rise from the dead.) Then the disciples went back to where they were staying.

Jesus Appears to Mary Magdalene

"Now Mary stood outside the tomb crying. As she wept, she bent over to look into the tomb and saw two angels in white, seated where Jesus' body had been, one at the head and the other at the foot.

They asked her, "Woman, why are you crying?"

"They have taken my Lord away," she said, "and I don't know where they have put Him." At this, she turned around and saw Jesus standing there, but she did not realize that it was Jesus.

He asked her, "Woman, why are you crying? Who is it you are looking for?"

Thinking he was the gardener, she said, "Sir, if you have carried Him away, tell me where you have put Him, and I will get Him."

Jesus said to her, "Mary."

She turned toward him and cried out in Aramaic, "Rabboni!" (which means "Teacher").

Jesus said, "Do not hold on to me, for I have not yet ascended to the Father. Go instead to my brothers and tell them, 'I am ascending to my Father and your Father, to my God and your God.'"

Mary Magdalene went to the disciples with the news: "I have seen the Lord!" And she told them that he had said these things to her.

Jesus Appears to His Disciples

On the evening of that first day of the week, when the disciples were together, with the doors locked for fear of the Jewish leaders, Jesus came and stood among them and said, "Peace be with you!" After he said this, he showed them his hands and side. The disciples were overjoyed when they saw the Lord.

Again Jesus said, "Peace be with you! As the Father has sent me, I am sending you." And with that He breathed on them and said, "Receive the Holy Spirit. If you forgive anyone's sins, their sins are forgiven; if you do not forgive them, they are not forgiven."

Jesus Appears to Thomas

Now Thomas (also known as Didymus), one of the Twelve, was not with the disciples when Jesus came. So the other disciples told him, "We have seen the Lord!"

But he said to them, "Unless I see the nail marks in his hands and put my finger where the nails were, and put my hand into his side, I will not believe."

A week later his disciples were in the house again, and Thomas was with them. Though the doors were locked, Jesus came and stood

Epilogue

among them and said, "Peace be with you!" Then he said to Thomas, "Put your finger here; see my hands. Reach out your hand and put it into my side. Stop doubting and believe."

Thomas said to him, "My Lord and my God!"

Then Jesus told him, "Because you have seen me, you have believed; blessed are those who have not seen and yet have believed."

The Purpose of John's Gospel

Jesus performed many other signs in the presence of his disciples, which are not recorded in this book. But these are written that you may believe that Jesus is the Messiah, the Son of God, and that by believing you may have life in his name.

John 20:1-31

The personal Stories of Redemption in the second part of this book are loving reminders that God does indeed work in our lives; none of us is ever beyond His eternal love and mercy.

We pray the Holy Spirit will move many people to have a new understanding of what God wants for us, what His Holy Forgiveness looks like, and to know—truly know—the blessed Hope found in His Holy Redemption.

Please, let's remember to pray for each other.

Part Two

Stories of Redemption

Michael H's Story

Thomas's Story

K.M.'s Story

Jamie's Story

Michael C.'s Story

Vicki's Story

David's Story

Verissa's Story

Middle Story

Jim's Story

Dennis' Story

Another Story

Pat's Story

Daniel's Story

Robert's Story

Vidal's Story

Luanne's Story

Epilogue

Stories of Redemption

1. "Out of the Depths" by Rev. Michael DeShane Hinton, M. Div. ...Pg. 159

2. "The Bent Tree" by Thomas M. ...Pg. 177

3. "Passing the Test" by K. M. Fleming ...Pg. 189

4. "My Story" by Jamie P. ...Pg. 203

5. "A Tale of Two Cities" by Michael C. ...Pg. 213

6. "Becoming One With the Spirit" by Vicki Manuel ...Pg. 223

7. "Jesus" by Dr. David Nelson ...Pg. 235

8. "My Story of Redemption" by Verissa Walber ...Pg. 241

9. "Grateful for His Mercy" by Luanne Nelson ...Pg. 257

10. "A Story of Transformation and Salvation" by James Mumaugh ...Pg. 269

11. "Hard Roads Can Lead Home, Too" by Rev. Dennis Kudlac ...Pg. 283

12. "Trust Him" by Luanne Nelson ...Pg. 291

13. "Redemption in a Hurricane" by Patricia Freeman ...Pg. 309

14. "Let Me Ask You a Question" by Daniel Holly ...Pg. 319

15. "Redemption" by Robert Schultz ...Pg. 331

16. "How Gratitude Got Me Through" by Vidal Cisneros, Jr. ...Pg. 339

17. "A Love Story" by Luanne Nelson ...Pg. 347

Epilogue ...Pg. 362

STORY ONE

"Out of the Depths"

By Rev. Michael DeShane Hinton, M.Div.

(1)
OUT OF THE DEPTHS

By Rev. Michael DeShane Hinton, M.Div.

*S*uddenly, I was falling, with a jolting snap let go into air and space and emptiness. There was nothing to grab, nothing to hold. Next, I was under water – then, fighting for my life.

> *The ropes of death surrounded me;*
> *the floods of destruction swept over me.*
>
> *The grave wrapped its ropes around me;*
> *death itself stared me in the face.*
>
> *But in my distress, I cried to the Lord;*
> *yes, I prayed to my God for help.*
>
> *He heard me from his sanctuary;*
> *my cry reached his ears.*

***

> *He reached down from heaven and rescued me;*
> *he drew me out of deep waters.*
> *~Psalm 18:4-6 and 16 NLT*

Five of us met at Lincolnville, Maine, for a cruise on Penobscot Bay. My son Justin, and our friends, Robin, Topher, and Terri were with me. Underway on Topher's cuddy cruiser, we enjoyed the sights of the New England coastline; fishing villages, old factory towns, boats of every kind, docks, and magnificent homes on the water. There were sea gulls, terns, puffins, an osprey, and seals. A porpoise was there, porpoising. The salty spray refreshed us and juicy sandwiches nourished us late in the day. Alas, we headed back to shore. The late summer sun sets early there and the North Atlantic is cold.

Justin's hat blew off into the water. Wanting to retrieve it, we turned about. On the pass by port we missed it, the boat's wake pushing it away. I suggested that we could get it from the swim platform astern, closer to the water. Topher backed to the hat. I climbed over the transom and used the swim ladder for a hold as we slowly approached. Just as I reached for the hat the ladder broke and I fell flailing into the drink.

It seemed that I was under water a long time. When I finally surfaced I could not swim back to the boat. I felt what I thought was seaweed or anchor rode wrapped around my leg. But I could not kick it loose. I could not kick at all! Something was terribly wrong and I asked Justin to help me. My older son is big and very strong. He yanked me out of the water and into the boat like a landed fish. What we then saw was truly gruesome, the mangled flesh of my left leg, hacked through to the bone, blood spewing out in pulsing splashes.

I knew immediately that I could die from this massive wound. I felt the life flowing out of me and there was little time. Urgently, I asked Justin to listen to me very closely. I asked him to tell my two younger children, Corinne and John, and older daughter, Alicia, that I loved them. I asked him to tell my mom and dad that I loved them, too. I hugged Justin close and told him how much I loved him. Convinced that I would die, I wondered if there was anything else left to say. There was not. I had said the most important thing. About to pass out I concluded, "I've got to go now."

Robin started yelling, "No, don't say those things! You're not going to die!"

"Well," I replied, "if I'm going to stay alive, we'd better get a tourniquet on this."

There was no rope on this boat.

There was no tourniquet in the tiny first aid kit.

I thought there might be something below decks so began to crawl toward the gangway but was pushed back and made to lie down.

Topher produced his belt. He handed it to me and stepped back, saying that he could not handle this!

I asked Justin, again, if he would help me.

My 17-year old son bravely replied, "What do you want me to do?"

I explained that the tourniquet would stop the bleeding. He would have to hold it as tightly as he could. Justin put the belt around my leg and pulled hard. But a fold of flesh left an artery exposed. So, we tried again. I arranged the various pieces of myself like a puzzle and slid the tourniquet in place.

Topher struggled to get the boat underway. Heading to port was slow going because the impact with my leg bent the propeller.

Terri suggested that we say the Lord's Prayer.

Lying on the transom seat, looking up at the blue sky and a few fluffy clouds, I believed that at any moment, despite our best efforts, I could die. A doubt emerged. It came from the deepest part of my soul.

It was a question that had tormented me my entire life. I had been an avowed Christian for 28 years and a Methodist minister for 25. I led many people to Christ and helped others to die in peace. But in that moment I wondered whether if I died the Heavenly Father would receive me.

As we began to pray, *Our Father...*

The sky went brilliantly white and then suddenly I was looking down at the frantic scene below. I was surrounded by darkness about 60 feet up in the air, peering through a round portal of clear vision with particles of light streaming past my face. I saw my own body in back of the boat, my son struggling to stop the bleeding and Robin holding my hand. I saw Terri praying while Topher drove the boat past brightly colored lobster pot buoys bobbing in the glistening sea.

Then I experienced a series of visions "up there," out of my body.

First, to the far right I was drawn to the image of a small boy. It was me! I was smiling as if I knew a secret. In a flash my entire life then unfolded before me – zip, zip, zip – an instant replay in a condensed version of my whole existence in this world, everything I'd ever experienced or done in life. After seeing my life so concisely I realized it had not been so bad. That sober assessment, not that bad, had a calming effect on me in antithesis to the chaos below and contrary to the last few months.

My circumstances had changed dramatically in the previous months, having lost my ministry as a Methodist pastor, the life I knew since the age of 19, having been betrayed by a liberal hierarchy of the Methodists. I was newly divorced after my ex told me that she did not love me anymore. I was already a deeply wounded man. Now this! But the review of my life "up there" was surprisingly simple. I realized in an instant that there was no reason for me to be sad or depressed. There in that trans-physical realm I saw clearly that I had experienced many wonderful blessings in my life. I realized in that moment of perfect memory that it was wrong ever to complain or to feel sorry for myself.

The next vision occurred to the left of the life review. I saw the faces of about 100 people. They were extremely joyful, looking right at me with beaming smiles. They were glad to see me! I did not recognize any of them but somehow knew that they loved me as if they were family, friends, and former church members that knew me, had prayed for me, and supported me. I could feel their love for me. It surprised me. It is one thing to be loved. It is quite another to feel it! I had never in my life felt love like that and have not since.

Then, I became aware of feeling absolutely at peace. The feeling of bliss that I felt is best described by the words of Scripture, *"God himself will be with them ... He will wipe away every tear from their eyes, and death shall be no more, neither shall there be mourning, nor crying, nor pain anymore" (Revelation 21:3-4 ESV)*. All the heartache and anxiety of my life was completely gone. I was floating in euphoric tranquility.

In the next vision, as if called to see something, I turned around 180 degrees to see that the particles of light were all converging at a point in the far distance, opposite the desperate scene behind me. There was a hole in the darkness, an entrance to what looked like a realm of light. Through the entrance I could see what looked like people walking around in there. And then there was a communication. It came in the form of a choice that was given to me. It came to me in a knowing that was in and around and through me, like a voice but not heard, a thought permeating the universe itself, pure and singular. The choice was either to go on to the light to be with God forever or to stay.

It was entirely up to me, the choice clearly before me, again, to go or to stay.

I turned back around to see everyone in the boat trying to help me and thought what a horrible thing it would be for them if I were to die in their arms. I could not bear the thought of them having to experience that, especially Justin, who was working so hard to save my life. They cared for me and I did not want to hurt them. I wanted to go back and be okay so that they would be okay.

Next, I thought of my two younger children, Corinne and John, who were 9 and 7 at the time, so beautiful and innocent. I wanted to be with them as they grew up. I wanted them to have a father. I did not want them to experience the tragic loss of their dad, something that would make them sad and something they might not understand at this stage of life because they were too young.

Then another thought came to me. I wanted to be a minister, again. It surprised me because I thought it was over! But maybe not, I thought, "up there." I realized that I wanted to be with God's people again as a leader and teacher and guide. I was not finished, yet. That's how the thought was formed, *you're not yet finished*, as if there was some destiny or task for me to fulfill.

I made up my mind quickly. It all happened very fast. I knew that the injury just sustained would affect my life. But I didn't know how much. What would happen to my leg? Could the doctors fix me? Would I be confined to a wheelchair? Would I ever play basketball again? I wanted to see the future. I looked to the left to see if there would be another vision, as if the answer would appear there. I became aware that I was not allowed to know; the future would remain a mystery and I would have to trust God to take care of me.

Then I heard Robin yelling at me not to go to sleep. I was back in my body in the boat just as suddenly as I had left it. But things were vastly different for me and have been ever since that day. There was a strength, confidence, and determination within me that I'd never experienced before. I had a deep and profound conviction that I would do whatever it took to live and to fulfill my life. I had received a powerful gift of faith.

I began to encourage Justin, who was distressed that the bleeding had not stopped completely. I could tell it was enough and told him so.

When we docked back at Lincolnville, a crowd had gathered. I heard someone say, "He's not going to make it." I smiled because of the confidence I felt that it was possible. Then I threw up!

At Penobscot Bay Memorial Medical Center in Rockport one of the nurses asked how long it had been since the accident. It had been almost an hour. She said that I would soon begin to feel it. She was right. Within minutes I was seized by a pain that was utterly devastating. Shock is exactly the word for it.

I tried to fight it. I wanted to stay awake. But the pain was too great. Passing out, I felt my spirit begin to leave my body, again. But I said, No, not again; stay with me. I was surrounded by Mainers and they would know what to do, I thought. So, I gave myself up to God and to His servants, and went to sleep.

Suddenly, I was aware of a being that came to me. It was a dark entity, not like the darkness devoid of light but substantive, like a piece of coal, cold, dry, and dusty, but moving, not liquid but slithering like a snake in mid-air. It had a head, body, and face. But the face was almost completely featureless; it was looking at me within an inch of my face, and up and down my body, creepy-like, but without actual eyes, and smelling me but it had no real nose. I thought that if this creature tries to taste me I'm going to be completely grossed out! Suddenly, as if it resented my thought, it seemed to emit a breath on me. That's when I became aware of its evil nature and intent. It was full of sheer malice. I could feel that it hated me and wanted to take me, to destroy me. It wanted me to die! And it wanted to drag my soul to perdition.

From within me, then, came an exactly reciprocal feeling of hostility toward this specter that it had for me. I said, sternly and, I felt, by my right, "Get away from me. Leave me alone. You can't have me. I belong to Jesus." When I said *Jesus* the demon vanished. I'm sure that demons are afraid of Jesus.

They got me stabilized at Pen Bay and sent me on a helicopter to Boston. I call it the Flight of the Valkyrie. Ask me about it later.

As I was wheeled through the doors at Massachusetts General Hospital the voice of a man ordered things done in urgent and authoritative tones. I saw the doors almost close behind the gurney and was out again.

I lost my left leg above the knee.

I did not know that there could be such pain. I was in the hospital for a month, had nine surgeries, and a dangerous infection. The antibiotics burned up the vessels in both my arms so they put a line directly into my heart. I was delirious with fever and had many disturbing dreams.

Mass General is extraordinary, a teaching hospital for Harvard medical students who saw me in waves of healing care every day. There were surgical teams, trauma counselors, and a pain manager. The nurses were angels.

My doctor was David Lhowe, head of orthopedic surgery at Harvard Medical School.

Dr. Michael Otto of Harvard, a leading cognitive behaviorist, visited with me, telling me how to avoid post-traumatic stress disorder in the wake of this injury.

As I prepared to be dismissed, a Jewish psychiatry student came to say goodbye, though it was his last day at the hospital and he had a flight to catch. We had a kindred spirit in accepting the challenge of faith in the midst of suffering.

Monsignor Thompson was Director of the Newman Center at Boston College. The bishop was dedicating a new building at the foundation, but the good father left celebrations early, wanting to catch me before I went home. He pulled his chair up close to my hospital bed and in humble, almost contrite terms explained to me how his faith had to become "practical" in order to deliver him from alcoholism.

What lesson can we take from this testimony for our purposes now?

What I learned in this near-death/out-of-body experience is that we human beings are not just bodies. We are not a bag of chemicals, or machines with parts and functions. We are body and spirit, that is, we have a spirit that intersects our body, creating the soul. God formed Adam of the dust of the earth and breathed into him (*ruach* in Hebrew is *espiritus* in Latin, either breath or spirit in English) so that he became a living soul (*psyche* in Greek). When Jesus raised Jairus' daughter, Scripture says that the girl's spirit returned to her. Jesus' body was lying in the tomb dead, but the Holy Spirit raised Him from the dead; Doubting Thomas saw His wounds and touched them! The injuries were healed and did not hurt him anymore. John wrote that as he "is" so are we in "this" world. One of the benefits of the resurrection of the Lord is that we enjoy the healing power of God. By his stripes we are healed because his stripes are healed in his glorified state.

The soul is comprised of our thoughts and feelings, which occurs at the intersection of body and spirit. So, at any given moment, our thoughts and feelings can be turned toward the lower nature, the body, or toward the higher nature, making us spiritually minded. If we always think about the body and its needs, then we are carnally minded. But if we adopt the spiritual perspective of the New Testament, our thoughts will be raised to high and holy things.

Now when we experience an injury or disease in life, it affects both our body and our soul. Physical illness or injury can affect our feelings adversely because we take it personally that we have to suffer. Conversely, an emotional hurt or disease or disaffection can make us physically sick. It works both ways. Have you heard of psychosomatic illness? But we have a problem, in our society, of focusing on the body only because we have become so secular and are not very religious.

Why is it that when a person is physically injured we hear sirens and people are taken to the hospital – we have a complex, advanced, and marvelous system of patching up bodies – but when we are hurt emotionally we often suffer alone? No one sees that our hearts are broken, that our feelings were involved in an accident, and that life or circumstances or some person ran over us with a Mack truck of abuse or neglect. The hospital takes x-rays and runs tests; police can take pictures of bruises. But hurt feelings are often invisible. Who takes care of that? Where is the emotional emergency room? What is the cure for our aching souls?

Similarly, what about the moral or intellectual emergency room? Where might one find the trauma surgeon to stop the hemorrhaging of a wounded spirit?

Now, the wonderful doctors at Mass General, and my friends Robin and Terri, who were both psychologists, were as equally concerned with my soul as my body. But that is not always the case. All around us are life's walking wounded, who suffer extraordinary emotional pain and distress. So, I want to share what I learned after the traumatic injury that I suffered that day.

Dr. Otto explained the Limbic system to me. The Limbic system is that part of the brain that remembers what causes us pain and pleasure. It includes the Amygdala, Thalamus, Hypothalamus, Hippocampus, Cingulate Gyrus, and Corpus Callosum. It deals with feelings, motivation, and memory. When we suffer an injury, the Limbic system is what flags danger for future reference. It is not the most primitive part of our brain but, comes in second for not being very sophisticated. It is simple-minded. Dr. Otto calls it a child that needs help, comforting when we are hurt.

When we are injured severely or repeatedly, again, either physically or spiritually, we can develop posttraumatic stress disorder or PTSD. This is how PTSD works:

1. The initial traumatic injury occurs.

2. The Limbic system, aided by adrenaline, remembers on an emotional level all the environmental clues that led to the injury.

3. Any similarity to the previous hurtful event, called a trigger, causes the Limbic system to believe simplistically that another injury is about to occur, so again it signals the fight or flight or freeze responses in order to protect us.

Now, the Limbic system is great for surviving evils in a hostile world. But after a traumatic experience the Limbic Child can take over our existence, and it builds emotional walls designed to keep us from being hurt. Imagine a medieval fortress with high, thick walls all around, a parapet on top, and towers at the corners. There's only one small, thick, iron-clad door in the wall. The Limbic Child stands at the door in full battle armor, guarding against anything or anyone that wants to come through it. The problem is that the walls, closed door, and armor, while helping us to feel safe, also keep out life, love, people, experiences, and many blessings that we might receive. How can we overcome these overwrought measures of the Limbic system?

Dr. Otto explained that we have an adult part of our brain that can help the hurting baby within to sort things out and be comforted. It's the largest part of our brain and it's what makes us human beings created in the image and likeness of God. It's called the Cerebrum. It's where language and reason operate. Knowledge is stored there, like things we learn in school and church and around the dinner table at home. It's the seat of wisdom, judgment, taste, and discretion. It holds the executive office of soul, that is, facilitating the choices that we make, and the preferences that we develop for certain people, places, and things.

The Cerebrum is more integrated than the primitive parts of the brain but there are identifiable "areas." One of them is the Prefrontal Cortex, or Frontal Lobe, where our unique personality develops; where our vision for life is formed; our dreams, goals, and ambitions are conceived; it supplies the imaginative element in problem-solving; music, art, and drama are appreciated there; all the finer things of life that make us internally full and rich; and it's where social sophistication is enjoyed in a thing called love, which is essential to, say, a happy marriage, effective parenting, or a strong church. In terms of Biblical theology the Limbic Child is carnal, the Cerebral Adult is spiritual.

Dr. Otto said that the Adult Cerebrum can speak to the Limbic Child, comforting and assuring it that the danger is over, and it's time to live.

For a number of years after the accident I had nightmares, full body spasms, and spikes of phantom pain. I was in constant, debilitating agony, barely existing in a very deep, dark hole. But I began to follow Monsignor Thompson's advice about making faith practical, clawing my way out of the depths inch by inch by prayer and discipline. I lived virtually as a monk, doing things through which God's healing power began to manifest in me. These are the things that I found helpful, which minister to the spiritual side of our nature:

1. As if returning to seminary I began to study God's word again, especially the New Testament in the original Greek. I became a student of Classical Culture the historical context of the NT.

2. I began to pray in a disciplined manner, reviving my use

of the Daily Office in the Book of Common Prayer.

3. Making better moral choices, I surrendered my ministerial credentials when a gay rights activist, in a fit of rage, smashed the chalice and paten at the big general meeting of the Methodist Church to which I belonged. I did not want to share ordination with sacrilegious people. I had been compromising with liberals my entire adult life. It was time to be true to myself, and to the Lord that loves me and died for me. There is no substitute for personal moral integrity. Going with that thought, though, and because of what I learned in prayer and study, I determined to undergo a strict moral renovation of my own life, which is an on-going project. I know that by grace there is victory over sin.

4. I sought more of the spiritual gifts. The charismatic gifts are where we find the miraculous solution to body/soul dualism. God is higher than nature. That is why we call him the supernatural God. Energy is superior to matter. Inanimate objects can be moved around, corrected, adjusted, and repaired by the power of God, which is what happens in healing miracles. Light (knowledge) overcomes darkness (ignorance) in teaching ministry. Life is greater than death. Goodness defeats evil every time it's tried. Prayer is the most powerful force on earth. Sacrifice gets things done. Faith moves mountains. Demons are subject to us in the name of Jesus. Love is the taste of heaven in this life that God wants us to have forever. The kingdom is within us. Grace is the divine activity that heals, frees, and forgives us in the name of Jesus Christ.

5. The ultimate triumph of the Spirit over carnality is the way of the cross. The cross completely disarms the fear and anxiety of the Limbic system by "accepting" legitimate suffering as the normal and ordinary experience of

human beings in this fallen world. The cross informs us of the true nature of the world. There was no one better in the history of the world than Jesus of Nazareth. He never did anything wrong but only what was good, loving, right, and true. And look what happened to him! The servant is not above his master. Why are we surprised when we experience evil, tested by fire?

I now sleep soundly through the night. I am free of narcotic painkillers! God did what drugs could not do. Only rarely do I have phantom sensations but I expect them completely to disappear in time. I feel twenty-five years old again and can't wait for the next day to dawn with the abundant life that God has for me.

God stands outside the fortress of our traumatized souls, knocking on the castle door, asking to come in, for he has a wagon load of blessings to give us. He knocks and from inside he hears us fearfully say, "We're not receiving visitors today."

But the Lord is persistent, knocking gently at the door. "Let me in; I love you with all my heart." Curious, we mount the ramparts to peer over the wall. Below we see our gracious Father with a big smile on His face, waving up at us. And we see then not one wagon but many, one right behind the other, full of good things, all in line, backed up down the road for as far as the eye can see, waiting to be delivered unto us.

DE PROFUNDIS is the Latin title for Psalm 130:

Out of the depths I cry to thee, O LORD!

Whatever depth of pain or sorry or injury you feel today God can meet out of his great love for you in Christ.

Michael Hinton is a missionary priest of the Diocese of the West, Church of Nigeria, Anglican Communion, and is planting a church in Lubbock, Texas. He earned the Master of Divinity from Asbury Theological Seminary in 1981. Rev. Hinton can be reached at www.christchurchlubbock.org

STORY TWO

"The Bent Tree"

By Thomas M.

(2)
THE BENT TREE

By Thomas M.

"Once a tree grows crooked, that's the way it's going to stay. People are like that too."

My mother truly believed this statement and repeated it many times to her children. I know this because I am one of them.

I grew up in a home where alcohol was hidden away in the coal bin. It was the elephant in the room no one talked about. My dad drank daily for years. When I reached adulthood, I came to realize my father was an alcoholic, just like his father and my great grandfather, or so the story goes. Although I was never beaten, ridiculed, mocked, or purposely made to feel bad, I have scars from my childhood that run deep and still surface from time to time.

I was a chubby kid growing up, it was called "husky" back then. Sears had a special line of blue jeans for kids like me. I suppose it's what stores label as "comfort fit" today. When I was really little, I had a crew cut and a big head. Strangers called me "Butch." To top off my misery, I had braces on my teeth complete with a metal around the head "halo" corrector, corrective shoes, and needed to go to a speech pathologist because I had trouble with "s" sounds. In retrospect, I think it had something to do with the braces on my teeth. I wasn't athletic in grade school. I had nice friends, and good grades came naturally for me.

 Bullying was different back then. Back in the 1960s, a kid could call you a name and ten minutes later he would share his lunch with you.

 My family moved into a new house right before the start of 5th grade. I remember this vividly because that was the summer when my dad had his "nervous breakdown." He was prescribed a cocktail of meds. I was afraid of him when his eyes looked drugged up. He looked like another person; he sure didn't look like my dad. I transformed into something like a dog looking at his master when he came home from work. I would try to acutely assess his condition and mood. This was one of the many new family survival traits I quickly learned in the aftermath of his breakdown.

As time went by, dad switched from the prescribed drugs to alcohol. He hid his bottles of vodka. I would search for bottles hoping I wouldn't find them, but I did. He had special places to hide his liquor bottles. Some were in the house and some in the car and garage. I don't know why I searched for them. They say selective recall is a form of denial. I don't recall telling my mom what I found. I never confronted him with my discoveries.

Mom must have known where he hid them; after all it is not difficult to tell if someone has been drinking.

Maybe I was hoping the bottles wouldn't be there after a while. Fifty years later, I still can't remember "why" I looked for them, I just remember looking in his favorite hiding spots to see if they were still there.

I remember sitting with my family on the hard, wooden pew at church on Sunday morning, silently gagging on the stale smell of alcohol and English Leather cologne. I've talked with other people who have gone through similar circumstances in an effort to unravel what happened to me growing up. I came to know the first trait a person often develops growing up in a dysfunctional family is denial. In denying any of it affected me, I had to "stuff" my feelings away. After all, I wasn't supposed to have feelings or confusion or anger or sadness. I was a kid. I was expected to be happy, so I kept any unhappy feelings to myself.

I denied I was broken. I didn't even know I was breaking at the time.

Growing up, I constantly sought approval from my parents,

my teachers, and my friends. I had a disproportional sense of responsibility, believing I could change or fix a situation if I "just did this or I just did that." In reality, I judged myself harshly because despite all of my attempts to change the situation, nothing I did worked. Consequently, I emerged from my childhood with a very low sense of myself. My self-esteem was shot from the get-go. I became terrified of abandonment, becoming a reactor rather than an actor in my own life. There was plenty of shouting in my childhood home; I became terrified of angry people and personal criticism.

I had an outrageous fear of abandonment. My mother frequently would "lose" me in stores. *On purpose.* Really. Usually someone would find me and take me to the police, or the store's "Return Department." In retrospect, I think maybe the "Lost and Found Department" would have been more appropriate. Either way, she always got me back. Strangely, I don't remember crying, I just remember her grabbing me by my wrist, with her icy stare, as she led me back to the car. These events happened before I even started grade school; I was 4 and 5 years old. My mother told me if I misbehaved she would call the police, and they would take me to a home for bad boys.

Since I was a child of the 60s, I decided I wanted to be like Dr. Spock on the hit TV series, *Star Trek*. He was smarter, stronger and had no emotions. Captain Kirk, on the other hand, used his emotions to his benefit and I couldn't see that happening in real life. I concluded that to not feel – is to not hurt.

As much as I tried to shut them down, I couldn't avoid it, I had feelings. Hidden deep down inside my Spock persona was fear, sadness, anger, and disillusionment. My friends had ok lives, why couldn't I?

Later, when I was in the fifth or sixth grade, my mother frequently would threaten my dad with divorce. My sister and I must have looked scared; Mom would tell us that she wouldn't really do it, she was only saying it to scare him so he wouldn't drink. Of course, that trick of hers didn't work, and he continued to drink.

I knew my family was messed up. Even so, I worried that it might breakup, and I would be shipped off to live with my aunt and cousins. My mom would scream at my older sister for a day or two before it quieted down. I continued to think that maybe, just maybe, if I was perfect, everything would be okay. I tried hard to be a perfect child/student. I became very good at it. I went off by myself as soon as I got home from school, I found solitary hobbies like model airplane and ship building; I learned how to entertain myself.

Interestingly, I never felt unloved, perhaps because we always expressed it with each other in spite of the craziness. How, may you ask? A hug, a kiss, and an "I love you" was commonplace. I just was never asked about feelings. I was a vigilant observer and based my "feelings" on the mood and actions of my parents.

Physically, I matured when I was in the sixth grade. I started doing pushups in the seventh grade and won a bet with my teacher by doing 50. I was navigating my life in a way I could stay out of trouble and excel. By the age of 15, I was a two-way starter on my High School football team and made Varsity as a sophomore. I dated a blonde cheerleader, became the class president, and an Eagle Scout. I was a happy, hardworking 15-year-old, as long as I didn't have to go home. I didn't think it affected me. I thought I could out-work any problem in life. All I had to do was work hard and avoid going home.

Dad still drank.

My dad, as long as I can remember, always seemed to be placating my mother one way or another. A bigger, fancier house, new furniture, a gleaming silver service for the sideboard, and so forth. You get the picture. He even got a face lift for her! He permed his hair. *Was this due to a guilt trip over his drinking? I don't know.* He did the family laundry on Thursdays, the day she got her hair done. Maybe he imprinted the martyrdom of marriage on me. If you earned enough points, maybe you could go fishing.

Then, at 15 years old, I couldn't stand it anymore. Tears in my eyes, I mustered up the courage to sit down on the couch with my dad and ask him to stop drinking. I was old enough to see he was destroying himself. I couldn't stand watching him do it anymore. I loved him. He was a quiet man who did not like confrontation. Miraculously, he stopped drinking for the next nine years.

My family never talked about any of it. It was almost as though the past was a neutron star black hole where nothing ever came out. "Forgive and forget," my mother often said. Years later, when she was in her 80s, she told me she found the "forgive and forget thing" in the Bible at the top of page 1,712. Of course, it's not in there anywhere – she made the whole thing up.

Nonetheless, sometimes I wonder if Dad's putting the bottle down for those years outraged my mother. The way I saw it, he wouldn't stop for her, but he did for me. I wondered if I was I being grandiose. I wondered if maybe it was God's timing and my prayers were working.

Dad started drinking again when I got married and left home. I really didn't think about it much, since our family didn't talk about feelings anyway.

Those old survival traits turned into dysfunctional thinking and acting. Perfectionism, control, the all-or-nothing perspective, and being judgmental slithered its way into my psyche. Some laid dormant, like a virus waiting to spring forth at the most inopportune and stressful time, while the others sprouted forth with little encouragement.

Perfectionism didn't seem to be me. I wasn't overly neat. My father would stress that I should put forth extreme effort and then be accepting of the results. He told me if I did my best, nothing more could be asked of me. More was asked, though. I kept striving, kept doing my best, kept working hard at school and my part-time jobs. I never learned how to slow down, how to relax, how to enjoy life. My dad told me kindness was the most important trait in life. I never relaxed; I was always on to the next thing.

I didn't understand it at the time, but when an alcoholic quits drinking, all that changes is the absence of alcohol in the house. The learned behaviors, the family pathos is still right there. Denial is a powerful survival mechanism. All the traits of an alcoholic family keep marching on.

Old patterns die hard. I met my first wife when I was in dental school; she was in undergrad, planning to go to law school. Our marriage lasted twenty-three years. We divorced fifteen years ago. At the time, I was crushed. I couldn't figure out what went wrong. Years later, after much soul-searching, prayer, and counseling with a Christian therapist, I came to realize I had indeed followed in the pattern of my parents' marriage. I repeated everything except the alcohol. I occasionally drank, rarely to excess. I had worked hard, cooked, even did the laundry. I had practically recreated my parents' marriage without realizing it.

My longstanding denial prevented me from seeing any behaviors on my part that were dysfunctional. I truly thought there was nothing wrong with me. I continued to strive to be the perfect person, the perfect worker, the perfect husband. I wasn't. Eventually, my first wife was treated for depression, like her mother, so I got a free pass to self-pity. I convinced myself she was mentally ill and I turned myself into the silent sufferer. Our marriage deteriorated. We divorced. She was out the door, and of course, I said it was her fault, since I hadn't learned to take responsibility for my part of the marriage. I played the part of the victim, as usual. Denial, avoidance, and shifting of blame. I whined to anybody who would listen.

I remarried and, eight years later, so did my former wife. Something was still wrong. My old patterns of thought and behavior were still there, like a software program that runs in the background until needed.

Over time, I realized I was an Adult Child of an Alcoholic (ACOA) with every single trait intact, firmly imprinted from my childhood. I came to realize if my mother's "bent tree story" was true, I was totally screwed.

My second wife and I had many heated discussions, putting it nicely. Any type of confrontation had always made me unbearably uncomfortable, and this was no exception. I thought I was being a kind man to her and could not understand why she was always so upset. I blamed our crumbling marriage on her.

I see now, she was fighting to save our marriage. In reality, she loved me very much; she was trying to "wake me up." It's clear to me now how the polite and fun me disappeared when we got married; my parents' marriage infiltrated every corner of our life. Hindsight is always 20/20.

For the first time in over fifty years, I realized I needed help. My second wife does not drink and hasn't for twenty years. I knew deep down inside I couldn't blame her for all of my problems. Lord knows, I tried. She would have none of it. I came to realize I could not hide behind her or anyone else any more.

After a lifetime of denial of feelings, blaming others for everything every time something went wrong, perfectionism and avoiding pain, I knew I had to do something different. I came to realize that if I offended someone, I could not go down my well-traveled road of thinking: "I didn't mean to hurt you, so don't be hurt."

The time had come when I had to stop blaming my parents and everyone around me for my own unhappiness. I realized I was doing to my second wife exactly what I had done to my first wife.

This new wife of mine was very noisy, though, and was not going to let our marriage dissolve without a fight. Or two. Or three. I know now it was her deep love for me that kept her from leaving. She saw goodness where I didn't.

Yes, family circumstances formed my patterns of thinking and behaving, but I can change.

After an epic skirmish with my wife, I agreed to seek help from that Christian marriage counselor I mentioned earlier. My wife joined me for a few sessions. He gave us marriage reading assignments and then suggested ACOA meetings and 12-Step recovery work for me. He handed me a small piece of paper with the location of a local ACOA meeting. The 12 steps should look familiar to anyone who has done a 12-step program, adapted for those of us who were raised in an alcoholic family.

It was there that I experienced a deep and profound spiritual awakening. I finally recognized, deep down inside, where my traits and character defects came from. I experienced a call to change, and I came to know I was not to beat myself up in the process.

I've completely turned my life over to God. He knows me. He created me. He loves me. I love my wife in a new way. I never meant to hurt her. Either wife, really. My new wife knows this. I now know she never meant to hurt me, either. All of it is wreckage from the past to take to the curb – and leave it there.

Redemption, by definition, is the act of being saved from sin, error, or evil. I know now first-hand that God can and will restore us to the person He created us to be. He does remove our defects of character when we ask Him. All of this happens in His time, sometimes quickly sometimes slowly.

I finally was ready to receive His healing, His grace.
The extended serenity prayer summarizes it well.

God, grant me the serenity to accept the things I cannot change
The courage to change the things I can.
And the wisdom to know the difference.
Grant me the patience with the changes
That take time.
Appreciation of all that I have.
Tolerance of those with different struggles
And the strength to get up and try again
One day at a time.
These changes take time. It's a joy-filled, although at times painful, journey to change how I think, how I process life.

The Bent Tree

I am not a bent tree. I am not the man I was 15 years ago nor am I the same one I was two months ago.

We all change, one day at a time, with God's Grace.

Thomas has chosen to stay Anonymous.

STORY THREE

"Passing the Test"

By K. M. Fleming

… (3)

PASSING THE TEST

By K. M. Fleming

I never had a church relationship with God.

My mother talked to me about Him, but I was never afforded a church-driven childhood.

We were largely Irish on my grandmother's side, and one would think I would've gleaned a Catholic upbringing with a pretty white dress for First Communion, but that wasn't us.

My reckoning was that an unyieldingly destitute life of farming, picking cotton, and eating chickens out of the yard in northern Arkansas had just driven the Catholic right out of them.

I wore pretty dresses and bonnets on Easter, and sometimes my Apache aunt took me to Lutheran services with her, but I never knew Him from that.

Rather, I just KNEW Him.

And I cannot explain how.

When I heard alcohol-fueled screaming emanating from the living room at night, I knew Him.

I knew He was there, and I clasped my little hands together and prayed for my Mother.

When my stepfather's unyielding hand burned my skin, I knew Him, and I asked Him to make me good … or take me away from there, for just awhile.

I knew Him my whole childhood and into my teens when I went to school still inebriated from the night before.

I was always drunk, always.

I knew I was bad, knew I was disappointing Him, but it just felt so damn good to be in a state where nothing mattered, my numb little cocoon.

He was always in my ear, keeping me one step away from harm.

At 20, I was an underweight wisp who woke up in unfamiliar houses and spent more than enough days wrapped in a sheet in front of a fan, trying to sweat the poison out.

Until I found myself pregnant, and an ill-conceived marriage followed.

I stopped drinking immediately and spent my days talking to my belly.

My Mother and I spent our days dreaming and chattering about this tiny one.

Every time the angel moved I was filled with promise for someone I'd give the world to ... but one day the angel went still.

She came into the world after a ten-hour labor, silent.

The room was dark, and I'd been given Demerol since there was no concern about hurting the baby.

It felt strange, oddly humiliating, like my birth wasn't important enough for lights.

It was a sad secret.

The nurse whisked the bundle to a table and examined it, and brought back a tiny daughter.

She was a diminutive red being, with long delicate fingers and a cupid's bow mouth.

In my delirium I held her tiny body, traced her tiny fingers, felt the warmth of her sweet head on my lips.

I said a thousand fervent goodbyes, and I watched as the nurse wheeled her out of the room, covered in a blanket that had held so many happy miracles before her.

The clouds came when I broke out of my stupor the next morning.

They came acidic and cross, pelting me with hot, stinging, unwelcome feelings of hatred.

At what?

I had no clue.

I was just filled with it.

I was humiliated… I couldn't even carry a baby to term without killing it.

My drinking had to be the cause.

It didn't matter that earlier tests indicated a possible problem.

My mother was my best friend, and she poured herself into my cause.

She gently led me to the counter in the floral shop, softly crooning over the tiny casket sprays in the book set before me.

I hissed angrily, and with hateful expletives, that I didn't care what was chosen, it wasn't bringing her back.

We buried my sweet wisp on December 6th, 1997. The day after my mother's birthday.

I remember the thundering silence in the cemetery, snow falling in big fat flakes.

I turned to look at her little casket draped in pink blooms one last time.

And at that moment I knew.

I wanted more than anything to cease to be.

I wanted to crawl into a hole, with my precious child, and just stop breathing.

To just hold her forever.

I prayed every night to die, until I remembered I could just end myself.

But I knew Him, and I knew it would hurt Him.

I clung to Him every single night, praying the same stale words every night until I fell asleep with sandpaper eyes ... please take my pain, please make my arms stop aching.

This went on for months.

My husband grew tired of my depression, my neediness, my anger ... and more often than not, I was left alone.

I was so lonely, and aside from my Mother, had nobody.

The grief was insurmountable ... it was gnawing my insides like demons clawing the wall.

While I went about my days soaking in a fetid pool of self-pity and petulance, a decision was made that I needed a stirring.

On the night that would change the way I would forever face every challenge or tragedy, I slipped into my usual fitless rest until my core was filled with an electric energy ... the energy you get when you reach the crest of a coastal hill and see the sea before you.

It was the familiarity that exuded the comfort and safety I remembered from having my beloved grandparents around, but leviathan in comparison.

Passing the Test

I was perched on my heels in front of my favorite statue of Jesus, twenty feet from where my child was buried.

This statue served as an earpiece for months, quiet and haunting in its mossy solitude.

This glow let me know at that minute that it was my Creator, and within a split second I'd asked Him a lifetime of questions that I don't remember.

I wasn't meant to.

I remember though, feeling the raw ache in my womb ... the umbilical, visceral pull of a million dreams that were out of my reach.

I asked "Will I ever love this way again?"

Yes.

I was told without words, it was conveyed cerebrally and I was aware the second I'd asked my question.

A heavy blanket was placed around my shoulders, and I woke up feeling more precious, more treasured, than I can ever recall.

I told my Mother about the dream and she was buoyant.

She hugged me and whispered, "That was God. He wrapped you in his love, and you're safe now."

The next few weeks I felt inherently special and handpicked, almost as if my favorite teacher had singled me out for praise in class.

The praise and its reward came in the form of a positive pregnancy test a few weeks later.

I approached this newest gift with guarded jubilation, too scared to say much out loud.

I treated my belly like a baby bird, thinking of nothing but its protection and well-being.

I was largely alone again, my marriage was nothing but a formality at this point, but my youthful ignorance assured me that everything would be fine, and besides ... I had my best friend, my mother.

She was struggling with her health but we still had shopping dates for my newest angel, revealed to be another daughter.

I gave birth to a healthy robust redheaded bundle of mirth during a January snowstorm.

I spent my days nuzzling her soft head, loving her till my heart hurt.

Every day I remembered my "dream" and how He provided.

Spring came and my Mother, who for years had forged through alcoholism, depression, and an abusive marriage ... started musing about God and Jesus more.

She'd never been particularly religious either, but like me, she'd always felt the hand on her shoulder.

"I want to get baptized one day," she remarked ... "and I think we all should."

It seemed an obvious gesture after my "dream."

I wanted to thank Him and serve Him, follow Him and raise my baby according to Him.

We gathered in our town's little brick Lutheran church and were made whole.

My Mother, who'd become so weak from still undiagnosed disease and worry, remarked to me one day shortly after ... "I feel so at peace."

I studied her face for a second, and she stared off into some painting only she could see, one that made her give a little sigh of contentment.

It unsettled me for a bit, but I brushed it off.

My restless feelings came back that summer.

I was laying next to my little daughter, just about to enter a hard sleep, when I felt more words.

The words came like the golden words in my dream, but they were not words I welcomed.

The words told me to *say Goodbye*.

Like a heavy cement block being dropped in a pool of water, my stomach fell.

Right away I knew I was being told, given the signs so many people pray for.

I thought I was going crazy.

I hid in my closet and cried.

I spent the next two weeks waiting for the next shoe to drop, looking over my shoulder, hugging my child and fretting over a million imaginary catastrophes that could befall her.

One sunny blue Monday I decided it would be a good day to take my little one to the beach for the first time.

We lived about three miles from Lake Michigan, and my sweet one looked so darling in her little yellow swimsuit with a tutu.

I called my mother and cajoled her to get my thirteen year-old brother and join us.

She was not herself that day and I could tell I was aggravating her ... she was "ornery" as she always like to say.

She didn't feel like driving over ... I told her I'd pick her up.

She told me she was tired ... I asked her if she wanted to miss her granddaughter's first beach day.

She wearily relented, and I strapped Faith in her car seat and sped to her house.

My younger brother bounded outside, ready to go, as my mother lagged behind.

She sat next to me and looked confused.

"Are you ok?" I asked her.

She looked like she was trying to solve a puzzle in her head ... but discontent, as if she wouldn't have felt any better if she'd solved it.

She told me she was fine.

I will never forget her demeanor.

I will never forget her face.

Now I look back and wonder if she'd heard the words, too.

A mile from the beach, under a brilliant azure sky, a pickup truck ran a red light and hit us at 65 miles per hour.

That sky watched me snap back to consciousness and witness the carnage of a life left in ruins once more.

It watched me shake my sleeping mother while I begged her to wake up and told her I loved her, over and over.

My Faith was safe but shaken, screaming so hard she could barely breathe, covered in tiny pieces of glass.

My brother sat slumped, unconscious next to her ... but he would survive.

A paramedic broke the news about my mother, and I turned mercurial, screaming that I'd killed her, as the driver of the truck took advantage of my disoriented state to place the blame on me.

I screamed so loud I lost my voice.

I purged months and years of pain in the back of that ambulance while the poor paramedic tried to calm me down.

I would never see my best friend again.

I was all alone.

I went back to my depressive state in the weeks and months after that day.

I was kicked like a stray dog.

I was hair-trigger volcanic one minute and falling into a deep sleep the next, ignoring my child while she played innocently in her bouncer in front of a *Teletubbies* episode I would rewind and play over and again, just trying to get more sleep in ... more hiding.

My marriage disintegrated, as a depressive wife who doesn't care to clean is not very appealing.

There were some who cared, though ... and pushed me to take care of myself and get on medication for my depression and PTSD.

I was coaxed back into driving.

He planted my name and my plight in their heads.

My life went on as surely as it always does.

We shake our old battle-weary cocoons and appear fresh and kissed by our Father, and live to do it over and over again until we are delivered Home.

My story doesn't end with some miraculous revelation that makes one break into goosebumps or cry.

My redemption all started with a tiny gift He gave me, a gift that called on me to hoe a straight row, and from there He went to work on me.

He spoke to me, and from there I knew He had been there all along, was, and would be.

Forever woven into the tapestry of my soul.

He showed me I needed Him, and would continue to need him in the tumultuous chapters that lie ahead.

He blew life into a tiny seed of urgency into my Mother's heart and she died at peace knowing the glory that awaited her.

Sometimes I sit and think about it and question why I was so lucky.

I'm not quite sure I know what would have happened to me if He had not come to me.

Before He spoke to me I was a wounded, knotted shell of a wild animal who welcomed an end no matter its form.

Some people wait their whole lives for what I was given … an assurance that they are heard.

My relationship with my Father has never been something that was cultivated through church or outside hands, but rather a childlike knowing.

I'm thankful for it; I've always felt it in my roots and never questioned it.

I spend my days now sunning myself in the brilliant glow of the light He provides … loving the family He's given me.

I try not to spend my days fretting over what could befall me because

He has shown me that I will emerge from the ashes battered but still good.

His tiny victor, war paint under my eyes and a soul of impenetrable stardust ... sculpted by His hand.

Impenetrable, because He stands behind me.

K. M. Fleming is a forty-something, married mother of 4. A high school dropout, she returned to school to obtain her GED; she'll ruefully regale you with a tale of how she missed an Honors degree by two points. She is a florist in the Great Lakes region, spending her free time writing and creating. She's also a mother to three herding dogs, three lazy cats, chickens, bearded dragons, a pair of doves, and a roomful of snakes, her favorite being a Western Hognose named Rasputin. She is driven by her love for God and her family and is a faithful, if somewhat crotchety, student of humanity.

STORY FOUR

"My Story"

By Jamie P.

(4)
MY STORY

by Jamie P.

B y the grace of a living and loving God, I have been clean and sober for over 19 years as of the date I'm writing this. I can state without any reservation that it was God and His Son, Jesus Christ, who miraculously got me sober, and because of his love and mercy, I am still sober. It has not always been that way, and I'd like to tell you about that.

Most stories of recovery tell how it was while we were in our cups (still drinking), what happened, and how we are today. My story must begin before that for you to understand God's mercy and grace in my life.

At the age of 18, I accepted Jesus Christ into my life. I believe I was a good Christian at that time. I read my Bible daily, went to church every time the doors were open for a service, and shared the Gospel with anyone when the opportunity presented itself. That was what the Bible taught me to do.

The time came when I was really interested in finding a girlfriend. I sought her out at church most of all, or in Christian settings. I dated a girl while in college, and we split up. I wanted to find another lady to date. One of my teachers at school made the suggestion of going to night clubs and looking there. As a Christian, that didn't appeal to me at all. But, I made the decision to go later on when I was really eager to find a girl. I didn't find a lady to fall in love with there, but in time, I fell in love with alcohol.

For a year or two, I drank responsibly and didn't get into any trouble because of alcohol. I would go to the clubs and have one drink and play pool most of my time there. I was never much of a dancer and still am not. I would play pool and talk a little to the people there at the club. Then one night, I had two drinks and was stopped by the police on the way home. I told the officer I had two drinks and he told me to be careful and let me continue home. I should have seen that as a sign of what was to come later, but it didn't register with me.

In 1978, I joined the Air Force and was stationed in Minot, North Dakota, at Minot AFB. During my training for that job, I drank responsibly for the most part and didn't get into any trouble in Denver at Lowry AFB. I did fall asleep while driving one day due to staying up most of the night before playing pool and snooker. My roommate and I went to tour the Air Force Academy in Colorado Springs, and I was tired from the night before. I should have said I wouldn't go, but we were going in my car and I didn't want to disappoint my roommate. We made it back to the base unscathed.

Then I was sent to Minot for my duty station. I met a lot of nice people there and some were Christians.

But my off-duty hours were spent playing pool and clubbing. I was okay for a while until a day in the dorm with my roommate and another service member. We were drinking beer, and I had my usual one. I was offered another one and drank it.

I remember to this day that a feeling of ease and comfort came over me, a kind of euphoria, and I continued to chase that feeling for 23 years. It made me feel very good, and I wanted that again and again.

I played pool and drank on my off-duty hours and on the weekends to start with since I was on the evening shift in the beginning. After a year and a half or so, I got into trouble. I wrecked my car driving while drinking. I was charged with reckless driving on that occasion due to the fact that I was immobile when the police officer found me. I had totaled my car by driving too fast and not being able to make a curve that had loose gravel on it. I went over an embankment, and the frame of the car was bent. Gone! A nice Cutlass lost due to alcohol.

After that incident, the Air Force had to discipline me. I couldn't be acting in that manner within the community, or on the base for that matter. I was reduced in rank and moved to day shift so that my superiors could keep an eye on me. I was taken from working on the airplanes, to the room where the electronics were stored after they were repaired by the technicians. It was a really boring job, and I hated it with a passion. I felt at that time that I should have been left on evening shift since that was when I would drink if given the time.

They gave me the time, and I drank. And did I drink! I stayed out most nights until the bars closed or close to it. I drove drunk and survived it. After wrecking the car, I got a truck, and it took a beating. I was in town one night drinking and headed to the place I was staying. I ended up driving down the sidewalk and drove the truck into a store window there in Minot. I remember people dodging the truck and when I went to put the brakes on, I missed and hit the accelerator. The front end of the truck hit the window and it came crashing down. I was arrested by the police. I don't remember the charges, but it was alcohol-related.

Not too long afterward, I was discharged from the Air Force with a General Discharge under Honorable Conditions. Failure to adapt is what my discharge papers read.

I went home to Texas in October of 1981, a bit disappointed in myself that I couldn't continue my service and be discharged honorably the following September. After getting home, I went back to my old job I left to go into the service. It wasn't too long before I was fired from that job due to alcohol-related tardiness and other issues.

What followed next was many years of the same. I hunted for a job, started it and was either fired or I quit. I was never satisfied with what I was doing for work. I continued to drink and spend my nights out in the bars playing pool and chasing women, which I never caught.

One night, a guy offered me a little white powder in the bathroom, telling me that it would wake me up, and I'd be able to play good pool. I later learned that it was cocaine and I started chasing that along with the booze. It was never as much of a problem as the alcohol because I couldn't afford it. Besides, drinking was legal and possessing street drugs was not! I wanted to stay away from getting in trouble again.

For the next nineteen years, I continued that lifestyle. I would go to the bars and drink, hunt for cocaine or amphetamines, and "party" as much as I could afford. During that time, I was arrested five times here in Texas. Three were misdemeanor DUIs (driving under the influence), and two were felonies.

I was arrested in the summer of 2000 for the last time. Part of my punishment was to spend thirty days in jail and serve eight years on probation. The prosecutor wanted to send me to jail for two years, but my attorney talked them into probation. Part of my sentence included going to a rehab facility for ninety days. I remember the person in the office telling me that and my reply was, "Do what?!" I still was not convinced that I had that much of a problem.

One day at the rehab center, I was sitting on a handrail going to the recreation room. It was about seven to ten days after I entered the facility and the alcohol and drugs had left my body. I remember thinking about what my life was like before and all the hurt I had caused myself and my loved ones.

I decided I wanted to change my life and the only way I was going to be able to do that was with God's help. I cried out to God, "God, please help me!" And I'm glad to say that He has every day since. I'm still clean and sober today.

My life is far from perfect. I struggle a lot and still have a desire now and then to have a drink. But I have learned that I cannot drink, not even one drink, because it will change the chemicals in my brain and the cycle of desire will be set in motion. I have many friends who are in recovery. They have helped me when I needed it. They've set me straight when I needed that, too. It's been difficult at times.

I didn't want to tell another human being my faults and failures. But I chose to talk to the pastor of our church at the time. As far as I know, he has held my confessions to himself. Recovery started on the day I entered that rehab center, September 27, 2000. But, true recovery started the day I called out to the Lord and asked for His help.

I have a lot of regrets. My father passed away while I was drinking. He never saw me get sober. I like to think that he knows I am now since he was a Christian and is sitting with God who knows all. Maybe God told him or Mother did when she went to be with them in heaven. Mom did see me get sober this last time, and I'm happy about that. I'm glad that my relationships with my brother and sister are on better terms than before, too.

I lost several vehicles during my drinking days, but more difficult was losing all those years to the nonsense. My work history isn't pretty. My criminal record doesn't allow me to work in some jobs, like security, for example. But I'm glad to say that those true friends I've had all my life have been supportive and never have turned their backs on me even when I was out there getting drunk. I still have friends from elementary school and high school who I keep in touch with through Facebook. But also important are my recovery friends; they are still keeping me honest and holding me up with support when needed.

Over the last nineteen years, I've had to lean on the Lord a lot. He has provided me all my needs and some of my wants. I've seen firsthand His provision for my shelter needs and food for my stomach. Bible verses have told me that He would do those things if I would trust Him with them through prayer. When I have doubted Him, He has still been with me through that, too.

One verse comes to mind as I end this story. It reads *"I can do all things through Christ, who strengtheneth me." (Philippians 4:13)*. It is through the strength I received from Him that I was able to get sober and stay sober to this day.

If you are reading this and don't have a relationship with God, I encourage you to know that He loves you more than you'll ever be able to imagine.

He loved you so much that He sent His only Son to die on a cruel cross. Jesus suffered the agony and pain we should have to suffer because of our sins. Then, after accepting God's forgiveness, we can have a relationship with Him and know the peace that comes from trusting Him with all our needs and desires.

Being a Christian isn't easy at times. The world scoffs and ridicules us at times. Some have even died due to their faith in the Lord, but we have the knowledge that God is on our side and watching over us. If you'll just say a little prayer and invite Jesus into your life, He will be more than happy to be your Lord and Savior.

It has been a privilege to share my story with you. I hope you've learned that God is mighty and able to save those who are lost in sin, and those of us that have been lost to sin even after having a relationship with Him. He is an awesome God!

Praise be unto God for His mighty works of love!

Praise be unto God for His mighty works of love! For all have sinned and come short of the glory of God. (Romans 3:23)

For the wages of sin is death, but the gift of God is eternal life through Jesus Christ, our Lord. (Romans 6:23)

For God so loved the world, that he gave his only begotten Son, that whosoever believeth in him should not perish, but have everlasting life. (John 3:16)

For whosoever shall call upon the name of the Lord shall be saved. (Romans 10:13)

I can do all things through Christ, who strengtheneth me. (Philippians 4:13)

But my God shall supply all your need according to his riches in glory by Christ Jesus. (Philippians 4:19)

Jamie P. has chosen to remain Anonymous.

STORY FIVE

"A Tale of Two Cities"

By Michael C.

(5)
A TALE OF TWO CITIES

By Michael C.

"Darkness cannot drive out darkness; only light can do that. Hate cannot drive out hate; only love can do that."
~ Rev. Dr. Martin Luther King, Jr.

Something I have found to be interesting is that we don't understand darkness until we experience the light. Through the nine months of our gestation and formation in the womb, we are in complete darkness, oblivious to the world around us. Then at birth, we are literally thrust into the light of day.

It is similar with my particular journey of faith. I had no idea how far I had fallen until an abundance of light pointed out my sinfulness.

"Everything happens for a reason.
Sometimes we're just stupid and make bad decisions."
~Unknown Author

In considering my own story, I had to contemplate the life of one particular Saint and Doctor of the Church, Saint Augustine. Most religious leaders avoid public introspection of their lives due to fears that it will damage their reputation.

One of the things that I respect about Christianity, especially our Holy Scripture, is that we are not presented with a whitewashed text. No, the Bible shows us that God has indeed worked through flawed people. From Adam and Eve, down through our day, flawed men and women have been and continue to be used to fulfill God's plan, bringing saving grace to the world.

> *"Forgiveness is the remission of sins. For it is by this that what has been lost, and was found, is saved from being lost again."*
> *~Saint Augustine*

Apart from Jesus himself, we would be hard pressed to find a perfect example of righteousness. This is especially true of the prominent players recorded in the pages of scripture. How many times did Abraham sin, yet he was deemed righteous? King David committed both murder and adultery, yet through repentance he is known as a friend of God.

The examples of history don't show that sin is okay or acceptable to God; rather, that we are able to find redemption in spite of our failures. Augustine had a rocky start in life, as recorded in his "confessions." His young life was filled with lust and illicit activities. Yet, he was also able to move beyond his failings, finding both forgiveness and redemption through the love of our Savior, Jesus.

We always tend to minimize our own shortcomings. Like most, I would have said about my youth, "I wasn't really that bad." However, in retrospect, knowing what I do today regarding God's contempt for sin, I cringe at my own arrogance.

Like Augustine (I've little in common with this illustrious man), my life can be divided into two metaphorical cities: The City of Man and The City of God. The two sides of my life are decidedly marked, on one side by my human failure, and on the other side by redemption in the name of Jesus. Nothing about my personal journey to redemption is worthy of being boastful. My failures are my own and any success I may have experienced are due to the grace, mercy, and providence of God.

As someone who has a measurable amount of influence within a particular church jurisdiction, I have, for reasons noted above, been reluctant to put words to my immoral conduct. I do so today so that some, who come across these words, may know that they too may find redemption from similar sins. Yes, and even the most egregious, the most conspicuously offensive.

Though I was raised in a non-Christian home, I did know something of Christianity growing up. This was due to the influence of my maternal grandmother. Growing up in my home, we had very little in the form of moral guidance besides being told to "be nice to your sisters, don't swear, and tell the truth, or else." The party lifestyle was prominent in my home. Drinking and smoking and partying to all hours of the night are my prevalent childhood memories.

We didn't go to church or Sunday school. It wasn't until I was about eight years old that I made it to Church when I tagged along with a school chum.

One Sunday morning, while listening to John 3:16, I made a tearful and heartfelt decision to become a Christian. I said the "Sinner's Prayer," and the Sunday school teacher proclaimed me saved. The problem was that after what should have been a momentous occasion, I had no follow-up or followthrough mentoring. As an adolescent boy, I had no idea what it truly meant to be a Christian. Shortly after that point, my friend moved away and I no longer had a ride to Church.

My life moved on from there with no seeming impact of saving grace. As I grew up, I continued to live like the world, following my parents' example of drinking and the party life. I was oblivious to things of the Spirit.

As I grew older, I attended a few churches on occasion. I usually had ulterior motives, like trying to get on the good side of my girlfriend's parents. You see, this church thing had no impact on my life or moral center at that time. The cute Bible stories of my youth rarely made mention of sin, or striving to live a sanctified life. I had no real concept of sin. I saw no need for anything referred to as sexual purity.

Basically, I was no different than any other typical teenager of my day. I was focused on doing what was right and pleasing in my own mind. Moral guidance was not even provided from my parents. Christian morality was not known. A sad observation, from later on: when I announced my engagement to my wife, we were asked "why not simply live together?"

Like most young adult males, I had one thing on my mind, on a regular basis. In a sense, I was encouraged by an interesting collection of pornographic calendars at my grandfather's house. Gramps even gave me a party hat with nude images of Marilyn Monroe. My teachers did not share my appreciation for such an artform when I wore the hat to elementary school.

I don't find it surprising that, like other young men, I had sexual experiences prior to marriage. We were in times described to be "the sexual revolution." It didn't really matter what we did or how many partners we had, at least that is what I thought. During this time of my life, I was firmly entrenched within the City of Man.

Even after I supposedly turned my life over to Christ, it didn't make a visible difference in my life. In Protestant Christianity, there is a concept that resonated with my un-formed faith: Once saved, always saved. This line of thinking falsely reassures us that there is nothing we can do to lose our salvation once we are "saved."

In my youthful ignorance and inexperience, that seemed like a green light to continue with life as usual. There is little as poignant and humbling as when we discover how wrong we can be!

As a young adult, I fully expected to marry the person I was sexually active with when I fell in love. Instead, two unthinkable things happened. My partner became pregnant and she decided her only choice was to have an abortion. I was just another one of the young men who rarely thought ahead, realizing there could be consequences to our actions.

Somehow, in the back of my mind somewhere, I heard a very small voice telling me that this was wrong. Rather than listening and voicing objections to what was clearly legal, I simply drove her to the abortion clinic.

I was listening with secular ears, firmly rooted in the City of Man.

A few years later, I hooked up with one of my high school sweethearts.

Even though we went to church together, we became sexually active. We did not see a problem with this, after all, sex between two consenting adults was legal so I thought it must be okay. In the midst of my emotions and lust, I never stopped to consider the consequences. You know what they say, those who don't learn from history are doomed to repeat it, and that's just what happened. I didn't find out about it until many years later.

I find it interesting how our sins catch up to us. We often live our lives refusing to count the costs. There are so many costs to sexual promiscuity. Even though I have been emotionally devastated by broken relationships, there is nothing that compares to the heartache of being told years later by someone you were in love with that they had an abortion without your knowledge.

Yes, some years after I was married to my wife, attending church, and even contemplating religious life, I had this bombshell dropped in my lap. It was during the time that I was deeply connecting with God, His moral truths resonating loudly in my heart and soul, I happened to run across my old flame in the middle of a department store, and she told me right there what had transpired.

I know how I felt at that time; I had feelings of guilt, shame, and anger. "How could she do this?" I asked myself in a moment of self-absorption. It took me quite a while before I could stop and consider the pain and guilt she must have felt. I cannot imagine the emotional turmoil she had to deal with.

How can we be so thick headed? Why does it take so many mistakes for us to get it right? For me it was thinking more about momentary pleasures than counting the potential costs of my choices.

The good news is, like Abraham, Moses, and David, I have asked for forgiveness and have been forgiven. I have dedicated myself to a life of faith and active ministry. There is nothing I can do to mitigate the emotional damage that has occurred due to my prideful lack of self-control. Due to my sinful actions (I could have said no any time along the way), two children lost their lives. They were literally sacrificed on the altar of my sexual avarice. Additionally, two women experienced what our modern society writes off as a simple medical procedure, which in fact, is a life altering emotional experience.

The only good news in this fiasco is that I have found forgiveness and even redemption from my sins. No. In my mind I find nothing to lessen my failures and the damage I've caused. In part, I'm writing to ask forgiveness from the two women who suffered as a result of my complete lack of impulse control. My prayer is that I will eventually be able to personally apologize to my two children who have preceded me into heaven.

In the end, the City of God became the dominant factor in my life. Despite having a Christ-centered life, I continually struggle to do the right thing. My temptations these days may be different; I still must consistently seek God's grace with a contrite heart. In all things the task before me now is to love God and be called according to His purposes.

My prayer is that this story will make a difference in the lives of some; that it will prompt more than a few to count the costs of their actions and seek first the kingdom of God before their own prideful lusts and desires.

Ultimately, it is my desire that God will use the words on these pages to bring many to an Authentic Faith and a Radical Transformation – being reconciled with, and redeemed by the love of God.

> *"Redemption is not perfection.*
> *The redeemed must realize their imperfections."*
> *~John Piper*

Michael C. has chosen to remain Anonymous.

STORY SIX

"Becoming One With the Spirit"

By Vicki Manuel

(6)
BECOMING ONE WITH THE SPIRIT

By Vicki Manuel

There may be a time in our lives when we'll experience difficulty and trauma; either physical, mental, or environmental. We will be introduced to ridicule, sickness, death, failure, judgment, and loss.

Some of us will experience more love than others; some will grow up not knowing what love is. Some will never feel like they belong, that they can't do anything right. Basically, all of those moments cause heartache.

See, the thing is, no matter what you are going through, someone somewhere has or is going through the same thing as you. We all have our journey in this life, and we all have a purpose in this life. Every person who comes into our life is for a reason, and for a season (some seasons are longer than others.)

Sometimes, we feel alone, deserted, and/or marooned on an island.

My life was full of moments that brought me heartache. It seemed as though anytime something was going right in my life, something horrific would follow. It didn't pay to be happy.

Due to circumstances along my journey, as far back as I can remember, I never felt completely loved. I felt as though I never belonged, never fit in, was never good enough, smart enough, skinny enough, or had the right words to say in the right moment. I even had friends who I felt just tolerated me. I felt as though I was a burden to society, that I would never amount to anything. I didn't have a sense of timing and I was forgetful. I was filled with anxiety, depression, shame, and fear, just to name a few.

As a child, I remember praying to God that He would change me, make me different. Create me so others would like me, to be smart, to have the right words, I just wanted to feel love and know that everything was going to be okay.

Instead, every morning I'd wake up and all I would see in the mirror was someone who had no sense of time, always late, could never remember anything, ugly and fat, was unliked, and when I talked it never made sense to others. I saw someone who always failed no matter how hard she tried. It was a lonely world for so long.

I experienced what death was like at ages 4, 8, 13, and 18. My grandma passed away first. The only memory I have of her was rocking me in a rocker at her house when we visited. I felt so loved. Next was my brother. I never knew him, I only saw him once in the hospital. He died of complications from pneumonia. He had been in the hospital from the age of three after being struck by a motorcycle. The motorcycle didn't kill him; it was all the "other attacks" he was under after that.

Then, my father died when I was 13; he was the only person who I felt actually loved me; and he died.

There were other deaths that happened before this that affected my mom, but I didn't know them.

Then, my mother died. I always felt as though her death was a blessing since she was no longer suffering. She had a mental illness, and she finally was at peace.

Food became my escape. I ate all the time but I rarely felt full. I see now I was just using food to fill the emptiness felt inside; I was hiding from the world.

As an adult, with all of these moments in my life and the negative affirmations rolling in my head, I learned how to live in numbness. My mind was riddled with negative thoughts I thought were true.

I learned to pretend to be happy.

If my surroundings were happy, then I was happy. Sometimes this worked and sometimes it didn't. Sometimes, I just separated myself from the world by isolating myself. There were times my anxiety was so bad, my body hurt. My anxiety had anxiety, and my fears became reality. I would feel so useless that I just didn't want to live anymore. I would default to my childhood and hear my mom saying "Why can't you be like "so-and-so?"

I would often think, I don't even know how to be me, much less them!

Believe it or not, I met my husband when I was 17. He loved me before I loved myself. He didn't even know the whirlwind that was filling my head. He knew I was afraid of heights, and he knew I had anxiety, but he didn't know about the burdens and the heavy chains I carried every day. To be honest, I don't know if he knows now. We have been together for 29 years.

Over the years I've worked in many different fields – a restaurant, retail, and child care. I never really thought about what to do in my life, I just allowed the universe to set its course. Things would just fall into place, doors would open, and I went through. Everything worked itself out.

My dad taught me to always see the good in everything, and my mom taught me keep my faith, so that is what I did.

Things started to change in about 2011, I don't know the exact date. I was working for the corporate world, low on the totem pole. I would talk to my co-worker and say, "There has to be more to life than this." It made no sense to me to work day in and day out with no purpose except to fill the pockets of the corporate world. My co-worker would always suggest that I go back to school. I didn't want to even think about that possibility, I still had nightmares about high school. It wasn't going to happen.

I grew up knowing who God and Jesus were. I knew God had rules for us that we needed to follow. I knew that Jesus was born and killed for us; BUT I thought God was always mad at me, just like a dad who grounded his child for doing wrong.

I could never hold up to the "laws of God," and I thought Jesus was like a long lost uncle who would come around when you really needed him and make things right, and then go home to his life when all was done.

Well, one day while I was praying, I prayed, "Lord, I know there is more to life than this, you have a purpose for me, what is it???" Well, He heard me and life as I knew it changed, and new doors opened in a totally different direction. I had to renew my mind. I had to let go of old habits, but at the time I had no idea what was going on.

I knew the "light" but I lived in the darkness. Jesus was like the moon in the darkness, always there leading the way and protecting me without me even understanding His love.

Over the next five years I did go back to school, I was baptized, I quit my job and continued along the new journey.

When I was almost 40, around 2011, I was diagnosed with a cataract in my right eye. The doctors weren't concerned. It was small and inoperable. Over the years, it got worse and worse. I didn't fret about it until 2016 when I developed a cataract in my left eye that got so bad I couldn't drive at night.

I was still thinking God was mad at me, and Jesus was a long-lost uncle.

I decided to allow the universe to open up doors and receive me through them. I just so happened to change jobs, and a co-worker told me how I could receive my operation for free. WOW! What a blessing. In the fall of 2016 I had cataract surgery on both eyes. It was a success, PLUS I didn't have to wear glasses full-time anymore.

I let go of a lot of things over the past five years but I hadn't fully let go of the negative nellies, fear, anxiety, and depression. January 2017, my right eye had side effects from the surgery. The first was a retina tear. My anxiety and fear went through the roof. The doctors fixed it in office and I went home. A week later at the follow-up, I was informed that my retina detached. What?! What does that even mean? My eyes were the only thing that I loved about myself, and now they were telling me that my eyes are rejecting me? Needless to say everything that I learned of God and Jesus on my own went out the window! I ended up having my retina detach again at the end of March.

Even though I was baptized in 2013, I never went to church. I never sought out a mentor. I never picked up the Bible. I never grew my relationship with Jesus. I still thought the old way. Although the universe would send me messages through Bible verses, they would just appear and I would have a new way of thinking. I gained a few friends who also believed, and we would encourage one another. I went through a few seasons, a season in the pit and a season of nothingness.

It wasn't depression, I had peace deep down within me. Both times God brought me out of them. Through the years I would get "words" to focus on which then became acronyms, and I would meditate on them until the next word would come to me. It was such a unique and amazing experience.

Surgery was scheduled and done; healing began. I had to rest until it healed. As the weeks went by I remember asking my husband "How do you go through life without worry? How do you let it go?" He replied "I just pray and hand it over to God." That just didn't make sense to me because, for me, when I handed it over it would come right back as though I was a magnet, and it was steel.

So, I prayed about it. New doors would open, and I would take them. One led me to a lady I didn't know at all. I know now God sent her to me. She called me out of the blue. We started having Bible study over the phone and she introduced me to God's amazing love, His grace, explaining to me that HE loved me more than life itself, more than the moon, the earth, to infinity and back!!! This was shocking.

Over the months, one door would open to another opportunity. I started learning how to shut doors behind me. I learned to let go of burdens and unlock the chains that had no business holding me back. I learned all of that was from the enemy; I learned it's the enemy's way of blocking me (us) from seeing God's true love.

I learned that I had to let go of certain "idols," which in my case was food. It was also hindering me from having a clear mind. In the springtime, out of nowhere, an old acquaintance contacted me and asked if I could watch her child. I agreed. One thing led to another, and one Sunday, while watching her child, God placed me exactly where I needed to be in a new church that would help me grow in my relationship with the Lord Jesus Christ.

Yes, my whole world changed in 2017! I fell in love with Jesus! As the love grew, the darkness diminished, the light started to shine like the sun on a beautiful sunny summer day. I let go and allowed God into my life.

The moment that I let go of all that old stuff, the nonsense, the lies, God refilled my mind with His promises, and the lighter I felt! The freer I became! (By the way, there are over 5,000 promises to us in the Bible.)

For the first time in a long time I felt true joy, true love; I felt alive!

I felt as though I had a purpose—because I did have purpose. I no longer have negative nellies constantly floating around in my mind. The enemy tries to distract me, but I have the word to chase the enemy away. Now, I focus on God's promises and His word to get me through trials and tribulations, to get me through each day.

Every day I pray that I live in the fruits of the Spirit so that I am able to shine His light through me for others to see. I was living in darkness because I never had that person in my life to show off His light. I know I had people praying for me because if I didn't, I wouldn't be writing this today. So, I thank the people who prayed for me.

Just recently, someone told me that religion was a disease, and I didn't know at that moment how to respond but if I had to do it all over again this is how I would respond:

Religion is a disease, a disease that is formed by man not God, but the

RELATIONSHIP that one builds and develops and continues to grow with Jesus is the most precious gift anyone can ever receive. HIS grace overthrows any disease, any negative spirit. For HE is life, He is life of yesterday, today, and tomorrow. He is the light that burns forever. The relationship that I have built with Jesus grows each and every moment in my life. Yes, life is hard but loving Jesus is easy!

How do you grow your relationship with God? Repent—ask for forgiveness, forgive yourself, forgive others, let go of the old beliefs and thoughts, be teachable, and live the best you can in LOVE. Love conquers all!

You know how I referred to how the universe was opening doors? That wasn't the universe, that was GOD! He was doing things for me the whole time, even when I didn't appreciate Him. He LOVES us so much!!

Remember: No matter how alone you feel ... YOU ... are NEVER alone! God is always with you! Call out to Him. He is waiting for you to receive HIM! You have a purpose in this life; you are valuable, God loves you, and He will forgive you when you invite Him into your life! You will be made new in Him!

Everyone has his/her own journey. We have no control over other's actions, nor do we have any control over situations that arise, BUT we do have control over our thoughts, words, and actions!

Live by example, live in love, shine that beautiful light that is within you. For YOU are a child of God whom HE loves so very much that HE wants you to have heaven on earth as well as in heaven long after this world is gone!

Thank you for reading. I pray, in Jesus name, that everyone who reads this is blessed with the experience of the grace and love of God, that you will always look to Him, no matter what situation arises. Amen.

Who is Vicki Manuel? I am the same as you. I was once so lost in this world I was barely holding on; I felt lost and broken. Three things kept me moving forward to where I am today...Hope, Faith, and always looking for the good in every situation. Along this journey I have received certificates as a Certified Health Coach, Happiness Coach, and Biblical Health Coach. Most importantly, I have accepted God's path, and He is leading the way. My passion is to help women to overcome health issues physically, mentally, and spiritually. This includes but not limited to losing weight, reversing disease, and growing your spiritual life in God our Father.

I lead a local women's support group called H.O.P.E. "Honoring Our Purpose Everyday." I'm also the owner of AromaNecklaces and More (handmade terracotta essential oil necklaces/bracelets)

https://squareup.com/store/AromaNecklaces

You can contact me at vickimwhc@gmail.com

STORY SEVEN

"Jesus"

By Dr. David Nelson

(7)
JESUS

Who is Jesus?

If He walked into the room right now, what would you say to Him?

When asked this very question, my response would be to hug Jesus tightly and to sob. A release, a total flood of emotions, where nothing is held back, and I know Jesus would understand. Jesus gets it. True empathy. Even though He is God, He was fully human when He walked this earth.

When his friend Lazarus died, Jesus was told by Mary, the sister of Lazarus, "Lord, if you had been here, my brother would not have died." Feeling her anguish, Jesus was deeply moved in spirit. Jesus wept. God and human. Human and God. Aware of what it's like to be human.

Jesus was joyful, exhausted, angry, disgusted, sorrowful, compassionate, frustrated, agonized, empathic, and forgiving. Doesn't sound like Jesus playing with children in the park all of the time chasing butterflies, does it? Rather, it sounds like Jesus immersed in the human experience.

Our experience. His experience.

The difference is this: We violate our divine purpose by sinning. He fulfilled His Divine Purpose. He never sinned.

Jesus felt temptation, hunger, pain, and joy. Just like us, he was tempted by Satan with promises of worldly power and goods. This is important; important enough that Jesus personally told us what happened to Him in the desert.

When a major auto magazine asked the question, "Who would you pick, from any person, past or present, to ride with you from New York to Los Angeles," a good percentage of those answering said, "Jesus Christ."

I can only imagine Jesus saying, "Let's open her up, and see what this baby can do!" or "Let's stop for a cheeseburger, I'm really hungry!"

Arriving in Los Angeles, He most certainly would go ballistic over the homeless problem, drug abuse, and all the meds given in the name of mental health care.

Anger, righteous anger. God and human. Human and God.

Jesus.

Naomi Ministry's Senior Pastor, David Nelson, is a man of compassion with a calm, gentle spirit. His perseverance and genuine humility spring forth from the tremendous adversities he feels he's been blessed to experience in his lifetime. A Doctor of Dental Surgery for 40 years, Dr. Nelson enjoys reading and gardening with his beloved wife, Luanne.

You can find David, usually with Luanne, preaching and teaching in groups both large and small—all for the Glory of Jesus Christ, their Lord and Savior.

STORY EIGHT

"My Story of Redemption"

By Verissa Walber

(8)
MY STORY OF REDEMPTION

By Verissa Walber

*R*edemption, so sweet the sound; but the cost, the price paid, is often untold.

Truth be told, I am very open about my testimony. I have written a book, *Angel of the Flesh*, sold on Amazon. I give it away to every new person who comes to Ministry of Living Stones, the church that I founded in Alaska, just so they know where I came from and how my Savior Jesus Christ delivered me from and freed me from the captivity of guilt and shame.

Thirty-four years, *thirty-four years* of hatred, bitterness, perversion, violence and addictions, my life in a nutshell the day the Lord stopped me from killing myself. I was hated as a child; my father's own sexual immorality created a division of hate between us. He didn't see me, he saw me as a product of adultery. I wasn't. I was his, but his adultery caused him to think my mother was cheating on him. Once the thought was planted in his head, my life was over for a normal childhood.

The beatings were daily; I still wear the whip marks. Even words slurring, falling down drunk didn't stop my parents from their torment. They could lay that weapon of choice across my buttocks, head, face, or whatever part of my body got in their way; experts in physical abuse rivaling the art of an interrogator. At the age of four, I hated my name, my body would course with fear the moment my name crossed their lips. One wrong word out of my mouth, or wrong move with my body, and I would get a backhand to the face, or my body would be sent flying into the closest wall or skidding across the floor.

Fear, constant fear, mixed with the smell of spilled grain belt beer, vomit, and urine. I recall looking at my mother, not looking for a kind look or a hug, never looking for love. I looked at her to gauge her glare, to gauge how angry she might be in that moment. My goal as a child was to avoid her sharp tongue and brutal hands. I was never able to please her, "dimwitted twit", "stupid," "lazy," were often the nice words she used when speaking with me.

Why? Why? Why? She knew the truth, I was daddy's daughter, but to keep the peace, to keep the anger from going to her—she hated me. I was the cause, in her mind, for her horrible marriage. My mother was a beautiful woman. A head turner was the phrase they used to describe her.

My father was considered handsome, or so *he* said. Everyone knows his type, life of the party, the good ole' boy; that was my dad. Of course, that wasn't the person I knew, I knew the foul-mouthed, angry, drunken man; he was quick with his fist and even faster with his belt. I could look at him, and it would be wrong.

The incredible part about what I have said so far—that is the "good stuff"; if only that is all that had happened to me. I am going to do my best to describe the fear and sordid lifestyle in which I was raised. I knew every creak of every floorboard, I knew the sound of the car door, and the squeak of the front hinge. The fall of the footsteps were the warning bells, the slurring words were the warning signals. Sleep for a child should be filled with sweet dreams, not so for me, I was constantly on alert for another scream, another yell. Deep, deep down, even without having experienced any other kind of lifestyle, I knew this way of living wasn't right.

I wasn't alone, but I took the brunt. I protected my younger brother to the best of my ability. He was born with crossed eyes that made him a piece of trash to our father. I felt badly for him, it wasn't his fault. I would hear the fights between my parents. "Look, how ugly she is. She is stupid. She isn't mine, you whore." It never stopped. "He has cross eyes, no kid of mine would have cross eyes."

I believed it was my fault. If only I wasn't so stupid, maybe he would love me. I hungered for his love or even just a pat on the head. The dogs received more affection.

Forays to the bar as a child were commonplace, day or night; warm or cold. We never got to go inside, we sat in the car for hours on end. Waiting, waiting for the torment we knew was coming. I recall one time when I needed to urinate; however, there was no way I was going to go inside to use the bathroom, and I couldn't open the door and pee on the sidewalk. If I would have, it would have brought them out and made them angry for having ended their drinking early. I held it. I held it until I was in pain. I held it until I squirmed. I held it until I couldn't hold it any longer. The urine began to leak out; then it gushed out. I wiped my butt all over the car seat to try and soak it up. I noticed my brother was doing the same thing. We huddled together to stay warm until our parents staggered out of the bar.

At home, I tried to get in the house without them noticing my wet clothing, but it didn't work, I went flying. They were yelling at me for being a baby, someone who needs diapers, but my brother made it in the house. I scrambled up from the pile of snow and ran into the house before the beating could begin. I looked for a pair of clean underwear but settled on the day before panties, at least they were dry.

The summer I turned five was a whole new experience. We were going to the farm, time to help the family. Summertime on the farm, hot hard work filled with new opportunities of horror. I understood fear, more than a five-year-old child should. I recognized quickly situations that would place me in a state of fear. To be honest, every day I walked in fear, there were just more fearful situations throughout the day.

One hot, humid day my father had the grand idea of dropping me into the water well with the bucket to get the watermelon that was chilling. I had to put the watermelon into the bucket treading water until the bucket was lowered and I raised to the surface.

One day I wasn't raised back to the surface, and I learned quickly how to do the survival float. The cold only got colder, the cramps in my muscles seemed insurmountable; hours later the bucket was dropped back down. Saved at last.

The summer dragged on; one afternoon, I rounded a corner and there they were ... farmhands. They were leering at me. Those men gave fear a new meaning; something sinister, evil, and I was about to be their toy. Threatening to throw me in with the bull, they offered to keep me safe by unzipping their pants ... five years old and performing fellatio. A silent rage began to brew deep within. I was nothing to them.

Harvest time was over, and I looked forward to school, my sister told me wonderous stories about the teachers and activities. Sure enough, entering my school years gave me reprieve. Just kidding. It was the beginning of a whole new torment.

The first day of school, my instructions from my parents were, "What happens in these four walls, stay in these four walls." There was no encouragement such as, do good, learn lots, or love you; just a blaring warning to keep my mouth shut about what happens in our home.

I wanted to read; I wanted to escape into the world of books like the ones that my sister read to me. However, when it came time to learn my letters, I was unable. I was not able to write them like all the other children. I would flip letters; the teacher would ask the students to read the letters on the chalk board and I would always mess them up. I would shout out a letter that I knew didn't make any sense and earned the reputation of a smart aleck. My dream to read was over. I got the attention I craved from my teacher but it wasn't the hug or adoration I craved. I didn't care, I wasn't getting beat and I wasn't being ignored.

My kindergarten year was a year of education for me in more ways than reading and writing. We had moved in with a friend of my father. His children became our babysitters and our new tormenters. The sexual assaults began right away; being raped, my mask became even more cemented. Treated like a piece of candy and tossed from person to person, gender didn't matter, they and their friends used me anyway their perverse minds could come up with and I never dared say a word.

My formative years were consumed in violent physical abuse, horrendous sexual abuse, and vicious mental abuse; and through it all, I wore my mask. My insides were in a constant state of fear and ready to take flight, but my feet wouldn't move. The craving for kindness was drifting away day after day until I was pretty sure kindhearted people didn't exist except in my mind. I would curl up in corners and pretend I was dead, hoping nobody would see me.

Silence is a killer. How many people have seen a situation that made them feel uncomfortable but believed it wasn't their place to say anything? How many children suffer at the hands of their caregivers but don't say anything because of fear? In the silence, the abuse continues, killing personality, innocence, purity, and sometimes life.

We never discussed the arguments or the ridicule that swirled around our home. I had wounds festering deep in my heart just waiting to erupt.

My father's mother was a Believer. She was kind to me and the times that I was able to be with her was a welcomes respite. I didn't know or even understand how she could believe in the God person; He didn't make my hurt and pain go away. Going to church with her was easy enough, after all, it was ingrained in me to sit still and say nothing. She taught me my first prayer "Now I lay me down to sleep, I pray the Lord my soul to keep ..." I wanted my grandmother happy so I prayed with her and I liked how it felt, so I would pray even if Grandma wasn't there with me.

The summer season was filled with wonderful times, much of it spent outside. My grandmother had a garden, and I helped her with weeding and harvesting, except for the eggplant. I hated eggplant and stomped on every single one. Unfortunately, my grandma told my father when he came out for a visit, for which I was soundly beaten to her horror; she never mentioned any negative thing to him about me the rest of the summer.

The end of summer ended up being another move, to another city. I had determined in my heart to find a way to run away from home. The city was building a new bridge across the Mississippi, it was a skeleton, but I knew on my roller skates that I would be able to make it across and be out of my nightmare. My brother and sister decided to join me, and determined, we set out. Oh, how the wind whipped across us, threatening to toss us into the river, but we stayed our course and gripped the steel girders moving ever so slowly across the bridge.

The sirens were blaring, the police were gathered as we disembarked on the other side of the river. We had been so focused on the crossing and escaping to our freedom that we didn't see the fire department gathering on the other side.

My heart sank as disappointment and fear filled it, replacing the spunk, grit and determination that had been there. The police officers took us home, my parents performed the perfunctory care and concern until they were out of sight and then the beatings commenced. They ended it with their standard phrase, "You fell down the stairs."

Over the years, my life didn't change, the towns changed, the houses changed, the schools changed, but my tormented life didn't change. I had my moments of happiness, short-lived, but they were scattered throughout the years and always away from home. Eventually, I had a teacher who made me feel valued; however, my reading never got any better. Today, it's called dyslexia. Back then, it was called stupid and lazy.

In my middle years, my father began to take me with him when he went to work. He was working as a chef; at first, I was terrified. I had no idea why he wanted me there; it became clear soon enough. I was to do his work. I learned how to de-bone chicken, cut up lettuce, rose radishes, and wash dishes. At the end of the week, the owner gave me $20.00. My first paycheck! It was in one hand and out the other right into the palm of my father's hand as "rent money."

Thirteen years old, I walked away. I walked right out the front door and figured I would never look back. I didn't know where I was going or what I was going to do. I did know that I was a hard worker; I figured I could work in the restaurant business because of my experience. I was almost 6-feet-tall with a terrific, solid body. I was mature and looked older than my years.

My first attempts at finding a job were a failure. I had to sleep in the park; but I refused to give up. I was so excited when I was hired for my first job. I had to lie and say I was 18, but I looked the part. I picked up waitressing quickly. I could not read or write but I could remember what people ordered without any problems. Freedom at last. I could go where I wanted, eat what I wanted, and do what I wanted without any fear of retribution. I didn't miss Junior High, I would have just gotten into trouble, so this life was much better.

One night after work, I was approached and raped by a young man. I was so free and yet the dregs of life still found me. During the rape, I went where I always went deep in my mind where no one else could go. I was able to block out the act happening to me but I never forgot the smell of his apple breath. After the act of penetration was complete, he knocked me out. I woke up in the dark, shivering in the cold. I made it home without seeing another soul. When I finally made it to bed, I still muttered my nightly prayer taught to me as a child, "Now I lay me down to sleep..."

My year of freedom was over the moment I got sick with pneumonia. Death scared me more than my parents; I couldn't pay my rent because I was so sick. I knew I needed help, and though I despised myself, I went to my father's job. He allowed me to come home after verbally degrading me and with the agreement I would pay rent as soon as I was well enough to get another job.

We moved to Seattle a couple of years later, and I got a job at Boeing. My family ended up moving back to Minnesota, but I stayed determined to make my way. It was during this time that I met Celeste, she became my sister in every way but blood. Celeste was a runaway and a blonde bombshell, whom had experiences in her past very similar to my own. We were kindred spirits and decided no one was going to control us. We would determine our future.

We left Seattle and went to Minneapolis. We were sixteen, ready to take on the world, and ready to move where the action was. It wasn't as easy as we had hoped; we struggled to find jobs. At one point we even gave in and asked our parents for help. My father's response, "too bad, so sad." I determined right then I would never ask them for anything again. Despite our struggles and poor living quarters, we eventually found employment and excelled. We were young, we were beautiful, and we weren't afraid to work.

We decided to move back to Seattle because we were tired of our landlord spying on us, making excuses to make his way into our apartment. Although, we made 75 cents an hour we often brought home a hundred dollars or more in tips. We were doing well for a couple of teenagers.

However, we had put up with enough perversion and abuse in our lives that we weren't going to live with it now. We left the apartment the way the landlord made us feel; we painted the walls black, left meat in vents and under furniture to rot. It felt good to be able to exact some type of revenge on the pervert. Our life of being victims was over—or so we thought.

Seattle, Emerald City—we hit the streets looking for employment the day we arrived. I saw an ad in a window saying win $100 as a stripper. We figured why not make some money dancing around in a bikini. It was easy money for a lot less work. Either Celeste or I won every night, plus tips. I figured men had used me all my life, now I was using them to succeed, to be accepted and to be happy. The irony of it all was lost on my young mind.

This was the beginning of the end for me. I loved the money I made, and soon Celeste and I were wanted across Seattle. We were money makers, and business owners in the adult entertainment world knew it. We still had to fight off a few of the men who thought they could take advantage of us, and we thought we were in control.

Along the path, we met all kinds of people with advice how to make money. One of them told us to head to San Francisco and learn the art of strip dancing. We wanted to be the best, so we went to the Mission District in downtown San Francisco.

San Fran in 1967, the height of Haight-Ashbury, hippies, drugs, and free love. I wanted to see, feel, hear, and experience everything but not on drugs. I grew up watching my brother strung out on drugs. Celeste, however, wanted to try some pot. I watched the change come over her and knew it wasn't what I wanted; I liked my perspective on life.

We did learn from the best and experienced some great adventures and great mishaps. However, we met our goal of becoming the headliners. Fame had its downside. While it puffed me, it was also very annoying. I couldn't have any quiet time. Celeste and I were having issues, too. Fame and attention had changed our attitudes, and we were starting to get on each other's nerves. Eventually, bored of San Fran, we left and meandered the west, ending up back in Seattle.

We looked for reputable strip clubs. The first one we auditioned for offered us a position immediately, and we took it. The money was good and the owner liked us, I could tell by his smirk. He offered us a place to live, and we were enthralled. Our first night had the crowds roaring and the lines started growing. We were making all kinds of money and thought we were rolling in it. Not only were we the dancers, we were learning the bar business. Being dyslexic I only had to be shown once. Mike, the club owner, was always buying us gifts, what we didn't realize is that he made sure he was paid back for those gifts by taking it out of our paychecks. The deception of who Mike was for me was sealed during the Christmas season when he handed out food boxes.

He never tried to take advantage of us sexually and plied us with gifts. He had us help him open other bars. I trusted him implicitly. However, all the while he was stealing money from us. He would have us robbed so we would have to continue to work for him.

Mike sent us to Alaska to open bars for him. I was done. I wanted my own bar. He had promised that to me for years, but I was no longer sober or drug free. I had a $1200.00 a day drug habit and drank a gallon of wine before I would even leave my apartment. My life of debauchery, and trying to run away from my past, caught up with me.

It had caught up with Celeste as well.

We ended up in Kenai, working for a woman with a brothel. We were the best, still. Men would fly in planes full of their buddies to see us. We dated famous people, we dated everyday normal people all the while we either were drunk or high. One day while in town, I saw a flier about a revival and I wanted to know what the heck it was about. One gal I worked with warned me to stay away from it, which piqued my curiosity even more.

The first night of the revival was like any other for me, I was drunk and high. Something weird happened during that meeting. I sobered up. The preacher man kept telling us about some man named Jesus and boom—I was sober. It was so incredible, I flew people in and told them we had to go to the revival drunk and high because we would walk out sober. We had the greatest party before the revival and walked out of it sober.

I had no idea what was going on. I didn't realize it was the grace of God. Nobody told me I had to go to church, nobody told me to buy a Bible and read it. I just knew when I walked in where the man was talking about Jesus I sobered up. My life got worse after the revival; I was depressed and angry.

One night I decided to end it all. I planned it out. Wearing my prettiest negligee, I propped myself against my pillows so Celeste wouldn't find my brains all splashed out on the walls. The .357 was in my mouth and I was ready to pull the trigger, when the Glory of God dropped on my room in the bordello.

He put His hand between the trigger and said, "You are mine."

In an instant, my life was ticker-taped, I saw the demon sitting on my chest urging me to kill myself.

However, it was the love, the realization that everything I knew was wrong and that Jesus Christ was real.

I began to yell and scream at the top of my lungs "He is real! He is real!" Celeste and four other ladies came running up the stairs to see what was going on and the power of God hit them like a ton of bricks, down they went under the power of God.

I walked out of the bordello, so did Celeste, and we would never looked back. Thirty-seven years ago, and I have stood on my faith knowing that God redeemed every sin in my life. No one can throw my past up in my face, it is my testimony.

I have endured the hatred of my past by the religious. I am understood by the common man on the street, the ones who can relate, the ones who battle their own demons every day. My childhood has been redeemed with every child I have helped. My youth has been redeemed with every runaway who has found their self-worth. My drug habits and drunkenness has been redeemed with every person who is born again and Spirit filled. God has used my life to start churches, schools, feeding programs, medical centers, and create jobs globally.

Jesus redeemed me, He paid the cost and He used every heartbreak and degradation in my life. He wanted me to be able to meet people right where they are, they can look at my life and know there is hope for them.

I haven't told you everything, just a few highlights. You can read my whole story in *Angel of the Flesh*.

This I know: Jesus is real, God is my Father, and the Holy Spirit guides me every single day since the day He met me. All sins are redeemable, you don't have to wait for perfection.

Redemption, so sweet the sound; but the cost, the price paid, is often untold. We didn't pay the price; Jesus did the day He hung on the cross.

Verissa Walber, AKA Vickie, is the Senior Pastor and Founder of The Living Stones in Sterling, Alaska.

Their website is www.AlaskaMinistriesoftheLivingStones.com

Verissa's book Angel of the Flesh *is available on Amazon.*

STORY NINE

"Grateful for His Mercy"

By Luanne Nelson

(9)
GRATEFUL FOR HIS MERCY

By Luanne Nelson

I am old. It surprises me. It happened so fast. But here I am, old. Not as old as my grandmother when she went to heaven. Not as old as Sister Mary Josephine, who made the best oatmeal cookies in the world and shared them while they were warm with the little second graders down the hall from the convent kitchen. I can still remember sitting at my desk picking out the raisins to enjoy separately. Back in those days, I wore a teeny navy blue jumper and a crisp white blouse and shoes with shiny buckles. Today, I prefer to be shoeless and wear a lot of black. I think it looks good with my usually messy blonde-gray hair.

I've had an interesting life. I think we all have, really. I wouldn't want to live it all over again although I wouldn't mind being 49 again. Maybe 49 for about three years and then pick up where I left off. I met the love of my life when I was 49. I know, I know. It took me long enough. David and I are still married,, which is a miracle in itself. I am not good at marriage. Good thing he is.

Speaking of miracles, I am going to share two of them that happened to me in my life so far. There have been many or I would be dead by now. In any event, here are two of my favorites from my blog:

The First Miracle:

THE SMOKING HOT NUN

I loved smoking cigarettes. I loved everything about it – the fire, the smoke, the rush, the air-art of jagged mountains that would fade in a breeze. At first, I used it as a prop on the stage of college life – journalism to be exact. A cigarette in hand, I instantly became an imaginary reporter in a dark and smoky room with a single light bulb suspended over my typewriter as I reported breaking news produced on the incoming newswires click click click click. My ashtray overflowed, each cig-stub representing another seven minutes spent constructing the perfect story.

I didn't graduate as a reporter; instead, I traveled, married and reared a few children. I raveled, married again (and again) and patched my life back together several times over. The blue smoke remained a constant. Cigs, you see, became my best friends. All twenty in a row – always there, always dependable, always pleasurable, always standing ready at attention like little white papered soldiers with tan boots in my flip-top box of life.

I smoked in Paris and felt tres chic. I smoked at the Vatican and felt like a racy little sinner. I becameAudrey Hepburn with her sleek little black cig holder as long as her neck. I was a fashion model using cigs to keep my weight down, punctuating my puffs with a spoonful of yogurt here and there and an occasional snickers bar to keep me going.

This went on for years – and years – and years. *I evened out at two-packs-a-day and kept that going for what seemed like forever.* There was a streak of time that I thought I was smoking three packs a day – turns out, other models were raiding my stash. I was relieved. Two was okay, three a bit excessive. Two going at one time was weird, but that happened sometimes, too.

I knew I was damaging my lungs but since I couldn't see them it really didn't matter to me. I imagined my lungs were blackening but honestly, I really didn't care. I could have swallowed a canary and it wouldn't have flown back out simply because I knew for a fact it would fly right past my lungs without so much as even noticing them. Then, they would get all tangled up in peristaltic action never to fly back up and out anyway. The canary test didn't apply, so therefore I was still okay.

Besides, my skin was still a healthy pink without wrinkles except for a few around the corners of my mouth like what nuns get from pursing their lips from being in the perpetual state of too much disdain. I related to the disdainful nuns and lit up another one. I wondered if I could smoke if I entered a convent.

Strangely enough, it was my molars that started to protest my lifestyle. "Every time you inhale, you are strangling a tooth. That's why you need so many root canals. You are constricting your capillaries and not feeding the canals," said my dentist. I really did not want to hear this. I could live with imaginary blackened lungs and a wrecked heart (heck, I lived through the heartbreak of a few lousy relationships, cigs were not going to do my heart in any more than it already had been done in.) But, my *teeth*? No one had warned me about that. All of a sudden, this was real and these root canals were getting expensive.

God has a marvelous sense of humor. I have to clue you in on something. I had fallen big time for the bearer of these bad tooth-tidings. Yes, I had the hots for my dentist. As a matter of fact, I was teeth over heels. I called him up and asked him out for coffee. My friends were going to duct tape my mouth shut to keep me from talking about him all the time. Anyway, I called him and he liked me alright and we were about to meet his Mother. The problem was this – his Mother lived almost four hours away by car.

Now, anyone who smokes knows the joy of smoking in the car on a road trip. Fine tunes blaring, the freedom of the open road with continual heavenly puffs of relaxation. Also, smoking helped to cut down on the snacking thus maintaining that svelte physique that had been in place for decades following that first puff ever (which, of course, was punctuated with severe coughing and the acute inability to breathe).

A road trip with my darling dentist with whom I was hopelessly in love meant – oh no! – I could not smoke during the entire trip. Four hours of rolling over ribbons of pavement without so much as a hint of smoky fun. This was a serious dilemma.

So, I took it to my girlfriends during a smoking break at work. What to do, what to do. How in the world am I going to pull this off? My little soldier-friends-in-a-box continued to stand at attention, expressionless, loyally remaining at my beck and call. One by one, my girlfriends snuffed out their smokes and went back into the building leaving me there alone to ponder (panic?) alone.

It's really difficult to tell you what happened next. Not because it's sad, rather, because it's just unlike anything I've ever said out loud - and, as you can probably tell, I talk a lot. I'm going to try to tell you though, so please bear with me.

I stood out there and lit up another one. I inhaled deeply. When I looked up, I saw a nicely dressed gentleman standing about an arm and a half's length away from me. I was startled because I had been deep in thought and didn't see him approaching. I vividly recall he had very kind eyes which softened the startle. He smiled and said, "I overheard you say that you needed to stop smoking." I thought to myself, what a nosy person – and an eavesdropper to boot! He continued, "I went through that a few years ago and haven't smoked since."

Thankfully, I was standing right next to the door that opened into the building in the event I had to make a quick exit from this stranger who had just barged into my life without being welcomed. This doorthought gave me comfort. Nonetheless, since I was curious, I politely asked him to tell me how he had been able to stop smoking. After all, that did seem to be the question of the day. He answered, "Pray often. Pray a lot."

Alrighty. Confirmed. This well-dressed eavesdropper was indeed just a holy-roller nutcase. I thanked him for his thoughts, told him I prayed a lot already and began opening the door to the building. He added this as I opened the door,

"Ask God to smoke for you."

"Flee!" my inner sinner shouted. I quickly opened the door. The stranger continued talking and added, "God loves you and doesn't want you to be sick. Smoking won't make Him sick – let Him smoke for you. Every time you want a cigarette, ask Him to smoke it for you." There was a sense of commanding urgency in his voice.

This, of course, stopped me in my tracks. I really don't know how long I stood there, but when I looked up, he was gone. I searched the area with my eyes and there was not a sign of him anywhere.

There is absolutely no way I could have thought this up on my own. It was way too weird. I had to admit that it did make sense, though. God could not get sick – He could take my addiction from me – relieve me – prevent me from getting sick – all I had to do was Ask Him to smoke for me. A strange feeling of protection, care and calmness – of love, really – swept over me as I opened the door and headed back to my work area.

I didn't say anything when I got back to my desk because the whole thing seemed just plain too big and too strange to tell anyone at work. I felt the need to sort and think and sort some more.

A few days later, on April 23rd, 2004, at 5:04 CDT (I looked at my car clock), traveling south on Oakland Avenue, I inhaled, exhaled and tossed my last cig out the window of my car. I looked in the rearview mirror and watched it bounce on the pavement. Yes, I littered in the throes of a Miracle.

It has been said that God chooses the biggest sinners and uses them to show His mercy and love. I have to agree, because I am far from holy and in the following days He must have smoked a few hundred cigarettes for me. The cravings became less and less as the days passed. It was totally amazing – I would think about having a cig (like every few minutes at first) and as soon as I asked Him to smoke it for me, the thought immediately was gone until the next time I wanted one. The times got further and further apart until I really didn't think about smoking at all anymore.

That was almost fourteen years ago. I truly do believe an angel visited me that day at work. Thank you, dear Lord Jesus.

And yes, I enjoyed a smoke-free road trip and did meet my darling dentist's Mother. Her son, David, and I are married now.

Hebrews 13:2 Forget not to show love unto strangers: for thereby some have entertained angels unawares.

And yet, Another Miracle:

BACK TO JESUS

Early in our marriage, David and I decided to relocate to Alaska. We had honeymooned there in summertime and it was both geographically spectacular and enchanting. Since we had married each other later in life, we figured the Land of the Midnight Sun would give us twice the life for the buck since it stayed light all day and night in the summertime. We could have two days in one! We hadn't considered the winter darkness and ended up driving home nearly six years later in June of 2013. There is more to it, but that's a different Miracle story.

While in Alaska, I injured my back. I was laid up in bed for two solid weeks barely able to move. When I was able to stand upright again, it was obvious my spine was severely damaged. When we got back to Wisconsin, I went to a doctor who told me she would be able to help me feel more comfortable, but the radiographs indicated that my spine was both curved and rotated and that the damage would not be able to be reversed. I went to her every week for "adjustments" for nearly a year.

The left side of my back was growing the "hump" that is common in scoliosis patients, even though I did not have scoliosis. One of my legs was shorter and I was fitted for orthopedic shoe inserts. My left hand tingled and my lower back often spasmed. It was getting to the point that I could not sit for extended periods of time. Walking stairs was a real problem.

I prayed for a cure. The days passed and figured I had used up all of my allotted miracles in this lifetime (the devil really likes to pull this lie on us, doesn't he?).

Meanwhile, a friend came to visit us from Alaska. Vickie* is one of the dearest and strongest women in Jesus Christ I have ever known. I truly am blessed with her friendship. She has seen the face of Jesus Christ who saved her life many years ago. While staying with David and me during an extended holiday in 2015, she noticed the pain I was in and saw the difficulty I had in walking.

Vickie happens to be an ordained minister. During her visit with us, she became our teacher (we didn't realize it at the time) and explained the Gifts of the Holy Spirit to us and how Jesus is with us today just as much as He was when we walked the earth with his disciples.

We grew up in Jesus Christ through her during her time with us.

One Sunday morning during her visit with us, Vickie and I were sitting at the computer watching the Livestream broadcast of the services of her ministry in Alaska when she turned to me and said, "I am going to pray for the healing of your spine." And she did. She laid her hands on my back and prayed in the Holy Name of Jesus Christ and asked Him for healing. I remember during one part of the prayer, she thanked God for all of His mercies and love, saying that if the ocean was the inkwell and the sky was the parchment, there would not be enough ocean or sky to fill with all of the praise for His Goodness.

When she was finished praying in His Name, she looked at me and told me to raise my arms above my head. I did. My back cracked and popped – loudly! – up into the right side of my head. It continued to pop and crack for the rest of the day. Thank you, Jesus! My back is straight! The hump is gone! My legs are the same length! I am healed!

Thank you, Lord Jesus Christ. Thank you.

Psalm 146:2 I will praise the Lord as long as I live. I will sing praises to my God with my dying breath.

Jesus Christ is my Savior and Lord. As you've read, I am a married to a very dear man. We have 5 children collectively (we both have had previous marriages which we've failed at) and most of our children do not speak to us. It breaks our hearts even though we stay focused and remind each other this is just another indication of the times we live in today. I know about unfairness in life. It is what it is, and I think every follower of Jesus' biggest hurdle is to not let our hearts get hardened and to not drown in our own tears no matter what.

Today, I am an ordained minister – my parish is on the streets and my congregation is a rag-tag group of warriors who have been healed just like me. We are Naomi's Street People. In the holy name of Jesus Christ, we continue to lay hands on the sick and the elderly – we've seen more Miracles and Healings in the name of Jesus in the last two years than in our entire lives.

I have heard His voice and I spend time with people who have seen His face. We are powerless without His grace.

Lord Jesus, please bless each and every one of us.

He said to them, "Go into all the world and preach the gospel to all creation. Whoever believes and is baptized will be saved, but whoever does not believe will be condemned. And these signs will accompany those who believe: In my name they will drive out demons; they will speak in new tongues; they will pick up snakes with their hands; and when they drink deadly poison, it will not hurt them at all; they will place their hands on sick people, and they will get well." (Mark 16:15-18)

*Note: "Vickie" is the author of the previous chapter, "My Story of Redemption" by Verissa Walber

"Grateful for His Mercy" appears here as printed in The Miracle Effect, *published in 2017 by FEW International Publications.*

STORY TEN

"A Story of Transformation and Salvation"

By James Mumaugh

(10)
A STORY OF TRANSFORMATION AND SALVATION

By James Mumaugh

The parable of the Prodigal Son, as told in the Gospel of Luke, offers a glimpse into the brokenness of each or our individual lives as well as our need for God's saving mercy and grace. It also exposes the truth of our corrupted flesh by the scourge of sin to which we were all infected with upon our conception.

It is a story of turning away and of turning back; a story of choosing to be held in bondage, beholden to death, and a story of discovering a much better path to happiness, peace, safety, comfort, and eventually complete glorious freedom.

My life has not been immune to the underlying truths in this parable of the prodigal son, and in many ways, it mirrors my own life story. This is my story. Maybe you can, in one or more ways, identify with it yourself to one degree or another.

I know for a fact that no one chooses to have same sex attractions.

Not upon wakening one morning and deciding, does one just choose this way of living only to be different; to live in a manner that rubs against the grain of the once accepted norms of society. I say, once accepted, because now, sadly, many of our once hallowed societal norms have not only become corrupted but also discarded as old fashioned and outdated.

Today, it's not only okay to live openly as a homosexual, but marriage between two men or women is now increasingly accepted and promoted as normal. As I stated earlier, though, no one chooses this orientation. Nor is it how we are born, and it is not how God created us to be.

If it's not a choice, and if God did not create us to be gay, then what could possibly be the cause or the answer behind the reason one is born into a homosexual orientation?

I believe, through many years of prayer and the guidance of the Holy Spirit, God has shed light on the answer. As Christians, we "know" God brought forth all creation in a state of perfection; unstained, untainted, and uncorrupted. We also know that at some moment in that perfect creation, pure evil slithered into the garden in the form of the serpent bringing with it ugly sin, and throwing complete disorder into what was God's once perfect creation. Sin is a demonic manifestation. It is a chronic infestation of the flesh that has the potential to cause death and the destruction of the soul.

Ever since that moment and until our Savior returns to restore Divine order, this world and all in creation will continue to remain in a state of disorder, tempted with sin. You and I and every other human ever alive and living now, being part of creation, experience this brokenness and suffer with sin in a variety of manifestations.

The prime example, the one that lies at the very root of all our disordered desires, is the corruption of our once perfect nature. Sin has not only distorted and corrupted all of creation, but has also attempted to destroy it. Our own human inclinations are not immune from the deadliness of sin; it has corrupted our choices and our abilities to choose right over wrong.

One glorious day, the one day which all the saints long for, our Lord and Savior Jesus Christ will restore the heavens and the earth and all of creation to its original state of perfection. It will be then when we celebrate in the restoration of creation and of ourselves. We will rejoice in being set free from any former inclination to sin and temptations will be a thing of the eternal past. Truly, on that day, Glory be to God in the highest!

Since the fall of man, each of us has made our own decisions, many of which are outside the will of God for our lives. God gave us free will to make our own decisions. It is a great gift but it cuts like a sharp blade both ways.

To have withheld free choice from humanity would have been for God, essentially, to have held us in a kind of bondage. We would have been chained into having no other choice but to worship Him. We would be little more than pre-programmed robots, not fully living children of His.

Homosexual desires are just one example of the result of our corrupted inclinations. Other examples of this corruption are the insatiable desire for wealth, uncontrolled greed, and the pursuit to dominate the lives of others, political influence and power, the inordinate desire for tremendous material possessions. Other deadly inclinations are sloth, gluttony, envy, and unjust uncontrolled anger. The most deadly of all corrupted inclinations (sins) is pride itself.

Disordered sexual desires, whether they be homosexual or heterosexual are both equally destructive. One is not worse than the other in the eyes of our Creator. Sexual sin is sexual sin. Sexuality is in itself a gift from God. In its proper expression, it is both holy and sacred. Our desires for love emerge from the heart and are, at the core, a desire to be reunited in the greatest love, the Creator Himself. Sexuality is how we share in God's planned creation through the miracle of birth; it's how we prosper and multiply as God's children. Our expression of love becomes the act of pro-creation. There is nothing wrong with the desire to find love and be loved as long as it does not degenerate into lust, whether inside and certainly outside the bonds of marriage.

It is not difficult for one to see the degree of corruption in our society today. There are acts of sexual relations between two of the same gender and acts between men and women that are outside the boundaries of what was intended. From the beginning, it was meant to be a consummate bond of loving union between only a man and a woman. One only need to look up the definition of the word "fornication" to see that this word clearly spells out exactly what it is.

Sadly, throughout the world, the sins of sexual immorality have become common place and are increasingly more so in our world today. The destructive result of this sin and so many others is appallingly evident in this world today. Marriage between two people of the same gender has now become accepted in many countries. The world now sends a message of acceptance for these relationships. Holy Scripture does not offer the same affirming message. Which authority are we to accept as truly valid? The world's authority or God's authority?

Therefore, gay marriage, even if authentic, loving, and monogamous, it is not what the Lord God ever intended the sacrament of marriage to be. I make no judgment, as I have not been given the authority to do so. I can only tell my story and where it has led me, to now hold the religious convictions that I now do.

I do not claim that those who are continuing in same-sex relationships, regardless how lovingly authentic they may be, are bound for hell. I do, however, firmly believe that they are putting their salvation in serious jeopardy. My hope and my daily prayer is that the well of God's mercy may prove to be so deep, that He "may" be able to look on their relationship as a tender heart's search to find love and receive love in the only way they knew how and not out of sexual depravity and as such, mercy and salvation may yet still be available to them. But, I cannot be certain of this. I can only rely on what Holy Scripture clearly spells out and am now compelled to accept this as Gods eternal truth.

Eternity is a very, very long time! I am not going to gamble with my eternal salvation.

I knew I was different from a very early age, as early as around 10 years. I was raised is a very solid Catholic, loving, supportive family. I went to Catholic grade and high schools. My six siblings and I remain close to this day. I had a wonderful father and mother, both lovingly devoted to all their children.

My parents have crossed over to the Lord. My siblings know about my story and that this lifestyle I once lived, now remains in the past.

As with any adolescent, the onslaught of hormones commenced. It was in high school that I found my attraction to other men shift into high gear, especially towards hunky, handsome upper-class guys. Even though I was not consciously willing to admit to my being gay, I could not deny that I found guys incredibly more attractive than any girl.

The thought of becoming sexual with a girl was simply repulsive while the thought of doing it with a guy ... that was a major turn on for me!

As I stated, in the middle of puberty, this was not an easy experience for a hormone charged teen. My Catholic upbringing and fear of several things kept me from engaging in sex until the age of twenty. By that time, I was truly like a soda bottle viciously shaken and I was ready to pop my lid.

My first encounter was in college. I wish I could say it was wonderful and thrilling but I had the unfortunate first experience of engaging with a guy who was not only creepy but not at all attractive. I found his number on a bathroom wall and called his number. It was only when he showed up in his car a few blocks from my home did I see he was one of the creepiest un-kept guys I had ever encountered. It was my first experience and it just kind of took place. I just know, if that guy is still alive this day, the poor man has not become better looking with age. Laughing about it now, but then ... eeeek! The guilt that soon came after that first time was because of my Catholic guilt. I do think my shame may well have been a little less intense if that first guy would have been much better looking. Just saying.

Other sexual encounters followed after that first horrible debut. And as I can now can look back on them as, yes, engaging in sin, (looking back at the humor in it), thank goodness at least they were with much better-looking, even really handsome guys.

The intense seductive, salaciousness of having another body like my own to touch and be touched by, and doing all the things that two men can possibly do with each other, and I did, flooded my life with incredible passion and desire. Sex was amazing. Yet, this is exactly what entrapped me and holds any one of us in bondage to the pleasures of the flesh. It is both a sweet and deadly poison. I can now say without any doubt or hesitation, the seductive pleasures are truly a trap. It gives the dangerous illusion of liberation and freedom when actually it only serves to enslave us and put us in bondage to the ... wages of sin and death (Romans 6:23). I was caught in the thralls of sexual pleasure and the thrill of doing it all with another person who had a body just like mine.

I had encounters in bars, and more intense encounters at times in the areas of some bars known as "dark rooms" (no pun intended), above or below the main bar. I fooled around at gay pride celebrations, basement bathroom stalls on campus, at shopping malls, and at the gay bathhouse, of course.

I met guys riding my bike in the park, the grocery store, public transportation, restaurants, and many other places. There were times when it involved more than just me and one other. It was all truly thrilling and exhilarating and for a while it was very addictive. Again, there is the trap, the bondage of the soul. I don't want to give the impression that I was a complete whore, certainly not as bad as some I knew, but I had my share, and for many years when I was in the thick of it.

I know the Holy Spirit was always there alongside me, right in the middle of it, when I was at my worst. I know this to be true, because there was often enough of this persistently nagging, little annoying, small, quiet voice in the back of my consciousness trying ever so hard to convince me that all was not as it should be.

Proof of this is when I was sitting in that basement bathroom stall of the campus library, which was a very active meeting point for a number of us college boys. I would be reading all the hot salacious, erotic scribbling on the walls and the phone numbers to call for "fun," while waiting for another dude to come into the stall next to mine. He would give the signal of tapping his foot, which one could see because the stall barriers did not extend all the way to the floor. One time, while I was sitting there reading the scurrilous messages, I was moved to write my own message on that same wall all those years ago:

"Oh Lord, if you could count our iniquities, who could endure them; but you, are forgiving, Oh God of Israel" (Psalm 130:3).

I know Whom it was who moved me to write that among all that other smut.

It was a message God was trying to get me to understand as well as any other guy who might see it. It was a message I wouldn't fully "get" for a good number of years but the fact that, right in the middle of the thick of it, clearly, He was alongside me.

I cannot pin it down to a singular, pivotal event as to what shifted in my life that caused me to begin, in small obscure ways, the process of turning around.

Repentance actually means "a turning around, a change of direction." I have come to learn by personal experience as well as what I have observed in others' lives, that the Lord changes each of us, degree by degree. It is not an instant process but a long period of learning and self-discovery. Only by fits and starts do we begin the process of returning to home to our Father. Like the prodigal children we all are to varying degrees, this does not happen overnight. How truly wonderful our God, our Father is!

He truly is a God of love, slow to anger and rich in kindness and mercy. Exodus 34:6, Psalm 103:8, and Psalm 146:8. Truly, thanks be to God all the more for how truly gracious He is.

This point of turning around involved a series of multiple undefined events, taking place in fits and starts over a span of twenty years. I never stopped going to Church even during the time when I was also going to bed with other men. I was truly living a double life;

attempting without actually realizing it at the time. I was trying to serve two masters at the same time; both God and mammon. True spiritual maturity causes one to realize this cannot be. You cannot serve two masters.

There was always, on some level, a kind of unease, a little annoying discomfort that I experienced even during the acts of passion, and after as well, that told me in then stillest, smallest voice, that something wasn't quite right; something was amiss.

It was the same voice that St. Augustine heard that pursued him. I feel a real closeness to him; a kind of brotherhood, for he too had lived and spent many years in fornication with women and had a longtime mistress outside of wedlock. I continue to ask St. Augustine for prayers, that God would do for me, what He did for him. I look forward to talking with St. Augustine one day and sharing stories of our similar weaknesses and youthful foolishness, and praising God together for saving us both.

I highly recommend reading, *The Confessions of St. Augustine* as an excellent and illuminating way for anyone to look more deeply into their own interior lives.

I love his quote in his book, "Oh Lord, forgive for how lately I have loved thee."

Like St. Augustine and many other great men and women of faith, God also pursued me, tracked me down and moved me to also accept His invitation to return to Him.

In closing, we absolutely risk our true happiness, our true joy and contentment, indeed our eternal freedom from sinful desires if we continue to view this world and all of its pleasures, whatever they may be, if we place them in higher importance than God Himself. *We are foolish, indeed in serious moral error, if we believe we can find more pleasure in the flesh than we can in the presence of the Lord.*

Jeremiah clearly warns us of this in chapter 17:5-6, *"Thus says the*

Lord: 'Cursed is the man who trusts in man and makes flesh his strength, (his contentment and pleasure), whose heart turns away from the Lord. He is like a shrub in the desert, and shall not see any good come.'"

This world one day will end, in one-way or the other, sooner or later. It will come to an end for all of us. Every human that has ever lived and will ever live is endowed with an eternal soul and that soul will exist long past this present life and this temporary earth. For one to argue against this truth is to place their soul in the greatest of jeopardy.

Each of us has an eternal life ahead of us that is far beyond this world and it will be in only one of two places. One is a place of surpassing happiness and joy and freedom. The other is of crushing desolation and despair and unending bondage.

There is suffering that one experiences in giving themselves over to Christ. It is the suffering of selfdenial for a far greater good that lies ahead (Romans 8:18).

As for myself, I make the decision to go through a light and temporary affliction now, and be done with it one day forever, rather than give myself over to the pleasures of this world which last only for a moment to find that I have not escaped suffering at all; and worse to find that because I placed a higher importance on worldly pleasures, over and above the Lord God, to find my suffering only beginning and without end. I would rather endure the light and temporary pain of self-denial and cry a little now rather than suffer and sob deeply forever.

May I continue to find the strength in God, my Savior, to have mastery over my disordered desires outside the will of God for my life and not have them have mastery over me. May you be so richly blessed to gain this same gift of life.

In closing, I leave you all with wisdom from the Book of Sirach 15:15-17, *"I set before you fire and water; to whichever you choose, stretch forth your hand. Before man are life and death. Whichever he chooses, shall be given him."* Deuteronomy 30:19 also relates to us a similar message. *"I call Heaven and earth to witness against you today, that I have set before you life and death, the blessing and the curse. So choose life in order that you and your descendants may live."*

May we all rightly choose to run the race that lies before us, and one day be given the glorious crown of victory in Christ Jesus.

I keep you all in prayer, my beloved brothers and sisters, in Jesus Christ.

James Mumaugh lives in Rogers, Arkansas, and continues to practice his Catholic faith. He enjoys good food, nice wines, good bourbon, and gardening. He tries to follow the example of Mary in living a chaste, celibate life and is doing his best to bring Christ to a world increasingly in need of His saving grace.

STORY ELEVEN

"Hard Roads Can Lead Home, Too"

By Rev. Dennis Kudlac

(11)

HARD ROADS CAN LEAD HOME, TOO

By Rev. Dennis Kudlac

Excerpts from: *Air Born Again – A Memoir of Flying and Faith by Deacon Dennis Kudlak*; reprinted with permission.
www.amazon.com/Air-Born-Again-Memoir-Flying/dp/0692704353

What about you? Have you walked some hard roads in life? Have you felt—maybe you still feel—as if your soul has left your body, that you are in exile from your own life? As you (may) have read, I've been there. Never in a million years would I ever minimize the suffering I've experienced or the bad choices I often made in response to pain. But I will tell you—in all honesty and sincerity—that, looking back, there was never a time when there wasn't some indication of God's presence through it all. It might have been a much-needed trip to Fatima to re-energize my faith, a flickering light in the living room, or the gift of a single rose. I fully believe that there is meaning in everything we experience—even those events that break our hearts. I also believe that the people who achieve real peace and joy in this earthly journey learn to accept life on its own terms. They adjust to it as it presents itself instead of allowing themselves to be crushed by its seemingly cruel indifference. Ultimately, a person's capacity to have faith in troubled times differentiates those who overcome from those who are overwhelmed. The willingness to relinquish control and leave ego behind when there seems to be little other choice is what separates the saintly from the insane. Listen to me: If you have walked a hard road, I understand. Believe me: It's no good to let life's hardships harden you. Trust me: Even though you may not feel it at times, God is—and always has been—walking that road with you. At any time, you can turn to him—and come home.

...So that's the way my life unfolded at this time. It was moment after moment of unexpected—but much appreciated—grace. I've learned that God loves giving mercy and grace to us. But the thing is, there were times I was ready for it and times that I wasn't. God is always ready and willing to give us gifts. In fact, he's eager to lavish them on us. The key is that we have to be prepared to receive them.

I believe that journey begins, not when you realize how much you love God, but how much God loves you.

Whatever success I've had in my career, whatever meaning my life has had, it is only because of the warm embrace of God's love. Over my twenty-six-year airline career and my twelve years as a deacon, I have learned that sharing faith empowers faith. I have also learned—quite well—that I am just a vessel meant to be used by God. I am committed to finishing the task God has called me to. But even as I write that, I know that it is "not I, but Christ" who is doing the work in me (Galatians 2: 20). He is the one who will complete the good work that He has ordained for me. Simply put, He's the master and I'm the servant. I just do what I do and try to bring faith to the people I meet. Christ's message to me was one of service: first as a pilot, then later—and now—as a deacon. In order for us to love one another, we must connect with others and find our true selves reflected in them—by putting them and their needs before ours. That's how I try to "be all I can be."

AS A BROKEN HUMAN BEING

Finally, as I've said, I've sat in a seat of suffering. Like many of you, I know what it means to be a broken human being. In John 5: 17-30, Jesus talks about how the Father is at work in the world, and He says something that startles those who first hear it. First, He claims equality with God the Father:

> *"'My Father is at work until now, so I am at work.'*
> *For this reason they tried all the more to kill him,*
> *Because he not only broke the Sabbath*
> *But he also called God his own father,*
> *Making himself equal to God."*

Pretty amazing! Scandalous to the people at the time, but perhaps just as surprising is that Jesus says something about his relationship with the Father: Jesus answered and said to them, "Amen, amen, I say to you, the Son cannot do anything on his own." The two things that I take out of that passage are this: first, that since Jesus is equal to God, there's no one better I can trust. Throughout my life, he is the one who has sustained me in my suffering, offered mercy to me in my failures, and steadied me when my life was spinning out of control. Are there some days in your life when you wish that God would move right in and take over for a while? Those times are when things are going haywire. And yet, the crazy thing I have learned (from learning the hard way) is that even when life is tough and turbulent, we resist turning the controls over to Jesus. Ironically, we are worried that we might lose control. We don't realize that it is trying to control our life that really puts us out of control! That's when we need to think about what Jesus said in the passage that I just quoted: "The son cannot do anything on his own."

If Jesus who is equal with God never did anything on his own, independent of his Father, why do we think we can? With all that I have experienced and endured, viewing life from my seat of suffering, I have definitely learned that I cannot do anything on my own! You've seen those great bumper stickers that say, "Jesus is my co-pilot," right? Well, I used to think those were pretty neat. I loved the sentiment. Then one day I heard someone make a great point. Jesus shouldn't be your co-pilot. He should be your pilot! Yes, that's absolutely right. Jesus should be at the controls. He should be in the seat of authority in your heart and life. When he is, your life—your flight of faith, I might say—will be one that glorifies God.

Deacon Dennis M. Kudlak, a permanent Deacon for the Diocese of Erie, is a retired Captain for United Air Lines. He's a hospice volunteer and is a volunteer "Angel Flight" Air Pilot. Angel Flight is a non-profit air transportation program, transporting patients who are facing medical & financial crisis with "free" air transportation. Deacon Dennis stays busy as a Chaplain at the Presbyterian Lodge, a Minister of Communion to the sick and home-bound and is an active member of the Pastoral Council. He is the coordinator for the Care & Concern Ministry, a Chancellor for the Knights of Columbus council #278, and serves as a Parish Stewardship council member.

His blessed marriage is 32 years strong, producing four children and 4 grandchildren. In his spare time, Deacon Dennis enjoys golfing, boating, camping, traveling, reading and writing. He is the published author of Air Born Again, *available on Amazon.*

STORY TWELVE

"Trust Him"

By Luanne Nelson

(12)

TRUST HIM

By Luanne Nelson

Joyful celebration surrounds the birth of a baby and this little one's arrival was no exception.

Meme and Pappap flew in from Pennsylvania excited to cuddle their very first grandchild. She was born on my birthday, a little more than one year after I was married. Her big blue eyes were alert the moment she was born, she seemed to not miss a thing.

The hospital's nurse was generous in her confidence in me, "Don't worry," she offered, "she's never had a Mom, so she won't be judging you. Just love her."

I did.

I still do.

Soft little strawberry blonde curls ringed her perfect face and tickled her neck. I remember taking her to see Disney on Ice when she was three years old. The person peddling peanuts and candy up and down the aisles of the auditorium stopped to offer some pink cotton candy. Our little girl politely said, "No thank you. I prefer green beans."

At home, she twirled and spun around on her head when she was thinking really hard, giggling while she read the newspaper upside down. She went to French Immersion School at five and could solve a Rubik's Cube in no time flat at six. Her favorite book was Good Night, Moon. She loved bright colors and foggy days. Trips to the art museum were frequent and fun.

Thirteen and a half months later, our second child arrived; a beautiful little brute weighing almost ten pounds. His baby face was bruised and his head was misshapen from the rough ride he had coming into this world.

This little one truly had a tough start in life. He had trouble taking his first breath and we almost lost him. We prayed frantically and he choked for a moment before catching his first breath.

He was a quiet baby who loved being wrapped snugly in soft blankets, being closely held. He was not interested in walking and saved his mobility skills for the day he could take off running. Dismantling objects was his favorite thing to do; alarm clocks, tricycles, anything mechanical littered the floors.

His kindergarten teacher called me one day saying she had asked each student the name of their favorite song. His classmates answered the usual, "Twinkle, Twinkle Little Star", "The Farmer in the Dell", and so forth. My son's answer? Anything Gershwin or Stevie Wonder.

I snapped photos galore. Shoe boxes filled with photos cluttered the closets next to boxes of crayons, finger paints, and wooden blocks.

Less than two years later, our third child was born. She arrived a few weeks after her due date, apparently completely comfortable where she was with no intention of kicking her way out. She was born talking. I am not kidding you. My doc did a midline incision and before she was lifted out she was chatty and cooing up pixie dust everywhere.

A sweet child, she liked everyone and everything. Her blue eyes were the size of saucers giving her a constant look of surprise and wonder. The third child born in three years, she quickly learned how to fend for herself. When this littlest one was thirsty, I usually was busy chasing her big sister and brother and would promise to get her something to drink "in a jiffy!" She taught herself how to shimmy up onto the kitchen counter, turn the water on, put her face under the stream of water and drink straight from the faucet. Self-sufficiency became her forte.

Her stuffed Kanga was her best friend. Although the smallest of the three, she was the noisiest. I can still see her lugging her French horn down the driveway after school. It was nearly her size. She was tenacious, tough, and oh so lovely.

The village's sidewalks unrolled into ribbons of adventure, perfect for afternoon strolls. We didn't have a double stroller, so two of the children would take turns teaming up in the seat part and the third would ride on the canvas roof.

I made their baby food from scratch, steaming veggies and fruits on the stovetop. We sketched pictures, finger-painted together, and watched *Mr. Roger's Neighborhood* on TV. We went on field trips to see dinosaurs on water towers and lily pads on ponds. Every museum was our playground.

Their Dad slept late and went to work noonish at the family's restaurant. He said taking care of children was a woman's job. I starched and ironed his shirts. I made him pastrami on rye with a slice of swiss and a small splash of mustard when he got home from work at midnight. He was a good man with an old-world heart.

Our children were baptized; I taught them how to pray. My husband did not join in because he was an atheist. This was news to me! He had told me he was an Episcopalian. We went to the mandatory marriage classes at church before our wedding; I had no inkling he was godless. One sunny summer afternoon, I was bringing cookies and milk to him and our eldest little one, who was about five years old at the time.

Getting closer, I heard her Dad saying, "Everything in the Bible is a fairy tale. Don't believe any of it. They are just nice stories."

I was flabbergasted and felt like I had been kicked in the gut. I protested. Don't get me wrong, he really was a kind man with a big heart who loved his children very much. He worked a lot and felt obligated to keep the family business going. His name was on the front door as the third-generation owner. He felt this was his destiny, his lot in life . . . he hated it.

He was so unhappy. I hoped he would find work he enjoyed. He never did, though, because he felt such a strong allegiance toward keeping the restaurant going. I watched him go through the motions of doing what he thought was right and sacrificing his own precious life in the process.

We rarely saw each other except over those midnight sandwiches and some Sunday afternoons. He was an avid Green Bay Packer fan, so those Sundays were reserved for the game. I took care of the children. I was exhausted and he was miserable.

We talked about moving to Colorado, away from the family business, and starting over. It became clear his allegiance was and would always be to the family business.

We divorced. We were just way too tired and unhappy to stay together anymore. When we divorced, I was thirty years old with three children under the age of seven under my wing. I had full custody when we moved closer to where I grew up. Six hundred miles of distance between the misery felt good; I was far away from my former in-laws, their restaurant, that very lonely life. I waived all rights to the lucrative family business during the divorce with this understanding: He would keep the family business . . . and I would keep the children.

During the divorce, my father-in-law told me I "could take care of the children while they were growing up but (he) would have them as adults."

Those words stung and I was confident he was wrong. It was an oppressive lifestyle, and I was relieved to get away from it.

I got into a treacherous short-lived relationship with a man who lied about who he really was; I was naïve and the children and I ended up in a shelter for victims of domestic abuse a few months later. He apparently had done this to women before me. I was his target; he used my children as leverage. He threatened to have my children taken away if I didn't do this or that. He was in a position where he truly could have made that happen. I was terrified and did whatever he wanted. I had never prayed so hard in my life. I did everything I could to protect and keep my children safe during the chaos. A stranger took my children and me to safety after seeing my blackened eye and bruises on my legs.

Have you ever been at a point in your life where you look around and all you see is wreckage? That's where I was at. One of my children looked at me at the women's shelter and reminded me, "Mom, evil never wins."

I can still see the earnestness in her eyes. Moms will do anything to protect their children, to keep them safe, to keep them in their care. I truly do not think there is a love greater than the love a Mom has for her children.

I was thirty-one years old, scrambling to get back on my feet, with nothing but trust in God to get us through this difficult time. He came through. He always does.

We moved into a cute little rental house a few weeks later. I passed my real estate exam and began selling homes. I also worked part time in the evenings raising funds for the local symphony, to earn extra money. We were blessed to know a wonderful Italian woman we'd met at church who took care of my little ones while I was working. I was not "street smart;" I was a naïve smarty pants. The devil really likes that combination. Intelligence doesn't matter when paired with lack of experience and insight. I begged God to protect us and to help me raise my beautiful innocent children. I struggled with finances, usually falling short at the end of each month.

Six hundred miles away, the children's Dad had met a young woman from Chicago while participating in a city pub crawl event. They married a few months later and had a child together shortly thereafter. I have to admit, I cried the day they married. Somewhere in the back of my mind, in my heart, I still believed he would leave the family business and we would start our lives over again in Colorado. We had even talked about it after we were divorced. He explained to me his concern that I would never be accepted back into his family. I realized nothing was ever going to change his mind.

I grew up quickly. I had to. Long gone were the days of sorority teas and Junior League. The privileged life I had while growing up was a distant memory. I daydreamed, reminiscing about an evening many years earlier. I remembered the night my Dad and I were enjoying a car ride together years ago. He asked me what I wanted to be when I grew up.

Joking, I flippantly answered, "A hood ornament on a Rolls Royce."

He was amused and chuckled; he was a kind man with a generous heart.

Later, I learned the ornament is called the Spirit of Ecstasy; an elegantl winged woman that looks like she's experiencing a constant headwind. Adventurous. The smart one. The overachiever. National Honor Society, Thespian Society, editor of the senior yearbook, and I had won a few beauty pageants, too. I had felt so strong and so smart and so ready to take on the world back then. When Dad and I arrived home, the conversation continued.

"Be a pharmacist," my Mother advised. "You'll want to have a family. Count pills. Go home at the end of the day," she said.

I dreamed of meeting a family man, marrying, and having a dozen children.

I recalled patting the folds flat on the pleats of my high school uniform's navy and white herringbone skirt. I straightened the shoulder pads in my blue blazer entering the chapel for the last time before high school graduation. We all looked practically the same: a gliding row of navy uniforms with crisp white blouses and Peter Pan collars. Cabled knee socks attached to brown penny loafers. Marching into the pews, we were a small blue army, a gaggle of girls. It seemed like forever ago.

Something caught me completely off-guard after the divorce. My former husband's family decided to act as though I no longer existed. Growing up in Pennsylvania, I saw how the Amish shunned a member who left their community. It was gut-wrenching and heartbreaking. I was living that shunning in my own life now. I reasoned I had publicly embarrassed "the family" by divorcing their son. Their name was a well-known one in the city; their connections were with people they considered to be very important. My former in-laws clearly decided to punish me.

A snow bird living in the southwest during the winter, my former mother-in-law would host an annual party for all of her grandkids when she was back in town for the summer. Christmas, Easter, birthdays, milestones in the children's lives would come and go without a card or a present in the mail. The aunts and uncles were busy living their lives and were silent, too.

Meanwhile, I struggled financially. The children and I lived on a shoestring.

Since moving back to Pennsylvania post-divorce, I drove to Wisconsin in the summertime so the children could spend a few weeks with their Dad per the divorce agreement.

During one of these trips I took the children to visit their Great Tante, a lively woman in her eighties who was the sister of their late great grandmother, Nana. She loved seeing the children, and I was doing my best to keep the lines of communication open however I could.

Tante's grandson stopped by during one of the visits. He and my first husband were cousins in a small, closely-knit family; their grandmothers were sisters. I knew him from family gatherings. He was fun; there was nothing prissy or phony about him. We started dating and married a year later. The children and I moved back to the Midwest.

This marriage never had a chance. Three years into it, a life-changing disaster of epic proportions struck. The phone call came early, before sunrise, one summer morning. The news was devastating. My first husband, the father of my three beautiful children, had taken his own life at the lakefront. We were all devastated beyond words.

Our children, who were nine, eleven, and twelve years old, were hardly old enough to even understand death, much less death by one's own hand. There are no words to describe the anguish.

Then, a few weeks later, I suffered a miscarriage.

I was forever entwined in a family who not only was shunning me, but now they were blaming me for everything that went wrong. They needed a fall-guy, a scapegoat. After all, if I hadn't divorced their son he would still be alive, right? We are all that powerful, right? My former in-laws and his widow called me on the phone and told me I was not welcome at the funeral home. They said they would send a limousine to pick up the children; I said no.

I took my children to the funeral home.

I stayed with them.

I dried their tears.

I held their hearts in my own.

I sat in constant prayer.

Then, I looked up the name of a Christian family therapist in the

Yellow Pages. I was a total mess at thirty-eight years old.

The aftermath was chaotic. A few weeks after their Dad's death, his widow claimed he did not have a will. I petitioned his estate in the courts on behalf of our children. Eventually, each child was awarded a small amount of money which cumulatively did not even match my attorney's fees. I remember writing a check to the attorney for seventy thousand dollars to cover all fees ... including my second divorce.

I was tired and broken.

Often, I felt like I was treading water, armless. There was too much water and not enough air. My former mother-and father-in-law falsely accused me not letting them see their grandchildren. They sued me for grandparental visitation rights three weeks after their son, the children's Dad, died. This news landed on the front page of the city newspaper. On top of grieving, their sharp tongues ripped through my heart and gutted it. They needed someone to blame for their son's death and I had become their very public whipping post.

My children and I went to grief counseling; we prayed; we had family meetings; we struggled. I was prescribed Xanax. The Xanax was a temporary fix, and I discovered the soothing effects of chardonnay to accompany it. I wanted the sharp edges of the pain dulled. It worked for a while . . . until it didn't work anymore. I had to face the grief and all of the suffering that went with it.

When my second husband and I divorced in the dark shadow of that tragedy, the children's teachers mercifully agreed I could keep the children home from school occasionally for mental health days. We worked on purposeful remembering. We put together photo albums and made dozens and dozens of cookies. We lived on a lake, keeping the doors open for their friends. We had dinner together every night and talked about what we learned that day. We always set an extra place in case a friend would drop in so they could just sit right down and join us, which happened often. Some evenings, the dinner place setting remained open and we agreed Jesus Himself was having dinner with us that night.

We planted and harvested three lovely vegetable gardens on the wetlands of our lake property. We went horseback riding. We went to church. We prayed together. I tried to make everything alright.

During a family meeting following their Dad's death, one of the children said, "We're damaged but we're not ruined."

Each one of my children grew up to be strong, beautiful, and very dear. I did my best with the information I had; I gave to them until I had nothing left to give.

After the youngest one graduated from high school, I moved into a small apartment in the city. I put the few earthly possessions I had left in some boxes and lined them up neatly against my bedroom wall. I shared a bathroom . . . and I shared my pain.

I stayed single for the next ten years. I considered becoming a secular sister. An aunt was a Franciscan nun, I researched the Franciscan lifestyle. I was in a chapel in a Franciscan convent when something extraordinary happened.

Midafternoon sunlight streamed through the stain-glass windows. I was practically alone in the little perpetual adoration chapel. There were a handful of ancient sisters sitting quietly in the surrounding pews. It was quiet and peaceful when I began my silent prayer. *Dear Jesus, Lord, keep my children safe, unbreak their hearts, heal them, heal me. . . please. Please.'*

I nodded off, or at least I thought I did.

When I opened my eyes, I was sitting at a table in an outdoor cafe, a huge umbrella covering the whole table shielding it from the hot summer sun.

I looked up and saw I was having lunch with Jesus. I sat up straight, looking down to make sure I was decently buttoned up.

A beggar approached our table. He was unkempt and dirty, bones protruding through his very soiled tattered garment. I reached to give him some food from my plate.

Jesus commanded, "No, don't do that!"

Startled, I looked up and said to Jesus, "But he's hungry! Didn't You tell us to feed the hungry, give drink to the thirsty, clothe the naked, visit the imprisoned?" I rattled off the corporal works of mercy straight from the Book of Matthew describing His own words from His Sermon on the Mount. Then, I realized I was arguing with our Lord and Master, Jesus Himself! I was embarrassed and stopped talking. I felt my face blush.

Jesus said softly, "Do not give him anything."

Totally confused, I asked Him, "I don't understand. Why not?"

Jesus said, "Because that's Satan. If you give him even the smallest piece of anything, he will keep coming back for more and more until there is nothing left of you."

I was trying to do the right thing, the holy thing, following His holy directions and I realized I had it all wrong! Thoughts swirled. I was caught off-guard, out of context, in a different dimension. I looked up at Him and asked, "How do I know when to give and who to give it to?"

"Trust Me," was His answer.

Immediately, I was delivered wide awake back to the wooden pew. I searched the chapel and thought loudly: "Wait! Wait! Don't go! Where are you?"

I realized, at that moment, I had no idea how to trust Him. I had no idea what it *meant* to trust Him. During my life, I had prayed, I performed the works of mercy, I had taught my children how to pray, I had gone to church religiously, and yet here I was–completely baffled.

Time passed. I lived a quiet life downtown, occasionally dating but mostly working. As part of the discernment process in considering religious life, I worked for a while with juvenile delinquents in a semi-secure setting. I was poor and spent many evenings ministering to people living on the streets downtown, praying together with them, spreading hope through His word. A few years later, all of my children, adults in their twenties, were invited to go on an all-paid-for luxury cruise with their grandparents and extended family from their father's side. Something strange happened during that cruise; my children came back distant and different. I asked what happened, but was left emptyhanded.

"From now on there will be five in one family divided against each other, three against two and two against three. They will be divided, father against son and son against father, mother against daughter and daughter against mother, mother-in-law against daughter-in-law and daughter-in-law against mother-in-law" (*Luke 12:52-53 NIV*).

I don't think there is a pain greater for a Mom than the agony of being shunned by her own children. Recently, I saw a photo of one of my daughters on Instagram. She was very pregnant. I texted her with a stunned message; she did not respond. She had her baby a few months ago; a beautiful baby girl. I saw the photo on the Internet; my first and only grandchild. I thought I would never stop crying. . . and praying. I prayed for God to send me someone to pray with and, again, He did.

Amidst the pain, God, in His infinite mercy and generosity sent me a loving man to be my husband and fold his hands with mine in prayer.

We share our joys and our pain. Sometimes, we fight; we're not perfect; but *always* we pray.

We find solace together in knowing God has all of us, including my estranged children, and all of our lives in His hands. He holds our broken hearts in His.

Deep breath.

I've been tracking down some old friends. I found one of my favorite college roommates on Facebook. She offered me more solace than she will ever know. When I told Mary about my kids, she quipped, "Who are we to say we are a better parent than God is?" Her words knocked the breath right out of me.

She's right. God's own children – each and every one of us – are sinners. I am one of them. We are not called to be perfect. We are called to do our best in His care. He does not punish us because we fail; it's in our repentance, our willingness to change – to do better today - that He has mercy on us. His love for us is complete, endless and humanly unfathomable. I know He loves me.

I realize now. . . I trust Him completely. Perhaps because all else has been stripped away but the right to pray and hope. It's a magnificent freefall into His care; knowing that no matter what, everything will be alright in the end. . . and if it's not alright, it's not the end.

The late great Eugene O'Neill said it very well. He penned, "Man is born broken. He lives by mending. The grace of God is glue."

When I stand back and squint my eyes enough to really see the whole picture –or, at least as much as I am supposed to see, I see clearly that we've always had exactly what we've needed every single day.

In the end of my first marriage, I had family to turn to.

In abuse, I had shelter and protection.

In loss, I held my children.

In desperation, I was given a someone to share the gift of prayer.

How could I *not* trust that every situation will be made right for His glory?

It's really true. It's true for each one of us in His care. He has always been with me. He never fails us. Ever. Even in our darkest, most human of moments.

Our Creator, our eternal loving Dad, paints the colors on the flowers and gives the birds their daily food. He loves us more than the flowers and the birds. I am confident He's keeping my maternal arms stashed in a safe place knowing I will need them again to hug all of my children someday. I know the end game. I will not let the adversary steal even one moment of joy in my life. He can't have it any more. I will not give even one little piece of my life away. No. God told me all about that one day . . . over lunch. I get it.

Trust Him.

"And we know that in all things God works for the good of those who love him, who have been called according to his purpose."
(Romans 8:28 NIV)

"Trust Him" appears as printed in "The Breakthrough Effect," published in 2018 by FEW International Publications.

STORY THIRTEEN

"Redemption in a Hurricane"

By Patricia Freeman

(13)
REDEMPTION IN A HURRICANE

By Patricia Freeman

A Christian doesn't automatically become a perfect obedient person at the moment he or she becomes a child of God and a follower of Christ. Just as we learn from our parents what is acceptable behavior from the time we are born until we leave home, we must also learn what God expects of us from the moment we are saved by Jesus' sacrifice until the day we die. We read the Bible, we learn what God's laws are, we pray and talk to God, we feel the internal presence of God's Spirit, we feel the love of God for us in simple (or not so simple) blessings in our lives, and even as we love Jesus for all His sacrifice and for all His day to day provision for us, there comes a time when we think or act like a selfish human and not like selfless Jesus.

No matter how much we love God and long to be all He wants us to be, our less-than-Godly human nature can win out over God's influence over us when we choose our will over His. Some days we are successful but some days we are not. We will not always respond to stress and pressures in a Christ-like manner. When we fail to have a Christ-like response, whether in thought or deed, that is our sin. No matter how much I wish to be Godly in all situations, my human nature draws me to fail, so it will always be a lifelong effort to meet His expectations, many times failing along the way, making me always in need of God's forgiveness and redemption, because no one is up to the task of being perfect.

My path of redemption started young, as a six-year-old girl, thanks to a mother who loved God and Jesus. Now, being a senior in my late sixties, I have had many years to try to learn what God expects of me and practice being Christ-like. As a teenager, I used to pray for wisdom, so I have always recognized the value of pleasing God and have grown in my desire to please Him, to make my thoughts and actions be acceptable to Him. But even in my growing desire to please God, my evil human nature has repeatedly prevailed at times, causing strife and problems in life, keeping me in sin.

I could mention countless hateful thoughts I have had that place me outside God's will and in need of forgiveness. I could mention some of the big decisions I have made that were guided by my human desires rather than God's desires for me. I have had two failed marriages for which I cannot place all blame on others. I have had serious breaks in relationships in which I had a hand in breaking. I have had financial troubles that resulted from not following God's teaching or leading. I can love God with all of my being and still fail to follow Him, yet He continues always to draw me back to Him, even after all these years. That "drawing" and my acceptance of His forgiveness redeems me from a state of being separated from God to a state of communion and relationship with Him.

I was in one such state of separation when Hurricane Ivan hit northwest Florida in 2004 and destroyed the first floor of my two-story home. I had been divorced only three months before. My meager income had been dependent upon occasional craft shows, for which I made and sold jewelry, and a part-time restaurant hostessing job. Maintaining a home without help of a spouse or a full-time sustainable income was highly challenging. When Hurricane Ivan stormed into my life, it brought with it the destruction of all of my income!

Before the hurricane hit, all residents in my town were required to evacuate the area because Category 4 force winds were expected as well as a huge storm surge. My home is on a natural bayou, so I, of course, found myself in a Tallahassee motel, hundreds of miles away, with my parents and my sister's family waiting out the storm. I shared a room with my mother and remember watching the news coverage of the storm on television at 3:00 AM, as my mother slept, as it moved over my home, as I prayed for God to safeguard my home.

The following morning, I remained at the motel while my sister drove back home to assess damages. She called to tell me to come back as soon as possible because all power was out in the entire northwest Florida area. Even all cell phone towers were down, and the area was susceptible to looting as there were no police patrols. Regular phone service was available in a few places but communication was basically out over the entire Pensacola region, as was electrical service.

I took time to buy supplies and extra gasoline in Tallahassee before I drove the four hour trip back home. When I arrived, I had to take a circuitous route through neighborhoods to reach my two-story home on the bayou because of the debris everywhere. It was quite shocking to see that all the homes on my short street were either totally blown away without a trace of anything or else shredded by the wind so badly one could walk right between wall studs. With one exception.

A large oak tree had been uprooted in my front yard and a very tall pine tree had fallen toward my house and clipped the corner of the roof, also breaking the main water main to my house. Thick tree limbs blocked the path to the front door. When I got past them, I could see all of my siding was stripped off of the first floor of the house and the heavy steel front door was gone. The garage doors hung in pieces, swinging from their chains. A telephone pole lay across the span from my concrete porch over to my neighbor's pool deck. There were gashes in the pylons supporting the house from the hits they received from pounding debris in the 20-foot storm surge wave that slammed through the area.

Everything stored on my first floor was gone, including interior walls, washed away, up the bayou, into the backyards of neighbors, even to several houses down the street at the end of the bayou. The stringer that supported the thirteen steps up from my now open-air foyer to the second floor was broken and the stairwell had sunk down about six inches. But when I got to the top of the stairs to view my main living space, it was almost as if there was no storm!

The water and food bowl for my dog was still where I had left it on the kitchen floor. Everything was in its place unmoved. The only interior damage I could find was a water leak in the ceiling over the living room where roof shingles were blown away. Even the tree that had clipped the front corner of the roof had caused no internal damage.

The initial inspection I took of the inside of my home revealed the first signs of God's grace. *My home was one of only two on my street with any livable space in it.* If I had had electrical power and water supply, I could have lived in my house immediately, with a few alterations. The fact that so much of my main living space was left intact was an obvious answer to my earlier prayers. So many on my street, or on the surrounding streets, had nothing left at all. In fact, some yards looked like a mountain of tumbled lumber or trash heaps where the storm surge had deposited debris.

In the chaos after the hurricane, I was in a mild case of shock and didn't think to ask God for help. I have always tried to handle things for myself and never really asked people or God for help for myself. All I could think was to put one foot in front of the other and try to contend with the most pressing matter in front of me at the moment.

My parents were not well enough to be out in the heat, and my sister's family had their own damages to deal with, so I, as a newly divorced woman, wandered the neighborhood and searched my home alone for something to salvage. In the weeks after we returned, God was to show me the size of His love and just how much He recognized my situation by inundating me with unsolicited assistance from one group after another coming down my street to help.

First, a couple with two young children stopped their Jeep in the street, where I was wandering and searching, to ask if I needed help. I mentioned the only problem I could see at the moment—the fallen trees blocking the front of the house. The young man immediately drove the Jeep to my house, took out a chain saw, jumped up into the branches and cut massive limbs apart to make the way passable. Another day, about a dozen senior men, some in their eighties, came with chain saws in hand to chop up and carry away the gigantic fallen pine and oak trees. Before they left, we gathered in a circle, hand in hand, and prayed together. A few days after that another group of about ten people came to remove layers of seaweed, pine branches and debris from my yard.

Once a day, as I worked sorting through debris around my house in what felt like a ghost town, no traffic or people moving along, no sounds or lights, a Salvation Army food truck would pass through neighborhood streets, announcing over a loud-speaker free hot meals to whomever could hear. There were occasional cars of people driving the back streets looking for people in need of ice or bringing fresh ice tea and sandwiches, a welcome change from the food truck or the MRE's (Meals Ready to Eat used by armed forces).

When some of my friends heard that I had lost my job because the business where I worked was shut down, four of them donated $800 to help with expenses. The young man who cut down limbs returned about a month later wanting to donate $200. I convinced him to take some of the angel pins I had made to give as gifts to his loved ones in return for his donation.

This was quite an adjustment for me to be on the receiving end of so much generosity. I had always been the one to come to the aid of others. I was overwhelmed by how many people had come, out of the blue, to help in so many different ways.

As I sorted through debris in the days to come, I stayed at my sister's home where we brought 4 or 5 large ice chests together on the tiled kitchen floor and filled them with all the items from our various refrigerators and freezers. We picked up a daily supply of ice from a distribution point run by National Guard soldiers where we also got gallons of water and MREs. Each evening, we cooked the food most in danger of perishing on their outdoor gas grill and drained the water from melted ice out of the coolers.

I was sitting at their kitchen table one day, staring at a tapestry of angels hanging on the wall, and read the verse featured on it from Isaiah 40:31, *"But they that wait upon the Lord shall renew their strength; they shall mount up with wings as eagles; they shall run, and not be weary; and they shall walk, and not faint."* I was compelled to find a Bible and read that chapter. When I had read it, I felt the Holy Spirit urging me to continue reading the next chapter. I don't remember how much more I read, but when I stopped, I had a clear message. God was telling me that now was the time to tell people who HE is, what He had done for me, how truly caring and cognizant He is for each of His children.

Even when life slams the breath out of us, God knows where we are, is always with us through the good and even the bad we create for ourselves, and stands ready to save us and give us all the great things He knows we need. He is almighty, He knows everything there is to know, and His resources are unlimited and available for our benefit.

God knew I loved Him but He knew I needed a closer relationship with Him after I had failed to regularly read His Word, the Bible, and talk with Him. I had disobeyed and ignored God's leadership in my life, for a while, and, in doing so, allowed my marriage to dwindle into divorce. He took the opportunity, in the chaos after the hurricane, to remind me, through a tapestry wall hanging and the kind deeds of strangers and friends, that He was still concerned for my needs out of His never-dying love for me and that He wanted my full devotion to Him and His plan for me.

Yet once again, God redeemed me from my own distance from Him and disobedience to Him to pull me into a personal relationship full of His caring grace. He forgave me for my failures. He taught me that I can admit I sometimes need help or have needs. He taught me that I can ask Him for things. I learned that help from others is one way He shows that He knows who I am and is aware of my needs and supplies them according to His riches -- which are limitless!

Redemption! What God is all about! And He is ever ready to repeat that process to bring us away from our world without Him into a richer, more peaceful and contented world with Him. *"And we know that all things work together for good to those who love God, to those who are the called according to His purpose." (Romans 8:28).*

I KNOW that God will arrange things for my good, even in hard times, because He has claimed me as His own, because I have claimed and love Him and want His plan to be mine.

"If we confess our sins, he is faithful and just to forgive us our sins and to cleanse us from all unrighteousness" (1 John 1:9).

Patricia Freeman is a single Christian woman who grew up under the influence of many Christian relatives, especially her mother, all of whom lived in the Bible Belt of the South. Her life has always been centered around Jesus Christ. Pat earned a Bachelor of Science degree from Florida State University in Education. Living mostly in towns around the South, she spent three years in Germany, but returned to her hometown in Northwest Florida, where she has lived for over thirty years. Her best little buddy, Buster Brown, whose dog dish was unmoved, survived the hurricane with her to live another eight years.

STORY FOURTEEN

"Let Me Ask You a Question."

By Daniel Holly

(14)

LET ME ASK YOU A QUESTION

By Daniel Holly

*A*re you lost, and don't know where to turn? Are you broken in one manner or another, and cannot fathom a way out of the mess you've gotten yourself into?

Sometimes, we get so wrapped up in our own "stuff" we don't realize how lost or broken we really are until we are found, or until the crystal clear light of TRUTH breaks through our spiritual blinders.

For some people, it takes much longer to see the light than others. That's how it was for me. It wasn't until I reached rock bottom that I woke enough to see the light and said, "I can no longer do this on my own." I had finally reached that place.

Years later, a friend told me that he had given up all hope for me. I went through three marriages, the loss of a son, and nearly drowning myself in alcohol; I still refused to wake up enough to grab for the brass ring of grace that God makes available to each one of us.

The good news is this: God never gives up on us, no matter how far we've fallen. He is always close at hand, ready to lift us out of our deepest despair. I know now God's redemption is always close at hand.

No, I did not grow up in a Christian home. I was born in Long Beach, California, in 1957. My mother was a non-practicing Catholic and my father did not profess any faith that I remember. My father left when I was 2, leaving my mother to raise 5 children on her own. When I was 4 years old, my mother remarried, and had 2 more children.

My stepfather was a member of the Mormon church. We became members of that church and, at the age of 8, I was baptized into the Mormon faith. In 1966, when I was 9, we moved to Ogden, Utah. My mother and stepfather did not go to church with us, but the children were required to attend worship service every Sunday. As I got older, I began to realize that what the Mormon church was teaching was not what the Bible taught. I knew, even at a very young age, that there shouldn't be conflict with what the church taught and what the Bible said.

Life back then never seemed to settle down to any sense of what I would consider normal. Once again, problems erupted in our home. In 1969 my mother left my stepfather, packed up the kids, and moved us back to California. That marked the end of my time in any sort of church for nearly 30 years.

From that time forward, I routinely told myself and others that I wanted nothing to do with any religion.

From my young perspective, I couldn't believe that any one of the world religions could be right.

Later on, I adopted the Karl Marx mantra that religion was simply the "opiate of the masses."

I couldn't believe that God existed, and there was no way that I was going to be accountable to anyone. Because of my beliefs, I had issues with authority figures. I never liked anyone telling me what to do. This caused me problems both in high school and the US Navy later on in life. We rarely spend much time in our youth thinking about our prideful motivations, do we?

As was the case for everyone else my age in public schools, I was being taught from elementary school on through high school, about the Darwinian "theory of evolution" and the "big bang theory." My teachers made it seem to be believable as the only "logical" reason for my existence and that of the world around us. No one dared to speculate for us that if the Big Bang Theory was true, what or who was the initial cause that produced that massive effect? Creation and intelligent design were, and still are, foreign to the secular educational process.

It was wild growing up during the age of the "sexual revolution." The mantra of "Sex, Drugs, and Rock 'n' Roll" rang loudly in my ears. As a result of cultural environment of those days, I had no one instilling convictions of sin (or right and wrong) in my life. My teenage years found me getting into all sorts of trouble. I ran away from home three times before I was 16, went to juvenile hall for stealing a car as a minor, I was arrested for breaking and entering and vandalizing school property, and became quite sexually promiscuous. I never gave it much thought as to whether or not I might be hurting the girls (and later on women) who I was having sex with. I was even responsible for at least one (that I know of) abortion, with no regrets at the time.

It didn't help that the at age of 15, I began my 22-year addiction to alcohol. Looking back, I find it kind of ironic being asked to write my own story of redemption by my partner in a few of my teenage raucous episodes. Neither of us had any spiritual guidance in our youth.

Looking back, it is fairly obvious that I only cared about my own pleasure. How many of those seven deadly sins were ruling my life? Starting with pride I was being driven by lust, and gluttony, just to name a few.

In addition to the sexual revolution back in the day, the 70s was also influenced by the "Jesus Freak" movement. It was in full swing. Everywhere I went, someone was trying to tell me that I needed Jesus. To me, this was ridiculous. I would not only ridicule them, I would do my best to make these dopes look stupid. It was easy to do. They tried to convince me that I would go to hell without Jesus as my Savior.

The problem was, no one could tell me why hell was so bad or why Jesus was so good.

No one who talked to me back in the day could defend his or her Christian faith, at least in any meaningful way.

They had no idea what 1st Peter meant, if they even knew what it said, (not that I understood back then). That said, I want to make it understood that I was not simply indifferent to Christ ... I was downright hostile.

The danger, in my mind was this: If God was real, then I was accountable to Him. Therefore, in my prideful way of thinking, there was no room for God – there could be no God.

God indeed works in His own time and timing. Though God indeed offers His grace to all men, I simply was not ready to receive it back then. It would have required me to accept the truth of 1st Peter.

Neither was I ready back in 1987, when my son was born. At that time, I was married to my first wife. She was a nurse; we had two little girls and a young son. Things seemed good enough, especially in relation to the family dynamic during my own upbringing, and my alcoholism was functionally under control.

When my son was about 18 months old, we noticed that as he tried to walk using his walker, his knees seemed to bend slightly backward. We took him to one doctor after another for the next 12 months, trying to get a firm diagnosis. We ended up at UCLA where a visiting doctor from France told us our son had a rare disease that affected only 1 in 400,000 people. He also told us that our son would not make it to see his 4th birthday. The news was devastating. One thing is certain, I didn't pray about it. *Why would I?*

Back to family dynamics: Shortly after we received the diagnosis, my mother-in-law spoke to her pastor about having my son baptized. I was not open to the idea at all. The pastor came and talked to us, and I was adamant that it was not going to happen. I told the pastor that not only did I not believe in God, but, that God was a sham invented by man to keep other men as compliant as sheep. This came as a bit of a shock to him. Like I said, I was hostile as well as angry. The problem was, just like those Jesus Freaks I mentioned earlier, even this pastor was unable to give any proof as to the validity of God – or any reason for me to believe in his fairy tales.

Well, the conversation went on and on despite my objections. Eventually the conversation expanded to include my wife, my mother, and my in-laws. I finally relented and allowed my children to be baptized at my mother-in-law's church.

As the disease continued to progress in my son's body, he lost all ability to move. I was working the graveyard shift, and my wife was working days so that there was always someone home with our son. We took care of him, changing his diapers and feeding tube as necessary. In 1991, twelve days before his 4th birthday, my son passed away.

In my anguish, much like many do, I started out asking the same question multitudes ask, how can there be a good and loving God who allows innocent children to get sick and die? Then in my tears, I cried and shouted out in anger at God, I cursed Him for taking my son away from me. It wasn't until much later that I realized how utterly stupid that was. How in the world can we truly be angry with someone or something we don't believe in?

Therein lies the atheist conundrum. At the core of our genetic makeup, we all have an intrinsic longing to understand our connection to the universe. Christians understand this connection to be "God," the creator of the universe. When we are in the midst of our grief, we cannot fathom the logic of a fallen world that has rejected God, and the subsequent need for reconciliation with Him.

As it normally happens with the death of a child, my marriage broke up. It didn't help that I was still drinking and that I had never given up my promiscuous ways.

It wasn't until 1994 that I finally quit drinking and was ready to admit that God actually existed. No, I still wasn't ready to believe in Jesus, and yes, I still insisted on being in charge of my own life and destiny – no matter the cost.

At the age of 40, I started going to church. My reasoning had nothing to do with God. I was going because the woman I was sleeping with wanted me to go. For about a year I attended, listening to the music and the sermons. I did not take communion because I knew it wasn't for me. Isaiah 55:11 says, *So will my word be which goes forth from my mouth; it will not return to Me empty, without accomplishing what I desire, and without succeeding in the matter for which I sent it.*

I didn't realize it at the time, but God's Word was working in me.

In 1998, the church I was going to hosted a "Why We Worship" seminar. The series ran Thursday night, Friday night, and all day Saturday. I went on Thursday night to listen to the music and the teaching and went home much the same person I had always been. I went back on Friday, expecting more of the same. As the band started the worship songs, I stood along with everyone else. About 20 minutes later, I felt an overwhelming desire to fall to my knees. I admitted to God that I was a sinner and that I was ashamed of what I had done in my life. I knew that I did not deserve mercy, but I asked Jesus to forgive me and to come into my life and be my Savior. Immediately I felt a weight lifted off of my shoulders and peace unlike anything I had ever felt. I knew that my sins had been forgiven and that Christ had come into my life. I was determined to live my life for Him and put my past behind me. I knew that I had to serve Him with all of my heart and soul and mind and strength, with as much passion as I had when I previously denied Him.

Following my spiritual rebirth, I have dedicated my life to being able to answer the questions that people ask me, the same questions that so many Christians couldn't answer when I was asking them. God has blessed me with a decent memory, ability to reason, and a desire to tell others of Him.

At 41 years old, I was reborn.

1 Peter 1 (1ˢᵗ Peter)

From Peter, apostle of Jesus Christ - To God's chosen people who live as refugees scattered throughout the provinces of Pontus, Galatia, Cappadocia, Asia, and Bithynia:

You were chosen according to the purpose of God the Father and were made a holy people by his Spirit, to obey Jesus Christ and be purified by his blood. May grace and peace be yours in full measure.

Let us give thanks to the God and Father of our Lord Jesus Christ! Because of his great mercy he gave us new life by raising Jesus Christ from death. This fills us with a living hope, and so we look forward to possessing the rich blessings that God keeps for his people. He keeps them for you in heaven, where they cannot decay or spoil or fade away.

They are for you, who through faith are kept safe by God's power for the salvation which is ready to be revealed at the end of time. Be glad about this, even though it may now be necessary for you to be sad for a while because of the many kinds of trials you suffer.

Their purpose is to prove that your faith is genuine. Even gold, which can be destroyed, is tested by fire; and so your faith, which is much more precious than gold, must also be tested, so that it may endure. Then you will receive praise and glory and honor on the Day when Jesus Christ is revealed.

You love him, although you have not seen him, and you believe in him, although you do not now see him. So you rejoice with a great and glorious joy which words cannot express, because you are receiving the salvation of your souls, which is the purpose of your faith in him.

It was concerning this salvation that the prophets made careful search and investigation, and they prophesied about this gift which God would give you. They tried to find out when the time would be and how it would come. This was the time to which Christ's Spirit in them was pointing, in predicting the sufferings that Christ would have to endure and the glory that would follow.

God revealed to these prophets that their work was not for their own benefit, but for yours, as they spoke about those things which you have now heard from the messengers who announced the Good News by the power of the Holy Spirit sent from heaven. These are things which even the angels would like to understand.

So then, have your minds ready for action. Keep alert and set your hope completely on the blessing which will be given you when Jesus Christ is revealed.

Be obedient to God, and do not allow your lives to be shaped by those desires you had when you were still ignorant. Instead, be holy in all that you do, just as God who called you is holy.

The scripture says, "Be holy because I am holy."

You call him Father, when you pray to God, who judges all people by the same standard, according to what each one has done; so then, spend the rest of your lives here on earth in reverence for him. For you know what was paid to set you free from the worthless manner of life handed down by your ancestors. It was not something that can be destroyed, such as silver or gold; it was the costly sacrifice of Christ, who was like a lamb without defect or flaw.

He had been chosen by God before the creation of the world and was revealed in these last days for your sake. Through him you believe in God, who raised him from death and gave him glory; and so your faith and hope are fixed on God.

Now that by your obedience to the truth you have purified yourselves and have come to have a sincere love for other believers, love one another earnestly with all your heart. For through the living and eternal word of God you have been born again as the children of a parent who is immortal, not mortal.

As the scripture says, "All human beings are like grass, and all their glory is like wild flowers. The grass withers, and the flowers fall, but the word of the Lord remains forever."

This word is the Good News that was proclaimed to you.

STORY FIFTEEN

"Redemption"

By Robert Schultz

(15)
REDEMPTION

By Robert Schultz

First, I must give thanks to God the Father, Jesus the Son whose name is above all names, and the Holy Spirit.

I remember from a young age having a reverence and fear of God. The only problem was my God was waiting to condemn me. Let me explain. Every child wants to know they are loved and valued. In my home my father was an alcoholic. I understood nothing of that when I was young. All I understood was that I got punished when I did wrong and I got punished when I did nothing wrong. I still remember the belt! I really could not understand why?

Even with that, I loved my father. In my mind, at the time, he was the image of my Heavenly Father. If I could not please my earthly father and be loved by him, how could I ever please my Heavenly Father and be loved by Him? This was my life. There was no where to run to, no one to talk too! I was certain if I talked to my heavenly Father, I felt he hated me too. All I knew from my earthly father was anger and wrath. I felt I had no worth or value to anyone.

Things got even worse when we went to church. I was Lutheran. I never sensed the joy of the Lord. All I sensed was the obligation to this God was fulfilled. Then I watched as the same people worshipping went out and got drunk and used the Lord's name in vain as if it were a joke. This made me feel even worse. If God cares about these people, what did I do to deserve His wrath? I had no hope; I was self-loathing.

Still, I had nowhere to turn. The only highlight of church was film that was shown every Easter Sunday. The film chronicled the events of Good Friday through Easter Sunday and the Resurrection. I remember sobbing; how could they murder Jesus who had done no wrong? At the same time, the resurrection did not mean anything to me. How could he accept me and love me? The image of my Heavenly Father was clouded by my earthly one. That was Satan's doing, but I did not know that at the time. I was without hope. I know all these things had to happen so he could save me and use me.

Time went on and so did the emptiness. I grew up and became angry. In high school I had enough. My rage and anger were vented on a football field. I can only thank God that is where he put me. I was going to make everyone pay for the pain I felt, and I did. Even my friends on the team knew I would hurt them. Now, my father came back on the scene. I was now his son. Even with all he had done before, this hurt the most. I worked for it; I paid the price for it, and he took the glory. Still, I was lost, hurt, and felt like nothing. I graduated, and life went on.

The next phase of my life was the military. I remember packing to go. My Godparents had given me a Bible on my Confirmation Day. I decided I would take it along and read it. I did, but at the same time, what good was this book if my Heavenly Father had already rejected me? I kept reading, got out of the military, returned home, and gotmarried.

I was married to Josie for 32 years. I have to be honest, when I took the wedding vows, I was afraid. I stood in front of Almighty God pledging my fidelity and faithfulness to Josie in whatever life might throw at us. At the same time, I was feeling He had turned His back on me. My feeling was validated soon after that. I didn't know it at the time, but what happened next was not from God; it was Satan at work in our marriage. It did not take long before Josie started pointing the finger at me; everything that went wrong in our marriage was blamed on me. To be honest, there was nothing major. When you already feel deserted by God and your wife turns on you, it kicks your life into another level of despair.

Josie was one of ten children, and one of her sisters married a man named Mike. One day, Mike asked if he could talk to me about Jesus. I said sure! He took me down the Roman road. I knew I was a sinner. I knew I could not help myself. I knew Jesus died for me. At that moment, John 3:16 came to life, *"God so loved the world that he gave his only begotten son for the forgiveness of sin."* God loved me the whole time, after believing all these years He hated me!

The icing on the cake was Romans 8:1-2, *"There is no condemnation to them which are in Jesus Christ, who walk not after flesh, but after the Spirit."* You mean, Lord, I am free? The answer was yes. In Christ Jesus, I was a new creation -- all the old things passed away and all things were made new. The same holds true today, every day.

This prepared me for what was ahead.

I mentioned Josie earlier. We had our struggles, all married couples do. You know when the Lord said the two become one flesh, it is more than consecrating the marriage. It is about the spirit of Jesus that unifies in love. That can be difficult.

Needless to say, after the birth of our children, Josie suffered post-partum depression. She attempted suicide three times. The last one I had to break down the bathroom door to save her. I was scared and asking her why, as the kids screamed in the background. She said she wanted to be with Jesus. I knew that was a lie straight from Satan. She got help, and for a time, she was better.

Then, more happened. Josie was diagnosed with colorectal cancer; she endured a colostomy, chemo, and radiation. I cried out to God. Honestly, I wanted to know why. Hadn't there been enough bad things happen in my life and now this? This was a ten-year ordeal. The cancer went to her lungs, and then to her liver. Finally, it led to her death.

Yet, the bright side is that the Lord touched her heart in a powerful way. In the midst of all of her suffering, she praised and glorified Jesus until she took her last breath. All I can say is, it is not what we face, it is Who faces it with us. He remains faithful even when we are not. Numbers 23:19, *"God is not a man that he should lie; neither the son of man that he should repent: hath he said and shall he not do it?"* In Titus 1:2, *"In hope of eternal life, which God, that cannot lie, promised before the world began."*

There is nothing that can separate us from the love of God. He has paid the price in full. He is your and my ever- present help. He brings joy into the darkest hour. He brings hope and power to defeat the enemy Satan. This is not about what we know, it is about Who we know, and that is Jesus. The enemy is defeated because of His love for us.

Take advantage of His word found in Holy Scripture. If Jesus could change someone as messed up as me, He will certainly help you. In the end, He desires none to be lost, no, not even one. He gives strength, hope, purpose. The victory has been won in the shed blood of Jesus. "Fear not! I am with you," He tells us in Isaiah 41:10. What I did not have with my earthly father, I have with my Heavenly Father. It is all about His mercy and grace.

He is so powerful that no one is out of His reach. In Christ Jesus all the old things have passed away, and all things are made new. It does not take great faith. It takes knowing you are a sinner, asking His forgiveness with a contrite heart, and accepting His gift of grace and redemption.

Get to know Him. You will be blessed and will never be the same again. I hope and pray you will accept the love, hope, and freedom only He can provide, in Jesus' name I pray.

Amen

Redemption

An Army veteran, Robert Shultz was born in Milwaukee and spent most of his life in Brown Deer, Wisconsin. He was blessed with a 32-year marriage when his wife Josie was called home to Jesus. Robert and Josie brought three children into this world: Joshua, Erin, and Andrew. A truck driver all of these years, he remains grateful for all the Lord Jesus has done. Robert enjoys fishing, hiking, and custom woodworking in his spare time.

STORY SIXTEEN

"How Gratitude Got Me Through"

By Vidal Cisneros, Jr.

(16)

HOW GRATITUDE GOT ME THROUGH

By Vidal Cisneros Jr.

If a fellow isn't thankful for what he's got, he isn't likely to be thankful for what he's going to get.
~ Frank A. Clark

"My life will not end like this. My family needs me and I have to follow my dreams and start now." That's the promise I made myself one evening, years ago.

I was sitting in my work truck on a road construction site that was the culmination of my dead-end career.

My dreams had faded to nothing, my marriage was stuck in idle, and my daughters only saw the remnants of the father they'd once known, when they saw me at all, which was seldom.

Riding on the power of that decision, I left my financially comfortable, soul-destroying construction career behind. I jumped into a success mentorship program, quickly discovering the power of personal development and opening myself to the idea that my life was in my hands.

I believed I had embarked on a journey that was waiting just for me. Then the unexpected happened.

I was quickly building momentum and learning the principles of building a successful business when my wife of seven years began to change.

She had gone so far into her new reality that it took all the courage she had to confess it all. "I'm seeing someone," she finally admitted.

All of the momentum I'd been building crumbled under the devastating blow as she hesitantly said, "There's more." A long pause, and then, "I'm pregnant."

At that moment I felt 100% shattered. I grasped for a straw of hope. "It's mine, right?"

One word blew that straw away. "No."

I still wanted her as my wife. I held on to that thought and tried desperately to make it work and win her back, but it was hopeless. As much as I prayed for a miracle, I had to accept she wasn't in the relationship with me anymore. It was time to let her go and move out.

Almost overnight, I went from new success to new distress. That year I spiraled into a deep depression and found myself sitting at bars and drinking more than I ever had. The rage I was trying to suppress came out one night in a drunken bender. In a high-speed chase one hopes to see only in a movie, I eluded a deputy sheriff twice, finally losing the officer but causing an accident and totaling my Jeep.

While, thankfully, no one was severely injured in the accident, I was a mess. Unsurprisingly, I was placed under arrest.

I'd worked with deputy sheriffs on construction sites and I had always respected the law. This behavior was out of character for me. I had to ask myself who I had become.

Sitting in that cell for four days straight not only sobered me up but also woke me up to the reckless way I was living my life. I hit rock bottom sitting in that cell, locked up with people who were on trial for awful crimes.

In those four days of incarceration I went through a wide range of emotions, but what I found was clarity in my mission and the passion that would pick me up from the deep depression I was in. I prayed. I fasted. I found inspiration in others' stories.

Most of all, the light was beaming brightly out from me again. I realized that I needed to forgive if I was going to move forward with my life.

Praying for everyone, especially for those who had created my nightmare, softened my heart and made things turn around faster than I'd imagined. Words, I learned, have power, and the ability of grateful prayer to change your life should never be underestimated.

I had fallen prey to alcoholism and depression. But now I held fast to my new vision. I would be grateful and wish everyone the best, including my enemies. I prayed for blessings for my ex-wife, her lover, and their unborn child.

Unfortunately, the day following the arrest, my name was plastered all over the news as a suspect in a high-speed chase. I was sentenced to six months for Driving While Intoxicated and Reckless Driving.

I saw the emotional effect my sentencing and conviction had on my family, and it was devastating to face six months behind bars away from my daughters when they most needed me. Although I thought this was the last thing I needed, looking back I realize it was, in fact, the best thing.

Those six months helped clear my mind from the nightmare and gave me the courage to accept professional therapy and get refocused. Most of all, it awakened my heart to a new relationship.

Before serving time, I had become friendly with a woman at work. Unbeknownst to me, she was also going through betrayal and divorce.

The similarity in our situations was eerie, and it was obvious to us that our becoming friends was no coincidence. I began to write her daily, and the closer we became, the more she was my ray of light in the storm I was living through.

She brightened my days with her letters and visits. She gave me hope, and it inspired me to keep going. In the outside world, the life I once knew was being pummeled to dust. But in my incarcerated world I found contentment in writing, drawing, singing in the choir, and inspiring others to chase dreams.

I learned something powerful – being incarcerated doesn't mean being unhappy.

I learned that, though life takes us through dark places, we can choose to believe in something bigger and have faith that your journey will take you to better circumstances when we serve a greater purpose that involves others.

When my six-month sentence was over, traveling on that bus back to my reality was surreal. I was returning, but with a new level of awareness for life. Learning from others' stories gave me insight into how powerful the principles I learned from my mentors really were.

I've learned that we all have the same twenty-four hours each day to sow seeds of abundance. And we can't receive greater gifts if we don't let go of the past ones.

It became obvious that I had been blind for many years to the power of visionary gratitude. I had taken so many things for granted for so long, including achieving my dreams. But by intentionally envisioning and being grateful in the now, it gives way to abundance in the future.

When I'm asked to speak to audiences about my story and how I persevered in spite of circumstances, I talk about the power of words, forgiveness, and blessings others through prayer, and why holding that vision of gratitude for what you have so that greater possibilities become real.

I've also been fortunate to see life from a new perspective through the program of Alcoholics Anonymous.

Learning how to live a 100% clean and sober lifestyle one day at a time has brought greater joy and impactful fulfillment, and I'm more than grateful for all I've learned from A.A.

Through the hardest moments, I focused on my faith and this mantra: Instead of waiting for the light at the end of the tunnel, be the light that sparks everyone on fire.

Vidal Cisneros, Jr. has been featured in Chicken Soup for the Soul: Think Possible, *and also has been featured in* The Huffington Post, Entrepreneur *magazine,* The Good Men Project, *NBC's* "The Morning Blend" *and has been featured at multiple book talks at Barnes & Noble Booksellers locations. Vidal hosts a top-ranked iTunes podcast which features* TEDx *speakers, best-selling authors, world-renowned consultants and inspiring entrepreneurs who share their stories of tragedy to triumph.*

Vidal owns and operates a digital agency that helps businesses and influencers amplify their message and grow their customer base through an impacting mission.

To connect, email: vidalcisnerosjr@gmail.com and go to vidalcisnerosjr.com

STORY SEVENTEEN

"A Love Story"

By Luanne Nelson

(17)

A LOVE STORY
By Luanne Nelson

I always ask what I should write about when I am in the shower. I've heard His voice – out loud – only once. Answering me this time, He said to my heart, "Write about that." Alright. I will. I knew exactly what He meant.

There was an unusual amount of rain that summer, small waves gently splashed against the shoreline. The pier was invisible, standing under about two inches of water. I sloshed a deck chair to the end of it and settled in. Lake water splashed over my bare feet. An iced bowl filled with cooked, peeled and deveined shrimp sat on my lap. My cigarettes and lighter were partitioned off to one side in the white porcelain bowl, safely tucked in a plastic waterproof bag. A bottle of chardonnay sat on the pier next to my feet, the wine glass in my hand waited to be filled.

It would have been a strange sight to any casual observer. It looked like I was sitting in the middle of the lake directly on the water. I enjoyed a fleeting thought about Jesus walking on water and wondered if He ever had a picnic with his apostles on a lake without the benefit of a boat. You know, just sitting on the water passing around plates of fish, figs, and unleavened bread while telling jokes. I dismissed this thought as sacrilegious and stopped thinking about it, since I knew for a fact Jesus was not a showoff.

I realized I'd forgotten to bring the perfectly rolled joint down to the lake. It was still sitting on the red checkered kitchen tablecloth up at the house. Oh well. At least I remembered to bring an extra lighter in my pocket in case the one in the baggie fell into the water. I ate a shrimp and tossed the tail in the lake. I thought about my life. I was 36 years old. The children were spending part of summer break with their dad and his wife. This was my time off, my summer vacation. A few years earlier, I had married their dad's cousin. Things were messy.

I was glad in a strange way that my replacement husband drank more than I did. I convinced myself I was in a good spot as long as he drank more. He hid his bottles of gin in the sleeves of his sweaters, I didn't do that. This, of course, allowed me to consider myself to be the suffering spouse of a flaming alcoholic. I went to group meetings and whined about how everything would be perfect if only he would just stop drinking. I sipped some more chardonnay and appreciated the cool water splashing over my feet.

As long as I was doing nothing but daydreaming on the pier, I seized the moment to critique my former husband's wife. She wore press on nails. I knew this because she apparently had popped one and I saw it sitting on the console of his Beemer. After giving him a wicked hard time about the tackiness of it, I continued laughing my derrier off and wondered exactly how and when I became so catty.

I tossed another shrimp tail in the water.

Deep down inside, I knew I was a dreadful mess. I imagined parts of me bobbing in the water next to the increasing number of shrimp tails and cigarette butts. An arm here, an ear there. Another shrimp tail floated by. I lit a cigarette and inhaled deeply.

A piece of lakeweed drifted by. I imagined a few of my sad thoughts attached to it, never to be remembered again. I waved at it with my pinkie and wished it a good journey. *Bon voyage, little green slimy thing with awful thoughts all over it.*

How had I gotten into such a predicament, I wondered. What was I going to do? I poured some more chardonnay into my pretty crystal wrong-shaped-glass. I reminded myself of that very important tidbit of proper etiquette dictating the fact that flutes were reserved for champagne; chardonnay belonged in a totally different shaped crystal vessel. This fork here, fish fork there, that spoon next to the others to the right of the plate. This thought made me smile to myself, recalling the things that used to be so important that were still so stuck in my head. The wine was working its magic. I felt delightfully fuzzy and warm.

There was a time in my life when I had taught charm school at a modeling agency. Saturday morning instructions and admonitions floated through my head: Stand up straight and what in the world are you thinking wearing blue eyeshadow? Tuck your hips under and keep your chin parallel to the floor.

I flicked another glowing butt into the air. A mini meteor of sorts.

He was a handsome guy, academic in nature, with a closely cropped beard and ocean blue eyes that sparkled with mischief most of the time. He was a doctor; a self-described "MudFud," meaning he was an MD with a few PhDs after his name. He was a brilliant man who admitted to sedating his brain with alcohol. His gin was medicinal, he said. He blamed his sporadic neuropathy on being hogtied during a research convention down south. He had misbehaved, the police got involved, and he landed in a jail cell tied up on the floor, face down. In the morning, the department chairman claimed him and bailed him out. Boys will be boys, the chair said. Later that week, before he headed back home, the mayor awarded him the keys to the city. I suppose the mayor felt it was a small, albeit adequate, reparation for bothering a conventioneer who happened to be a visiting physician from a large medical college. It worked; sparkle man had it framed and put it on his desk, bragging about it for years.

Little did we know; we were both already seriously destroyed when we re-met during that very hot summer years ago. While my children were visiting their dad and his tacky wife, I was out and about town visiting old friends, including blue eyes - my soon-to-be next husband. While I was visiting his grandmother, who was the sister of my first husband's grandmother, her eyes lit up, and it was clear she was about to put a great new idea into motion.

She reached for the phone and called someone. "Guess who's in town?" she said. A few minutes later, handsome MudFud walked through the door. We saw each other at family gatherings over the years and had chatted occasionally. It was nice to see him again.

He was in his thirties, staying at his parents' house. His mom and his dad had died way too soon. Their clothing was draped on the cloth hangers in the master bedroom's closet. His mom's hats still sat on the top shelf of the entranceway closet waiting to be worn, and his dad's boots were on the floor waiting to be stepped into. He explained to me he just didn't have the time to go through everything and clean it all up, even though his parents had both been gone for nearly a decade.

You never would have guessed, looking at either one of us, how wrecked we truly were; even we didn't know it. On the outside we looked just dandy. People said we made a stunning couple; he with his burled walnut pipe and me with my mane of messy blonde hair. He was book smart, I was street smart. We both were clueless.

A few years earlier, I had barely escaped a treacherous relationship after my divorce. I had landed in a shelter with my children 600 miles away, out east, in my home town. The monster was a wildly abusive guy who lied to me about pretty much everything. He was a smooth talker; I believed him. I learned a lot. Life can kill you if you're not careful. There are landmines everywhere.

So, the brokenhearted man who felt orphaned, and the brokenhearted woman who had just been damn near dragged and left for dead in Dante's inferno, fell in love and agreed to make a go of it. Give it a whirl ,of sorts, we said. After all, we figured we were both intelligent people who believed in God, had gone through some awful things,

A Love Story

and came out on the other side of disaster alive. We decided to elope, sending postcards from Colorado to our family and friends to announce our wedding. A few years later, I found a box of old wedding announcements in the attic from his first marriage. I scratched out his first wife's name, wrote my name in the margin and mailed them out to a handful of friends. We made lemonade out of lemons, all the while stuffing our mouths with sugared cookies.

The children loved him, and he adored them right back. Let's face it, their dad and new stepdad were related, so there was an instant bond. We truly had so much fun together. We all sat together at grade school basketball games, football games, and Christmas pageants. We were quite the trio. Sometimes, I sat in the middle of the two of them. I suppose we looked strange from the outside for anyone who knew our story. We didn't mind. We would go out in the parking lot and smoke together during half-time or intermission.

We took the children to Disney World in the middle of the winter. The following summer, we vacationed in Colorado, foot skiing on the leftover snow in the mountains. One time, he made a makeshift Haitian flotilla-looking craft out of the pontoon boat after the canopy ripped. I nearly died laughing.

When my littlest one received her first Holy Communion, he was right there in church with us. He was not a religious man; rather, he was a scruffy guy with a loving spirit. His Godmother was my children's great aunt. Sitting in the pew with his aviator glasses on, he reached into his pocket to grab his pipe. I whispered to him, "You can't do that in here!" He smiled that spectacular grin of his that did me in every time. He loved razzing me. He loved me, and I loved him right back.

Three years into this marriage, the unthinkable happened. A life changing disaster of epic proportions struck. The phone call came early, before sunrise, one summer morning. The news was devastating. My first husband, the father of my three beautiful children, the cousin of my dear husband, had taken his own life at the lakefront. There are no words to describe the shock, the anguish, the raw pain.

Our children, who were nine, eleven, and twelve years old, were hardly old enough to even understand death, much less death by one's own hand. Their beloved dad's life was gone, he was nowhere to be found, ever again. The suffering was palpable. They searched his closets and looked under the beds. He had to be there somewhere. It was gut-wrenching.

A few weeks later, I suffered a miscarriage. Then, I broke.

The next two years were miserable. I tried my best to balance a ship without a rudder. No sails. No wind. Sometimes, no air.

Hadn't I done everything you told me to do, God? I had gone to church (almost) every Sunday, I had been faithful in adversity, I had kept my chin up and made the best out of bad situations, I had my children baptized and drove them to Catholic school every morning, picking them up at the end of each day. I had prayed together with them. *I was doing my best, God. I remembered, You had sent me an angel to let me know there is life after this one. Where are you, God?*

My world went dark. Very dark.

The doc prescribed Xanax. Chardonnay rounded some of the sharp edges of intense grief. The doc decided I'd had enough Xanax after a few months. My husband was drinking more, and so was I. The more we drank, the more we fought. We had loved hard and fought with passion before this happened. It was different now. There was a heaviness in the air that was suffocating our marriage. We were mean to each other, and we got meaner to each other every day. The children were suffering. We were all suffering.

Extended family needed someone to blame, and I became that person. After all, he would still be alive if I hadn't divorced him, right? Aren't we all that powerful? If I hadn't had the audacity to marry his cousin, everything would have been alright, right? I felt like running into the wilderness with everyone else's sins on my back and shaking all of them off. The scapegoat. Pour me another one. Please. It's all too heavy.

A Love Story

Although we did not realize it at the time, from the start we both had a hidden, deadly cache of landmines in our hearts. Over the next year, we routinely stepped on each other's mines enough that eventually we blew each other's hearts to smithereens. Later, we detonated whatever we had left during one of the cruelest divorces ever. Even our attorneys were appalled.

There was nothing civilized about it. He said he hoped I would end up living out of my car with the children and I told him I had the dogs killed, even though I hadn't. We never stopped fighting long enough to realize what we were really doing was trying to kill the demons inside ourselves. Misplaced outrage. Heartsickness. Alcohol is not called "spirits" perchance. People - like us - unleash them with every sip. Amazingly, even through all of this, I still thought he was the one with the drinking problem, not me.

After five years of marriage we parted ways, angrier than hornets, and didn't look back.

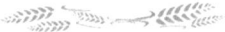

Well, there I was, lights out. Dark. Divorced again. Dead inside. Dank. Dreary. Destroyed.

I was sure I had used up all of my chances as far as my relationship with God was concerned. I had to sleep in the bed I had made for myself. It was an ugly bed. That is what I was taught, and I believed the lie.

Confidence in myself was shot. I began to look to everyone around me for approval. I knew I was no longer good enough. I knew it. I was wrecked. If I forgot this for even a moment, my family reminded me.

I want you to know, I can count on one hand the number of times I was actually inebriated. I just wanted that sweet buzz going so I didn't have to feel the pain. I drank my chardonnay at home. I didn't go to bars. This didn't make me any better than the next sot, it just meant I drank in solitude. I didn't have to hide bottles in the sleeves of my sweaters. It didn't matter. I was angry all the time. I was furious at God. I wondered if He even saw me anymore or if He even cared enough to look at me, mess that I was. I figured even if He did catch a glimpse of me, He probably looked the other way, thoroughly disgusted.

One day, I was shocked to realize I could not stop drinking even though I wanted to. I, believe it or not, had still considered myself to be a social drinker, one who was going through a rough time. The fact that I was drinking alone simply meant I didn't want to talk to anyone.

I figured I would want to be with people again sometime later, when I was in a better mood. I had alienated my friends, anyway. I had become a miserable, self-loathing, self-pitying pain in the neck.

Denial is a strange thing; while in it, I had refused to connect the dots until I got to the point I couldn't stop drinking. Good God Almighty in heaven! I had a sudden realization that my life would not have been any better even if my husband had stopped drinking. It wasn't his fault. I realized he could not have stopped drinking even if he had wanted to. I realized I could not stop, and it had nothing to do with willpower. Nothing. I realized he didn't love his gin more than he loved me after all. He couldn't stop, either. *Oh, dear God in heaven, help me!*

I tried to quit. Every day. For nearly a year. Every. Single. Day.

There was the day the alcohol stopped working. I would have a glass of wine and it made me sick, literally. I broke out in hives. I had a constant headache. I thought I had a brain tumor. It never dawned on me maybe I was hungover. I supposed being buzzed for a few years would do that, right? *Please God, wherever You are – I need to sober up. I don't want to die like this.*

I remembered there was a place, about an hour away from where I lived, called Holy Hill. I knew miracles happened there. Pilgrims from all over the world trekked to this designated holy place, leaving their crutches behind, hanging in rows on the Miracle Wall. I thought, *I will go there and put my wine glass on one of the crutches.* I had a plan. I felt hope for the first time in a very long time.

So, I started out early one day and drove up to Holy Hill. I kneeled at the altar and prayed my heart out. I confessed my sins. I apologized to Him for being such a mess. I begged, truly begged, Him to be there, to hear me, to heal me. *Please please please, take my ugly bed, my mess, my old self, and make me new again.*

I drove home and opened a bottle of merlot. No miracle for me. *Of course not,* I thought. *Why would He bother with me after all I've done? Said? Thought?*

Daily, I continued to do my morning supply inventory. I needed a 1.5-liter bottle of chardonnay daily, even though it made me sick. I was living in my own hell. I learned to say, "God help me." I said it a lot. I figured if I said it enough, He might feel sorry for me and in His pity for me He would help me. This went on for months.

"God help me."

I remember walking into my living room, standing in front of the fireplace right after I said this for at least the thousandth time, and then, I heard HIS VOICE – out loud – HIS VOICE said,

"You don't have to do that anymore."

I dropped to the floor. Not because I wanted to - rather, because I could not stand myself upright. I knew I was in the presence of the Most High God! At that moment, all of the pain, the tears, the heartache, the sorrow, the embarrassment, the rage, the misery, the grief, was pulled right out of me. Gone. This extremely crushingly heavy burden was – lifted! He healed me! He really and truly healed me! Just like that!!!

I was on the floor, a blank canvas. *Lord God Almighty, write my new life on me however you want me to be ...* and this is the first thing He did: *"Take away her thirst."* And, just like that, my thirst cravings were gone.

It has been twenty years since God relieved me of my alcoholism. In the weeks following the Miracle, I prayed a lot and came to realize a few things:

I came to know that everything happens in His time, not mine, not ours. He knows the map of our hearts. Every single one of us. We are His children. He knows every hair on our heads. He knit us together under our mother's hearts. I know He loves me – and you.

And that prayer I prayed that day at Holy Hill? I now call it my "Brat Prayer." He knew very well my deeply rooted character defect of arrogance. Piecing it all together, I realized that had He lifted my sickness from me up there on the Hill that day, I would have taken some of the credit because "I" drove there and He heard "me." I would have missed the whole point.

I know now, He was not punishing me by delaying the Miracle for a later date, He knew I needed to learn to be humble, I needed to be prepared and ready to receive His generous Miracle. He wanted me to learn the difference between humility and humiliation.

I came to know - and it still takes my breath away to this day - that when I am at my weakest, I know the magnificent force of His strength and the loving touch of his tender mercy. God's grace is sufficient to see us through, no matter what.

As time passed, I have to admit I started to look for my former husband in crowds of people at museums, in stores, and at the mall. He was nowhere to be found. Last year, I sent a friend request to his new wife on Facebook. She spammed me. I figured he was either still pretty angry about everything or he had just decided to forget everything

A Love Story

that happened. I wondered if he was still drinking. I wondered if he was alright.

I did hear from him last summer, during his season of death, in a very spiritual way. He let me know he needed my forgiveness in order to pass through the gates of readiness; to be able to love completely into that forever place we call heaven. He let me know he knew he had hurt me. In all fairness, I knew I had hurt him, too. I completely, without hesitation, forgave him. I've asked him for his forgiveness, too. He tossed a glittering wrapped present of forgiveness to me from heaven.

I truly hope he is having fun now playing with our loved child who was never born; the child we miscarried shortly after his cousin's suicide. I secretly named this little girl Annie Maroney. I think she was a little girl. It was his favorite name, the name he affectionately used to call me. If our baby was a little boy, I am certain he's named him after himself, just like we had agreed.

Life goes on.

Who am I today? I am a forgiven woman, I am humbled, I am relieved, I am restored. I have been made new. I am renewed daily in Him, and I am strengthened by His Word. I am a Warrior. I am a Survivor completely and totally because of His Grace and Mercy.

I am a married woman, married to a good man who loves me and protects me now. I know I am strengthened by our prayers together. My husband is the head of this house, I am the heart of this home. I am a mom. I am a grandmother. I am thankful for what I have, for what I am today in Christ. God gives me exactly what I need today, saving the rest for later, in His time.

I am God's servant. He is my King, my Master, my Savior. I am no longer a slave to anything or to anybody.

Today, I know I am enough.

I am His.

"And we know that all things work together for good to those who love God, to those who are called according to His purpose" (Romans 8:28 NKJV).

Luanne Nelson is an ordained street minister with Naomi Ministries. A #1 Best Selling Author, she shares stories of her trials and victories through the healing grace of God and encourages other men and women to share their stories, too.

Luanne's stories have been published in several books including: The Miracle Effect, The Breakthrough Effect, and The Identity Effect. She is featured in Comfort for the Grieving, Holy Whole and Fit, and A Few Words on Your Identity in Christ, collections of devotionals published through FEW International Publications.

Her recent chapter about "Aging Gracefully," is included in the Amazon #1 New Release 2019 edition of Natural & Organic Healing: Your Ultimate Guide to Health & Wellness.

You can find Luanne, usually with her beloved husband David, preaching and teaching in groups both large and small – all for the Glory of Jesus Christ, her Lord, Savior, and Best Friend – forever.

Please visit her website at www.LuanneNelson.com

Epilogue

*There's not much else to do except think up worse case scenarios
while being held captive in a dental chair during a root canal.*

Jiggle to the left and I know I'll definitely end up with a hole in my cheek;
swallow the pooling saliva in the back of my throat and
there is a good chance of choking which would end very badly
as I convulse violently ruining the procedure losing an eye
after knocking the glasses off of my face frantically trying to breathe
and then finally dying right then and there a maimed and bloody mess ...

There is no adjusting the little paper napkin thingie draped over my chest,
because I fear accidentally tapping the endodontist's arm
startling his concentration, resulting in a mishap of a different sort.
Not a death, definitely maimed, though.
One of us will end up maimed.
I just know it.

I think about the consent form I signed on the way in
and suddenly realize why it's so long and so comprehensive.
Downgrading the carnage, I am certain that at the very least,
I will end up with a useless tongue
and a mangled inside of my cheek
because the anesthetic is not going to wear off.

Ever.

I remember that part of the consent form vividly.
"Numbness could be permanent ..."
Oh, God. I should have braved it without the shot.
It couldn't have been any worse than this, right?

It's only a tooth. Way in the back.
I am more of a carnivore anyway. I really don't need the grinder molar
he's working on way back there.
I think about farmers plowing the back forty in the heat.

Focus!

Maybe I should just make some guttural noises
and they'll let me go to the ladies room and I will just leave instead
get into my car and drive home and forget the whole thing.
Send me a bill, please, and gee I am so sorry I had to leave I felt sick.
I wonder if the anesthetic is wearing off.
The right side of my tongue is a big dead marshmallow.
I am certain I'm screwed. I wonder if I leave if they would let me
come back later to have it finished since I'll never need another shot again
for the rest of my life since I am one of the ones
who is permanently numb.

I imagine talking to myself in the rearview mirror at the next stop light
to see if my paralyzed mouth is noticeable during speech.
I remember I've forgotten to pluck the rogue hair on my chin
that has been resprouting since it first
showed up when I was twenty.
One of my kids named it the billy goat hair.
I wonder if the dental assistant has noticed it. It's on her side.

I know, I'll say another Our Father.
Really really slowly this time so God doesn't think
I am repeating the same prayer over and over.
I know He doesn't like that.
He hears us the first time.

Maybe that's why the shot is not going to wear off,
He's mad at me for swearing so much at my husband last night.
God, you saw the whole thing, he was being really unreasonable.
Please return the feeling to my mouth after this procedure
and I promise I will only say nice things from now on.

I am terrified of dentists.
So, what does God do? He brings me one to marry.
So, I do.

God has a great sense of humor.

Remember that.

Romans 8:28

John 14:6

www.ingramcontent.com/pod-product-compliance
Lightning Source LLC
Chambersburg PA
CBHW030103240426
43661CB00039B/1474/J